USING MICROSOFT ACCESS XP

A How-To-Do-It Manual for Librarians

E. Sonny Butler
Timothy R. Napier

**HOW-TO-DO-IT MANUALS
FOR LIBRARIANS**

NUMBER 120

NEAL-SCHUMAN PUBLISHERS, INC.
New York, London

Published by Neal-Schuman Publishers, Inc.
100 Varick Street
New York, NY 10013

Printed and bound in the United States of America.

The paper used in this publication meets the minimum requirements of American National Standard for Information Sciences—Permanence of Paper for Printed Library Materials, ANSI Z39.48–1992 ∞

Library of Congress Cataloging-in-Publication Data

Butler, E. Sonny.
    Using Microsoft Access XP : a how-to-do-it manual for librarians / E. Sonny Butler, Timothy R. Napier.
        p. cm. — (How-to-do-it manuals for librarians ; no. 120).
    Includes index.
    ISBN 1-55570-442-5 (alk. paper)
    1. Microsoft Access. 2. Libraries—Automation. 3. Database management. I. Napier, Timothy R. II. Title. III. How-to-do-it manuals for libraries ; no. 120).

Z678.93.D33 B89 2002
005.75'65—dc21
                                                                2002029390

CONTENTS

LIST OF FIGURES

CHAPTER 7 FORMS

CHAPTER 8 DATABASE STRUCTURE

CHAPTER 13 LINKING WITHOUT SWITCHBOARD MANAGER

CHAPTER 14 SECURITY

CHAPTER 15 WORKING ON THE WEB

PREFACE

E. SONNY BUTLER

The most-used computer programs in the world today are database management system programs. Anytime you use an Internet search engine you are searching a database of some type. Certainly in this era of information gathering, and with such a wealth of information available, it is even more critical that librarians understand how to retrieve and organize information in a timely and cost–effective manner. *Using Microsoft Access XP: A How-To-Do-It Manual for Librarians* is written to assist the busy professional in developing applications to retrieve and organize information for libraries.

My earlier two books, *Using dBASE Version V for Windows: A How-To-Do-It Manual for Librarians* and *Using Microsoft Access: A How-To-Do-It Manual for Librarians*, demonstrated how librarians could take more control of their information management using popular database–management systems. *Using Microsoft Access XP* expands on that base and adds several chapters for using the latest version of Microsoft Access XP (2002). Microsoft Access was selected because more libraries prefer this database program. Its interface is seamless with the other popular Microsoft Office applications such as Word, Excel, and PowerPoint. Creating databases with Access XP also allows for information to be shared via the Internet or an intranet. This is done by creating data access pages that are a special type of Web page that allows users to combine the features of a dynamic HTML (DHTML) document with data stored in either a Microsoft Access or Microsoft SQL Server database.

This manual is designed to assist librarians in programming unique applications that meet specific library needs. It does this by demonstrating how Access can be used to meet library needs in case after case. The examples cover designing the database, adding entries, enhancing the structure, preparing reports, querying the database, and printing results.

Applications software can change more rapidly than we as individuals can assimilate. I find that software is becoming more difficult to use rather than less difficult. That said, we information specialists are expected to know how to use and often how to teach an amazingly broad array of information tools ranging from word–processing programs to online catalogs to Web browsers. There are so many different programs and services providing access to databases of all descriptions that it is almost impossible to stay current with all of them.

This How-To-Do-It Manual is designed so that you can learn the fundamentals of using Microsoft Access XP and how the program can assist you in managing your library's data. If you need advanced instructions, it will be easier to consult and understand a more comprehensive instruction manual because you will have mastered the fundamental concepts; thus, you will feel more comfortable with not only Microsoft Access but with the database concept after using this manual.

All instructions are current with changes through Microsoft Office XP Professional version with Microsoft Access.

HOW TO USE THIS MANUAL

- Chapter 1 goes over the basic functions of working with Windows, describes terms such as multitasking, and shows how to use the menu and tool bars.
- Chapter 2 covers the basics, defines some useful terms, and leads you through the steps for database objects, database design, and using the database wizard.
- Chapter 3 discusses designing, saving, modifying, and closing the table.
- Chapter 4 discusses entering, finding, and deleting records.
- Chapter 5 teaches you to sort and index data fields within your database and presents some of the advantages and disadvantages of each method.
- Chapter 6 explains how to create and modify queries.
- Chapter 7 shows you how to create forms, modify forms, modify table records using forms, and using sub–forms.
- Chapter 8 discusses database structure with relationships, tables, and queries.
- Chapter 9 explains advanced queries.
- Chapter 10 follows that with reports.
- Chapter 11 shows you how to create and use macros.
- Chapters 12 and 13 discuss creating and modifying using the switchboard, which is a useful tool and allows you to do some interesting things with your database.
- Chapter 14 deals with some of the security aspects of Access and Chapter 15 provides information for working with Access on the Web.

ACKNOWLEDGMENTS

I have enjoyed working with Tim Napier on this project. Tim was a student at Eastern Kentucky University and I was his advisor and professor in a couple of his CIS courses. After he graduated we stayed in touch and worked on another database project. When the opportunity presented itself to update the Access book for Neal-Schuman, I asked Tim if he would like to participate and he gladly agreed to. We have updated and added several chapters to this edition and it has been a pleasure working with Tim on this project. Tim and I appreciate Neal-Schuman and Charles Harmon for allowing us the opportunity to update the book to the XP version of Microsoft Access.

Finally, thank you for consulting our book. We sincerely hope you will profit intellectually, personally, and professionally from the knowledge derived. Please feel free to forward your comments to the publishers and they will forward them to me for review and updates.

1 WORKING WITH WINDOWS

OBJECTIVES

Microsoft Windows is a graphical user interface operating system. Graphical User Interfaces (GUIs) work with your application, in this case Microsoft Access, to control the basic operation of your computer. This brief overview will assist you in learning some of the basic skills you will use in Microsoft Access. We will discuss how to start Windows and how to use the mouse to start Microsoft Access in the Windows environment.

1.1 STARTING WINDOWS

Windows is usually automatically started, or launched, when you turn your computer on and it boots up. It becomes apparent quickly what a graphical environment looks like when you see the icons that represent programs on your screen. As a graphical interface, Windows uses pictures and symbols, known as *icons*, to replace the many arcane commands of the previous Disk Operating System (DOS) environment. Windows allows you to run more than one application at a time; for example, you could be using Microsoft Word, Microsoft PowerPoint, and Microsoft Access at the same time and switch between them. Running more than one application at a time is called *multitasking*.

To begin, turn on your computer. You will see some technical information on the screen while it boots. In the Windows environment, CONFIG.SYS and AUTOEXEC.BAT files are replaced by files known as .INI files. These files go beyond the scope of this book so I will not discuss them, but I feel it is important that you know of their existence for your future use of Windows because there may be a time you will need to edit some of these files. When you turn on your machine and it "boots up," a screen

1

that is called your *desktop* appears. The metaphor here is an actual desktop with items placed on it. You have a **Start** button on the bottom left of your screen (you may change locations if you like, but for now let's use Windows the way it installs), which I compare to the drawers in your desk. If you click on the Start button and point your mouse to **programs** you will see other files available such as Accessories, Microsoft Access, Microsoft Excel, Microsoft Word, etc. (see Figure 1.1).

Figure 1.1 Programs Menu

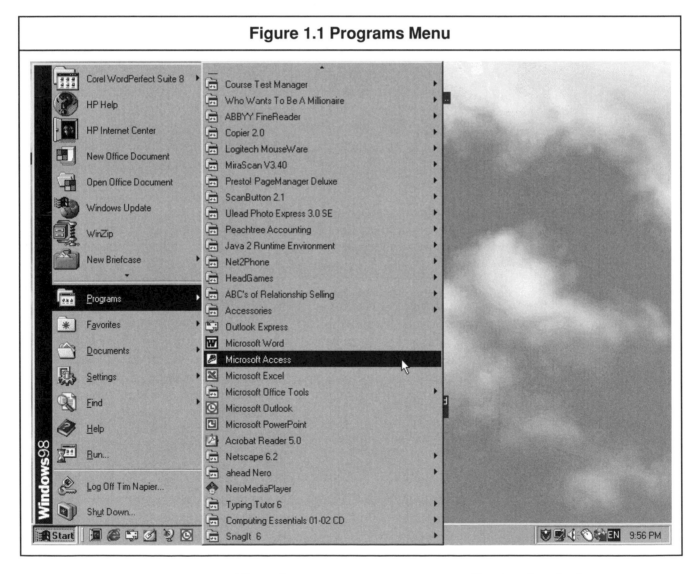

From here, you may open any application by placing your mouse on that program and *clicking the left button once*. The application will open for you to begin use.

1.2 MULTITASKING

A very useful feature of the Windows environment is the ability to open multiple applications and go back and forth between them. For example, if you are doing an inventory of publications or searching a database looking for specific information, and you wish to include some of the information in MS Word, you can open both MS Word and MS Access and, by using the task bar at the bottom of the screen, switch between the applications or use another technique that involves the <Alt> and <Tab> keys. Let me explain this technique briefly. After you open all the applications you will be using, hold down the <Alt> key and press the <Tab> key. You will see a window pop up with the name of one of the applications you have opened. Holding the <Alt> key down and continuing to tap the <Tab> key will result in other applications appearing in the window in the middle of your screen. When you arrive at the application you need, release the <Alt> key and that application will open. You may use this technique whenever you want to move between applications, or you can use the task bar at the bottom of your screen if you are using Windows 98, ME, or XP.

1.3 SAVING FILES

Any documents or databases you create are stored in the computer's *Random Access Memory* (RAM). RAM is temporary storage space that is lost when the power to the computer is turned off. To store or save a document permanently, you need to save it to a hard or floppy disk or some other type of storage device. You need to save your database files often to insure that you are able to retrieve them if an accident occurs or the power to your computer is disrupted. Saving files using MS Access is discussed further in different chapters that pertain to specific functions of building tables and using MS Access. Figure 1.2 shows you an example of what MS Access's file menu looks like.

1.4 CLOSING AND EXITING APPLICATIONS

When you have finished working with your open applications, you should save, close, and exit the application(s). If you do not save and close applications appropriately, you run the risk of losing your data. Figure 1.2 illustrates the menu used for closing and exiting MS Access. When you save, close, and exit your applications, you may then exit Windows. Windows has a **Shut Down** button on the Start Menu that will close any remaining open applications and prepare the computer for turning off the power.

Figure 1.2 Closing and Exiting Applications

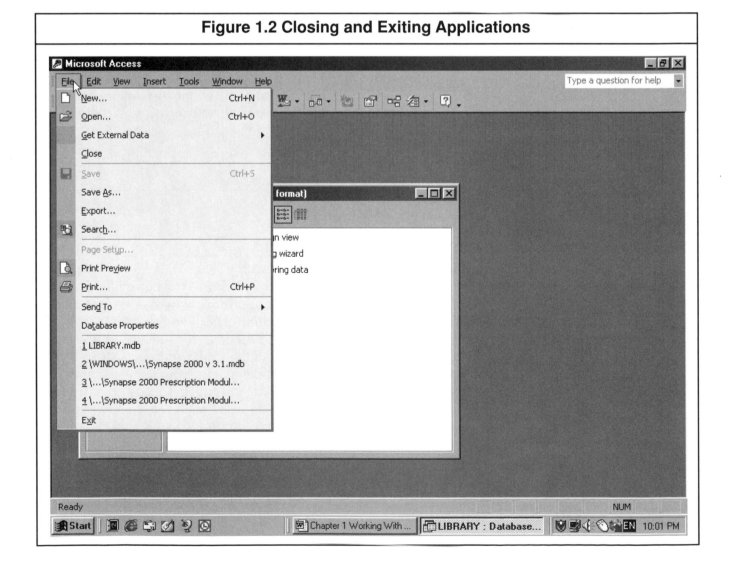

2 DATABASE BASICS

OBJECTIVES

2.1   DATABASE OBJECTS
2.2   DATABASE DESIGN
2.3   DATABASE WIZARD

In this chapter we are going to discuss what a database is, the components of a database, and how a database can assist you in your work. We will cover the basic terminology of a database and give you a better understanding of how databases work. Before we begin, here is some important information you need to know about the program used in this book.

The database program we are using is Access 2002. This version of Access is also compatible with Access 2000. More specifically, if you create a database using Access 2000, you can also use that database with Access 2002. Also, if you create a database with Access 2002 you may be able to use that database with Access 2000. By default, Access 2002 will create a database using the Access 2000 file format. This allows you to open the database in either Access 2000 or Access 2002. A database created with Access 2002 using the Access 2002 file format, however, will only work with Access 2002.

Now that you understand some of the basic compatibility issues involved with Access 2002, we can move on.

2.1 DATABASE OBJECTS

WHAT IS A DATABASE?

A database is a compilation of information related to a particular subject such as an inventory list or a library catalog. The information is stored in tables and is accessed with the use of forms, queries, and reports.

Databases allow you to save all related information in a single location instead of having to perform updates to several files. A well-designed database helps eliminate the possibility of data-entry errors as well as data redundancy. The term *data redundancy* means that you have the same data stored in more than one location.

Next, we are going to discuss the different objects that make up the database. These objects are used to store, retrieve, update, and report data. We will even discuss how you can post your data on the Web.

WHAT IS A TABLE?

A table is a database object used to store data. Each table stores data about a particular topic. Tables use rows and columns to store the data.

The rows in the table are called records. Each record pertains to a given person, product, or event. Therefore, a table consists of related records.

The columns in the table are called fields. Each field contains a specific piece of data in each record. Therefore, a record consists of related fields.

Also, each record must be assigned a unique identifier. This is a field in each record that uniquely identifies that record. This is also referred to as a primary key.

WHAT IS A FORM?

A form is a database object that is used to interact with a related table. You can access the data in the table with a form to add, update, and delete records from the table.

By using a form, however, you eliminate the possibility of accidentally deleting several or even all of the records in a table by pressing the wrong key. A form usually will only display a single record at a time.

Forms usually consist of controls such as labels, text boxes, list boxes, combo boxes, etc., that allow you to interact with the data stored in the related table. When creating forms, you will determine which type of control is appropriate for the data you are accessing. Different types of controls give you more manageability in what data you want in your table.

WHAT IS A REPORT?

A report is a database object used to display information stored in a single table or several tables. The report is bound to one or more tables either directly or by the use of a query. Reports, like forms, consist of controls that are used to display information. You can customize your reports using headers and footers, by sorting your data in ascending or descending order, and by grouping your data by categories.

WHAT IS A QUERY?

A query is a database object used to retrieve information stored in a single table or several tables. When you use a query, you are asking the database to retrieve information that you need. The data retrieved by the query may be displayed in a form, report, or data access page. Or you may choose to just display the query results in the query datasheet view.

There are several different types of queries in Access. Examples of queries include: select, parameter, crosstab, action, and SQL. In this book we will look at the first three types of queries mentioned here. Therefore, we will give a brief explanation of these types.

A select query is the most common type of query. It retrieves data from one or more tables that can be displayed or modified.

A parameter query returns information from one or more tables based on input that is entered into a dialog box when the query is run.

A crosstab query allows you to redesign your data for easier analysis of the data.

WHAT IS A DATA ACCESS PAGE?

A data access page is a type of Web page used to view and modify data stored in a database. This gives users access to a database via the Internet or an intranet. You want to be very careful about what data you allow to be accessed with a data access page. Remember, those who view the data can also change or even delete the data.

WHAT IS A MACRO?

A macro is a database object used to automate a task or set of tasks that perform an operation. Examples of operations include opening a form or printing a report. Macros don't actually have anything to do with maintaining the data in your database; however, macros are used to make working with that data a much easier task.

Now that you understand the different objects that make up a database, we will take a look at how to design a database and the different ways to create a database. Remember, a database is used to store, modify, and present information to make your work easier.

2.2 DATABASE DESIGN

HOW DO I DESIGN A DATABASE?

Before you create a database you will find it very helpful to spend time designing the database. You should specify the purpose of the database, the tables needed, the fields that belong to each table, the primary key for each table, and the relationships between the tables. You should also give some thought to the output you desire from the database. By understanding what information you will need to retrieve from the database, you can better determine how to design the tables and their relationships.

PURPOSE OF A DATABASE

This should be an easy question to answer. You obviously want a database that will meet the needs of the users. You should, therefore, ask those who will be using the database what they need the database to do. It is always helpful to understand what types of forms are used to gather data and what types of reports are used to present the data. This will give you an idea of what the user needs from the database and also the current process of gathering data and outputting information.

WHAT FIELDS DO I NEED IN THE TABLES?

Include all fields that are pertinent to the subject of the table. For example, a customer table would include information about each customer. This information is stored in the table in the form of fields.

A field is the smallest piece of data that will be stored in the database. Examples of fields include names, addresses, phone numbers, etc. Remember to break fields down into their smallest components. For example, if you want to store a person's name, you would not store their entire name in one field. You would break the name into smaller components such as first name, middle initial, and last name. The same principle applies to addresses. You would break the address into smaller components such as street address, city, state, and postal code.

WHAT TABLES DO I NEED IN THE DATABASE?

Each table contains data about a different topic. Only fields related to that particular topic should be stored in that table. Make sure you don't store the same data in separate tables. This is what is called data redundancy.

Data redundancy makes your database very unreliable. If you

have the same data stored in separate tables, then you would have to update the same field in each table where it was stored. This is almost impossible to keep up with. That is why you need to spend time listing the fields and deciding which tables they will be stored in before you actually start creating the database.

WHY DO I NEED A PRIMARY KEY?

A primary key is a field that uniquely identifies each record in a table. Primary keys are necessary to link the tables in your database. A primary key is linked to a foreign key in one or more related tables and this creates a relationship between the tables.

A primary key must contain a unique value. Since the primary key is used to link to other related tables, the primary key cannot contain a null value. A null value essentially means that the primary key field is left blank.

HOW DO I CREATE A DATABASE?

There are essentially two ways to create a database. First, you can use a Database Wizard. The Wizard allows you to select the type of database you want, and the database objects and their relationships are defined for you. This is helpful if the type of database you want to create is listed in the Wizard's selections. Second, you can create your database from scratch and define your own database objects and their relationships. This is a better choice if you need flexibility in your database. In this book we will spend our time creating a database from scratch and defining our own database objects and their relationships. Just for your information, however, we will discuss the Database Wizard briefly below.

2.3 DATABASE WIZARD

HOW DO I USE THE DATABASE WIZARD?

Here are the steps you follow to create a database using the Database Wizard.

1. Click the **New** button on the toolbar to open the **New File** task pane (see Figure 2.1).

Figure 2.1 New Button

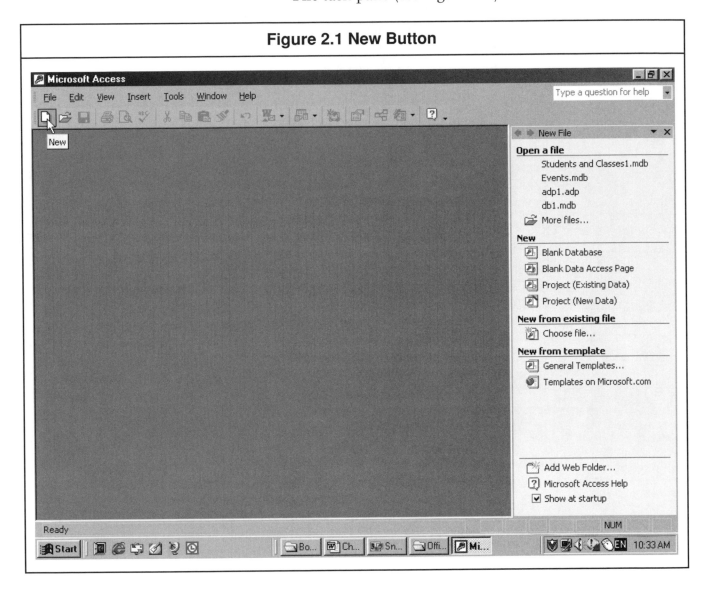

2. In the **New File** task pane, click **General Templates . . .** under New Form Template to open the Templates window.
3. Click the **Databases** tab (see Figure 2.2).

Figure 2.2 Templates Window

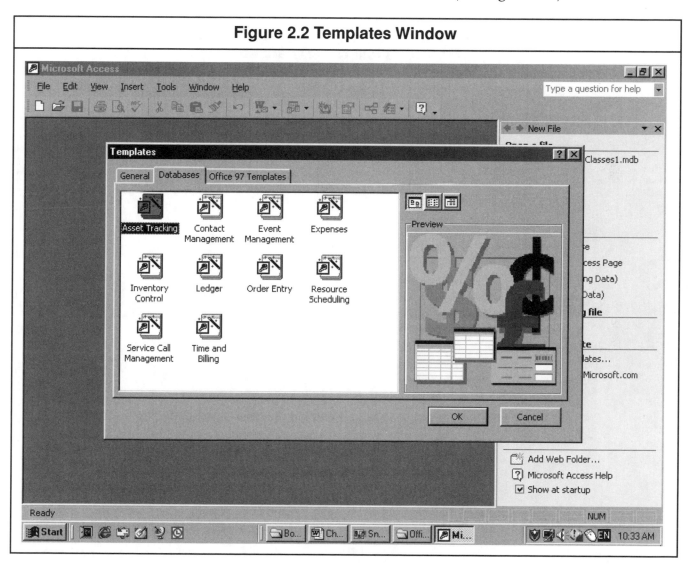

4. Click the icon for the type of database you want to create.
5. Click the **OK** button.
6. In the **File New Database** dialog box, enter the name and location for the database (see Figure 2.3).

Figure 2.3 File New Database

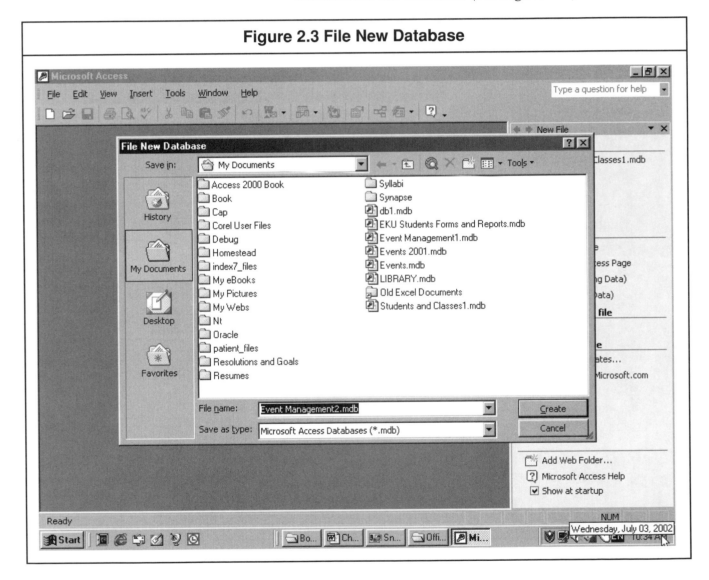

7. Click the **Create** button.
8. Follow the remaining instructions in the Database Wizard to finish creating the database.

The Database Wizard creates tables, forms, reports, etc., relevant to that particular database. After the database is created, you may still find it necessary to modify some of the objects that were created using the Database Wizard. It is important, therefore, to know how to add, modify, and delete objects and relationships.

In the remaining chapters we are going to look at creating, modifying, and deleting the different types of objects. We will also look at how to enter, modify, and retrieve data. Along the way we will discuss database design and even how to post your database on the Web.

Let's get started.

TABLES

OBJECTIVES

3.1 DESIGNING THE TABLE STRUCTURE
3.2 SAVING THE TABLE STRUCTURE
3.3 CLOSING THE TABLE
3.4 EXITING ACCESS
3.5 OPENING ACCESS FILES
3.6 MODIFYING THE TABLE STRUCTURE
3.7 USING THE TABLE WIZARD

Data is a valuable resource to libraries. Libraries need to store, manipulate, and retrieve many items of information about each publication they own as well as about each registered borrower. Organizing, creating, maintaining, retrieving, and sorting such data are essential activities. One of the many tools available to accomplish these tasks is the Database Management System (DBMS).

Most people use databases to manage their lives, although they don't refer to them as database systems. A database is simply a collection of information, or data put together in a usable form that can be retrieved. A dictionary, card catalog, reference index, client file, or overdue list is an example of a database. Software programs such as Microsoft Access that instruct computers how to handle data are called database management systems. As a professional librarian, you will use database technology to organize your inventory of publications. A database can contain different types of data such as printed, audio, video, or any other item(s) that you must maintain and account for in the library.

The most important step in designing a database is defining the problem(s) to be addressed. Once you have defined the problem(s), you then need to decide what data you need, what kinds of data should be grouped together, and what relationships exist between the groups of data. If you start designing the program before you have a clear idea of the solution, you have a very good chance of solving the wrong problem, just adding an unnecessary report, or leaving out something important.

Changing the actual structure of the database is not difficult. For example, if you include unnecessary data, it will not be too difficult to delete all of the unnecessary information. If, however, after you have entered a few hundred records you discover that you have left out something vital, it can be difficult and time consuming to add the field to the database structure and then enter the actual data.

In the chapters that follow, we will be developing a card catalog and a circulation record for a small, fictional library called Manchester Memorial Library. The library's users come from two separate towns with separate ZIP codes. We will enter information on several users and several books from the library and then manipulate this information to demonstrate some of the features of Access.

When you create a database in Microsoft Access, you can use several types of objects. *Tables* are the basic type of object, in which you define which data go together and then enter the data in the table. *Queries* are objects that retrieve specific records from the table. *Reports* are objects that present the data in formatted, printed form. From now on, we will not use the term *object*; instead, we will indicate which type of object we are using.

The database we create will be called **LIBRARY**. The tables we will be working with in our library database are the **Books** table and the **Library Users** table.

Many libraries get their bibliographic information from the Library of Congress or another bibliographic utility in Machine Readable Cataloging (MARC) format. The MARC format tapes provide more information than we will need for this tutorial. If you get your cataloging information from this source, you can choose which MARC tag fields you want to use. If your library grows and you want to use more of the available cataloging information, Microsoft Access will accommodate additional fields.

Let's start thinking about the **Books** table. Each piece of information (for instance, author, title, or publisher) about a book is called a field. You will need to decide the length and the data type for each field. To keep from duplicating data fields/items, you need to define the purpose of each table and then identify each piece of data that is to be stored in each table. In Microsoft Access, the data types are: Text, Memo, Number, Date/Time, Currency, AutoNumber, Yes/No, OLE Object, Hyperlink, and Lookup Wizard.

3.1 DESIGNING THE TABLE STRUCTURE

Open Microsoft Access by clicking on Start, Programs, and then Microsoft Access. You should see a blank Access screen with the Menu bar, Database toolbar, and any other open toolbars (such as the Formatting toolbar) at the top of the screen. At the right of the screen you see the Task Pane which is a new feature with Access 2002 (see Figure 3.1).

Figure 3.1 Viewing the New Database Screen

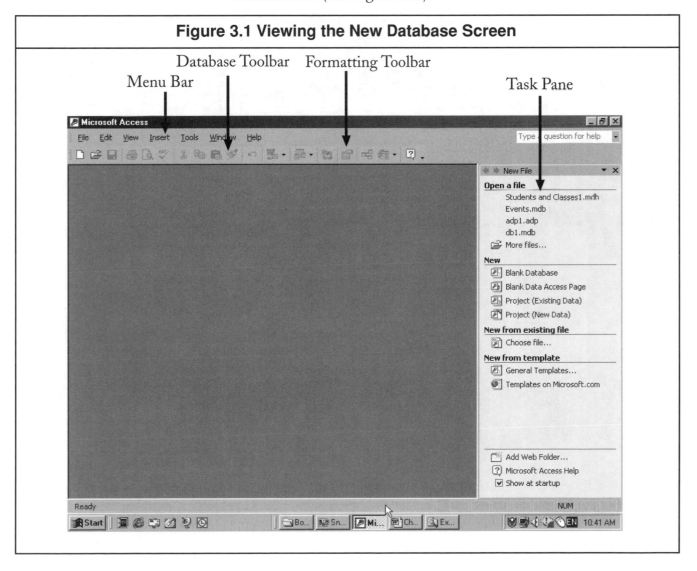

First, we will create the structure for the table **Books.**

1. Click on **Blank Database** on the Task Pane. Notice that when you move your mouse pointer over the currently active items in the Task Pane that each item is displayed with a blue underline.
2. Type **LIBRARY** in the space labeled File name. Access will add the file extension **.mdb** where needed (see Figure 3.2).

Figure 3.2 Database Name Screen

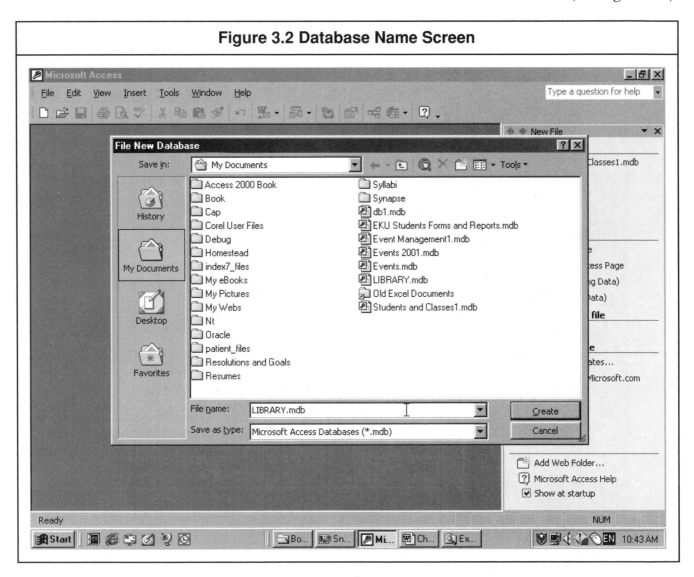

3. Click on **Create**. The screen you see now allows you to define which kind of object you want to create: **Tables, Queries, Forms, Reports, Pages, Macros,** or **Modules** (see Figure 3.3)

Figure 3.3 Create New Database

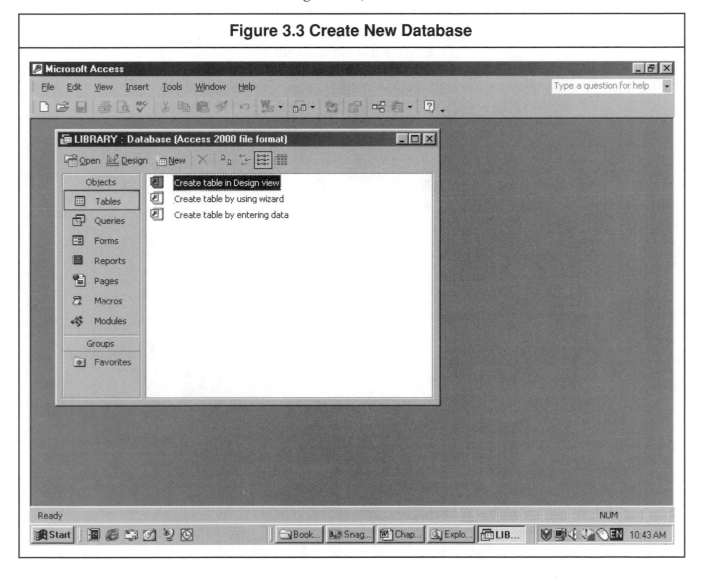

4. Click **Tables** to select it (if it isn't already selected).
5. Click **New.** You will see a screen asking you to choose how you want to create your new table.
6. Click on **Design View.**
7. Click the **OK** button (see Figure 3.4).

Figure 3.4 New Table

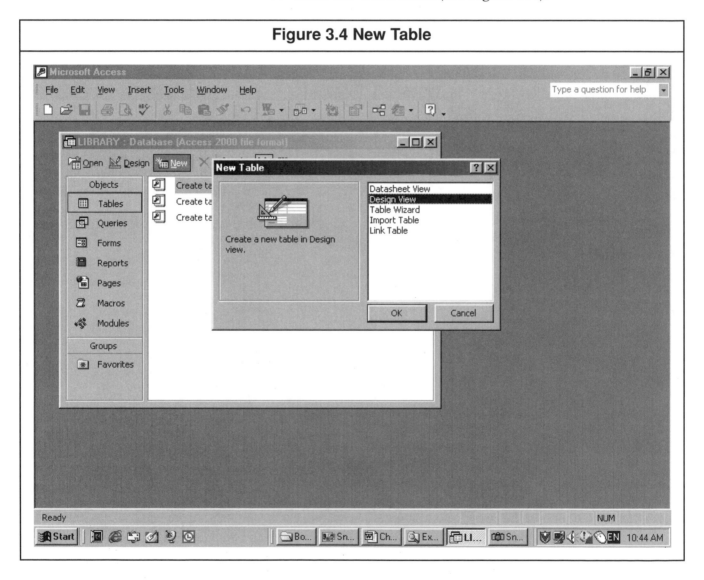

Now you should see the screen for defining the structure of the table (see Figure 3.5).

Figure 3.5 Design View

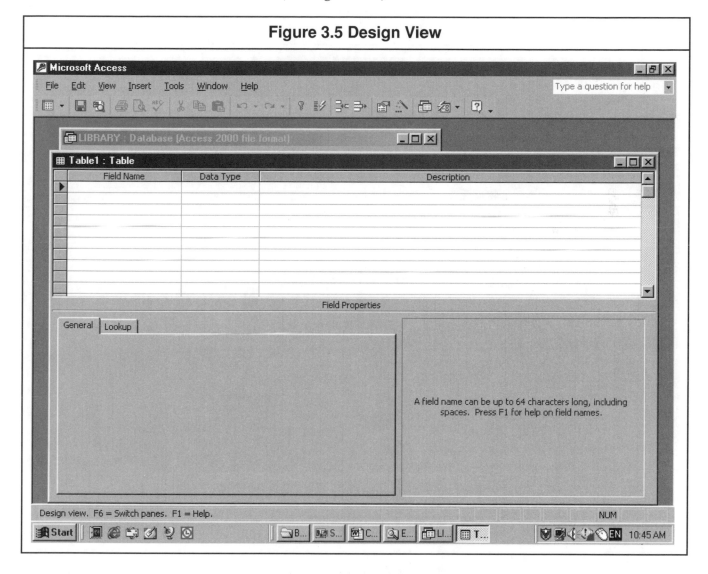

8. In the Field Name space for Field 1, type **AccessNo**.
9. Press <Enter>. The cursor moves to the **Data Type** box.
10. Click in this box to reveal an arrow at the right side of the box.
11. Click on the arrow to reveal a drop-down list with your options for the **Data Type**.

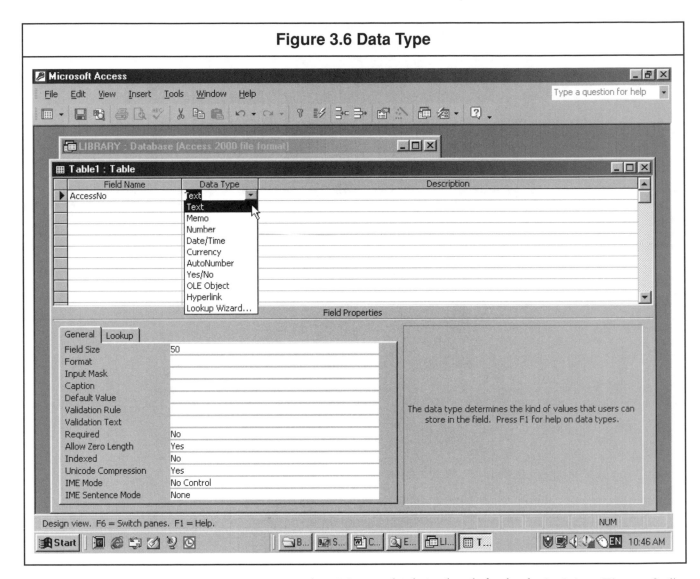

Figure 3.6 Data Type

12. Select **Text** (which is the default choice) (see Figure 3.6).

Note: You must assign a data type for each field. The data type determines what field values you may enter for that field and what other properties the field will have. In Access, you assign one of ten data types to each field. A drop-down box holds a list of choices appropriate for that particular space. The space usually has a small arrowhead to indicate that there are more options. Click once on the arrow to reveal the choices and then click on the one you want.

- **Text** – Use for field values containing letters, numbers (that are not to be used for calculations), spaces, special characters, or any combination thereof. Text fields may be up to 255 characters long. You should assign the text data type to fields in which you will store names, addresses, phone numbers, postal codes, or social security numbers.
- **Memo** – Use for lengthy text and numbers, such as long comments or explanations. Stores up to 65,536 characters. Our application could use the memo field for storing an abstract of a publication.
- **Number** – Use for data to be included in mathematical calculations.
- **Date/Time** – Use for dates and times.
- **Currency** – Use for currency values.
- **AutoNumber** – Use for sequential numbers that are automatically assigned to each record as it is added. You can specify sequential numbering or random numbering. This guarantees a unique field value so that such a field can serve as a table's primary key.
- **Yes/No** – Use for values that can be Yes/No, True/False, or On/Off. Use this data type for fields that indicate the presence or absence of a condition, such as whether a book has been checked out.
- **OLE Object** – Use for data from other application programs that support Object Linking and Embedding (OLE) such as Microsoft Word and Microsoft Excel. This advanced feature involves inserting objects from other programs, including pictures, sound, or any other type of data.
- **Hyperlink** – Use for hyperlinks.
- **Lookup Wizard** – Use for a field that allows you to choose a value from another table or from a list of values by using a combo box.

Now that you are familiar with the various data types, you can enter the appropriate type for each data field.

13. Press <Enter> to move to the next space. This is the description box, where you can, if you choose, enter a reminder to yourself of the information this field contains. For example, if you have a currency field, you may wish to remind yourself this field is an overdue fee currency field and make that notation in the description.
14. Using either the tab key on your keyboard or the mouse, move the cursor to the Field Properties area below these boxes to further define the field (see Figure 3.7).

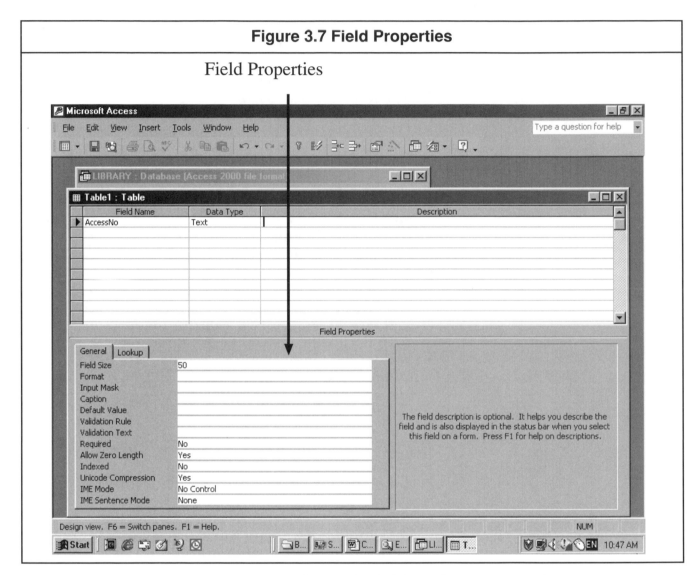

Figure 3.7 Field Properties

15. Change the field size from 50 to 10 for AccessNo.

There are several Field Properties for each Data Type. Some commonly used Field Properties for text fields include:

Field Size – Field size determines a field value's maximum storage size for text and number fields. The other data types have no field size property, either because their storage size is a predetermined fixed size or because the size is dependent on the actual value stored (e.g., a memo field).

Format – Allows you to specify how to display the data (e.g., (999) 999–9999).

Input Mask – Restricts data entry to the appropriate type and format required for the field. If you wish, you can create an input mask for the customer phone field that will automatically add the parentheses and hyphen to the phone number (see above). If you notice a similarity between Format and Input Mask, you are correct. Try each property and see which you prefer.

Click on each of the property boxes, and look at the box on the right side of the Field Properties area for hints and definitions.

Before we leave this section on table design, we will define the AccessNo field as the primary key field. This concept is used in Relational Databases, discussed fully in Chapter 10. If you do not create one, Access will create one for you. If you are starting a library and using Microsoft Access to catalog it from the beginning, using an AutoNumber field is the best way to assign accession numbers. We are assuming, however, that the Manchester Memorial Library already has a catalogued collection with accession numbers assigned, so we must create this field.

In the rest of the fields we are defining now, leave the last three properties (Required, Allow Zero Length, and Indexed) at the default value of **No**.

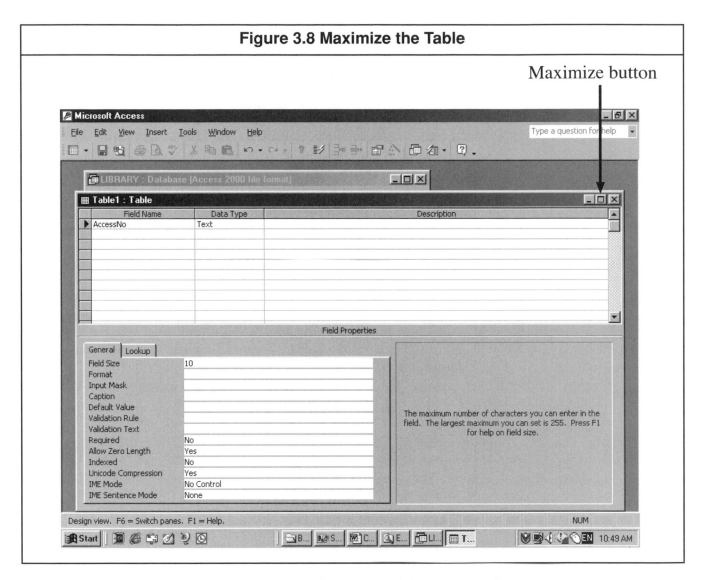

Figure 3.8 Maximize the Table

Maximize button

16. Click on the Table maximize button (see Figure 3.8).
17. Repeat steps 8–15 to define and enter the remaining fields (see Table 3.1).

		Table 3.1	
Field Name	**Data Type**	**Description**	**Field Size**
AccessNo.	Text	Primary Key	10
Title	Text	Publication Title	50
Subtitle	Text		50
Author	Text	Primary Author	30
Author2	Text	Second Author	30
Others	Text	Other Authors	30
Others2	Text	Remaining Authors	30
Place_Published	Text	Location of Publisher-City, State, Country	50
Year_Published	Text		4
Call_No	Text		20
ISBN	Text		12
Subj_1	Text		50
Subj_2	Text		50
Subj_3	Text		50
Checkout	Yes/No		
User_No	Number		10
Date_Due	Date/Time		
Notes	Memo		

You should now have all of the fields defined for the table (see Figure 3.9).

Figure 3.9 Table Structure

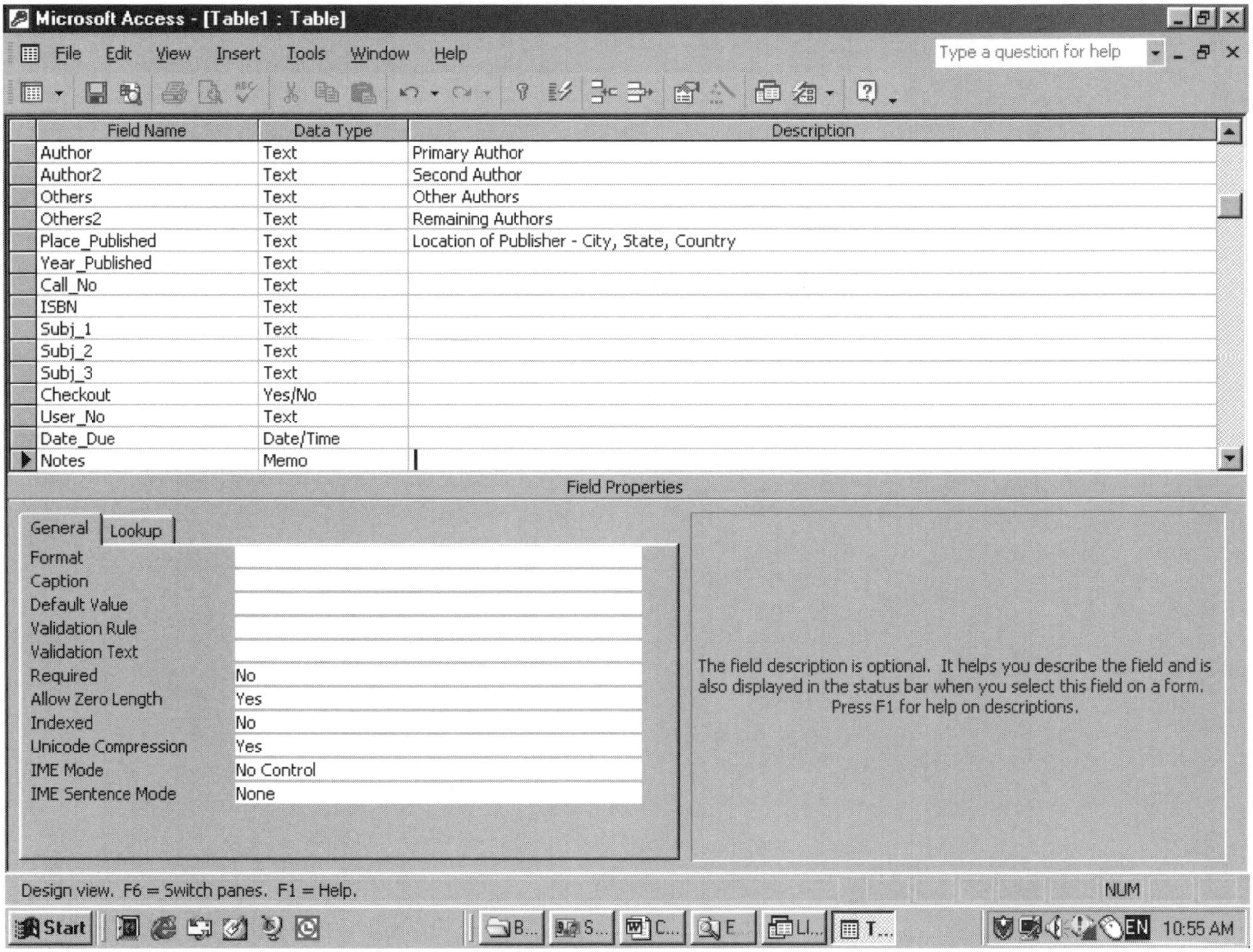

You will notice that the first few fields no longer appear on the Access screen. In order to see all fields, you will need to use the scroll bars on the right side of the screen. Before we save this design, we need to make sure we have specified the **AccessNo** field as the primary key field.

18. Scroll to the **AccessNo** field and click in the **Field Name** for **AccessNo**.

19. Click on the **Primary Key** in the tool bar above the screen. You should see a small key symbol placed beside the **AccessNo** field (see Figure 3.10).

Figure 3.10 Primary Key

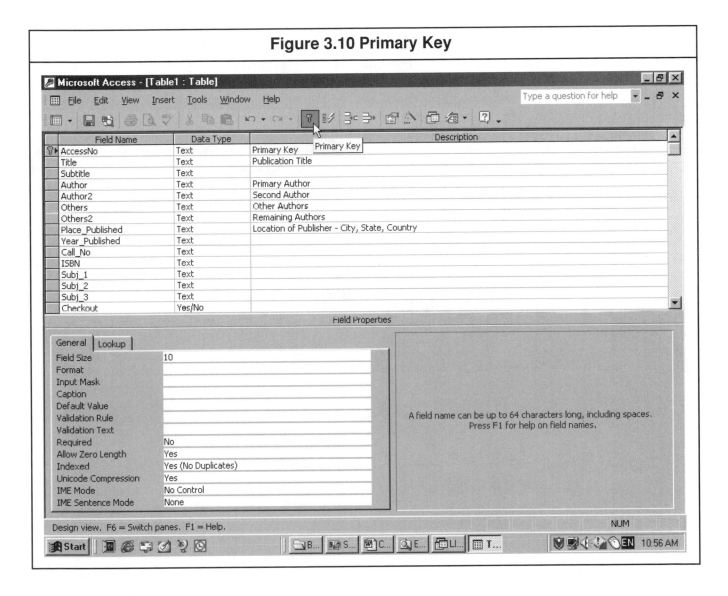

3.2 SAVING THE TABLE STRUCTURE

Now save your table structure.

1. Click on the **Save** button in the tool bar or go to **File** on the menu bar and select **Save**.
2. Access displays the box in which you name the table. Type "**Books**" (see Figure 3.11).

Figure 3.11 Saving the Table

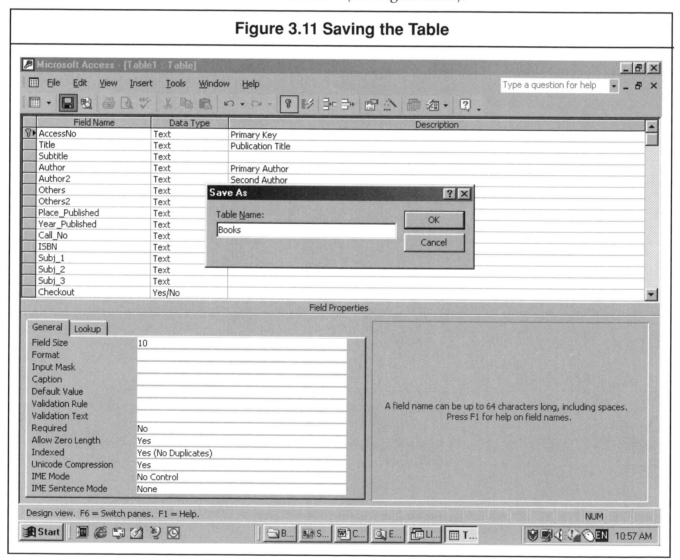

3. Press <Enter> or click on **OK**.

The **Save** box in this case is different from other **Save File** dialog boxes you usually see in Windows programs. There is no way to specify a disk drive or other information besides the name. In

Access, this table is considered part of a database (called **LIBRARY.mdb** in our case), and all the tables, queries, reports, etc., are considered part of that database. Disk drive and directory information are only entered when you save the database as a whole.

3.3 CLOSING THE TABLE

The Access file structure has now been saved. You may start entering records, close the file, or exit Access. If you decide to close the file do the following:

1.   Click on **File** on the menu bar.
2.   Click on **Close** (see Figure 3.12).

Figure 3.12 Closing the Table

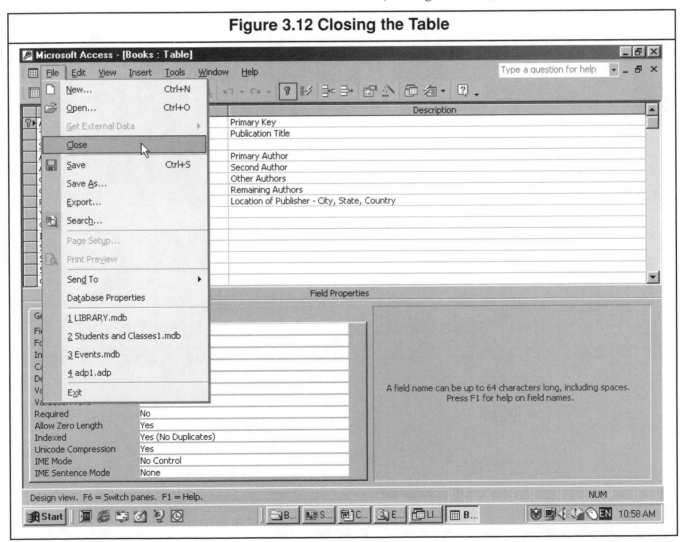

3.4 EXITING ACCESS

If you want to end your Access session, do the following:

1. Click on **File** on the menu bar.
2. Click on **Exit** (see Figure 3.13).

Figure 3.13 Exiting Access

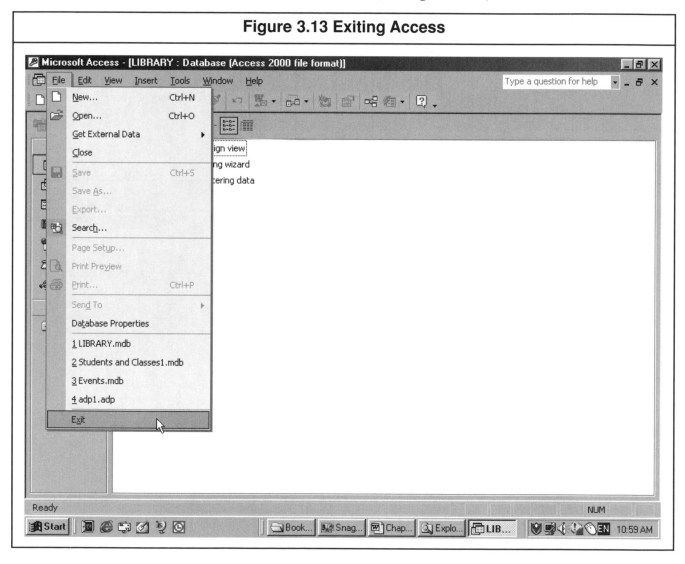

3.5 OPENING ACCESS FILES

If you exited Access in the previous instructions, you now need to reopen Microsoft Access so you can start entering records. You should see the same blank Access screen as when you started (see Figure 2.1).

1. Click on **LIBRARY.mdb** in the **Open a File** section on the **Task Pane**.

The **Library** database now appears with the **Tables** object selected. You should see the **Books** table listed.

2. Select the **Books** table (if it is not already selected) (see Figure 3.14).

Figure 3.14 Selecting a Table

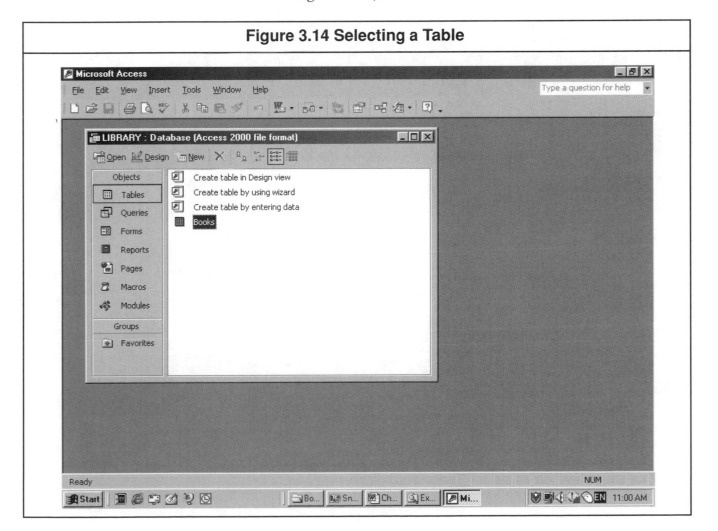

3.6 MODIFYING THE TABLE STRUCTURE

Now suppose that you start entering your books (records) into the **Books** table and you quickly encounter a book that has two authors, an illustrator, an editor, and a publisher, each meriting separate entries in your catalog. You will need to modify the table structure, which is quite easy.

    1. Click on **Design** in the **LIBRARY** database list (see Figure 3.15).

Figure 3.15 Select Design Table

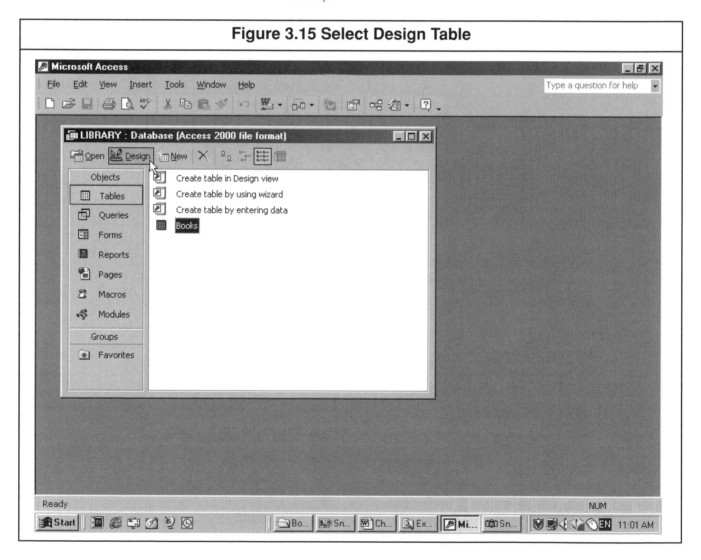

    2. Now you will see the screen displaying the database structure that you saw before when you designed the table.

We want a field for a third person whose name we want associated with the book in the catalog. Since we want this field to appear in a logical place in the structure, we will insert it near the other name fields.

3. Click on the field name Place_Published.
4. Click the **Insert Row** button (see Figure 3.16).

Figure 3.16 Insert Row

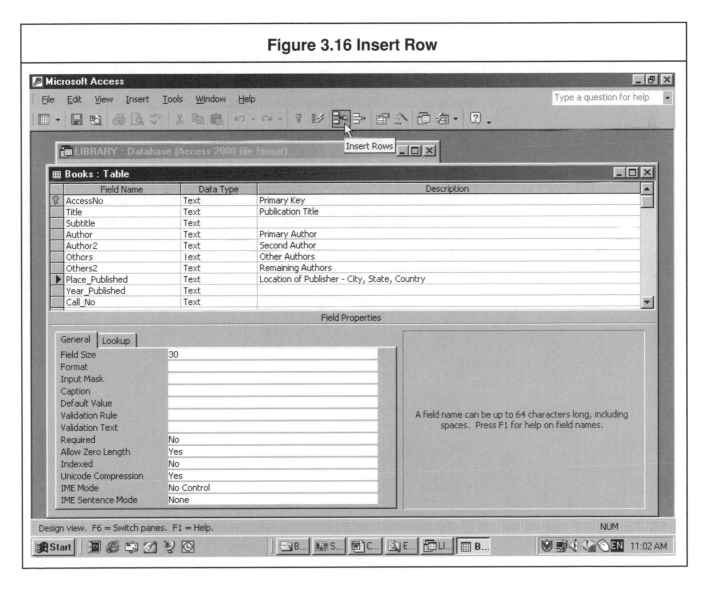

5. Enter the following field information into the table:
   Name: Others3
   Data Type: Text
   Field Length: 30

6. Save the modified structure by clicking on the **Save** button on the Standard Toolbar.
7. Close the Design screen by clicking **File** on the menu bar and then clicking **Close**.

3.7 USING THE TABLE WIZARD

Next we will use the Table Wizard feature of Access to design a table for library database developers.

WIZARD

Wizard is the name of the Microsoft suite of products that comprise an online tutorial. These tutorials will lead you step by step through most any process, such as building a table, creating a report, etc. We will not review Wizards in depth in this book because they are self explanatory when activated. You are encouraged to try using the Wizards for various aspects of database construction, as they can clarify questions for you and give you additional information on the process you are using.

1. With the **Tables** object selected, click on the **New** button (see Figure 3.4).
2. Select **Table Wizard** from the **New Table** dialog box. Then click on the **OK** button.

The Wizard displays a list of possible database tables. There are tables for business and for personal purposes. Each sample database table includes a different list of possible fields.

3. Make sure **Business** is selected and then choose **Customers** from the **Sample Tables** list (see Figure 3.17).

Figure 3.17 Table Wizard

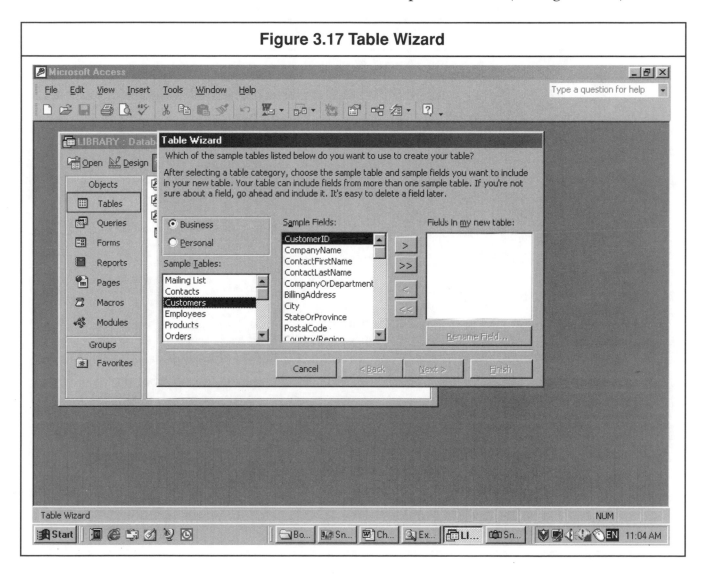

4. From the Customer list, choose these fields (see Figure 3.18):

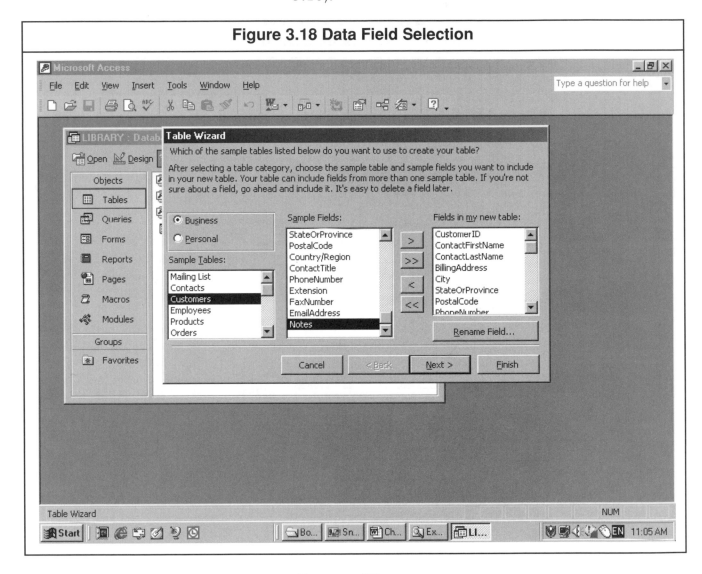

Figure 3.18 Data Field Selection

CustomerID
ContactFirstName
ContactLastName
BillingAddress
City
StateOrProvince
PostalCode
Phone Number
Notes

5. Now click on **Next**. Enter **Library Users** as the Table name. Click **No, I'll set the primary key** (see Figure 3.19).

Figure 3.19 Table Wizard Name and Primary Key

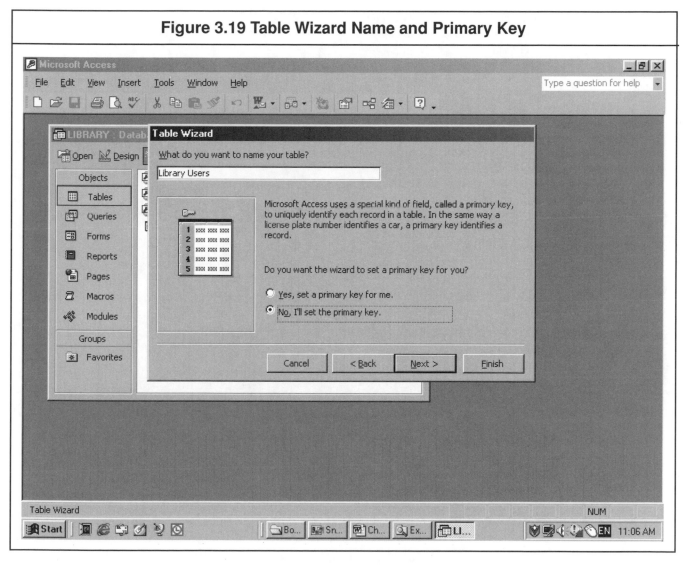

6. Click on **Next**. Access displays a screen where you set the primary key. The first field on the list, CustomerID, is the field that is unique to each library user, so we will use it as the primary key. Since the library already has a list of users with numbers already assigned, click the choice that says **Numbers I enter when I add new records** (see Figure 3.20).

Figure 3.20 Primary Key Field

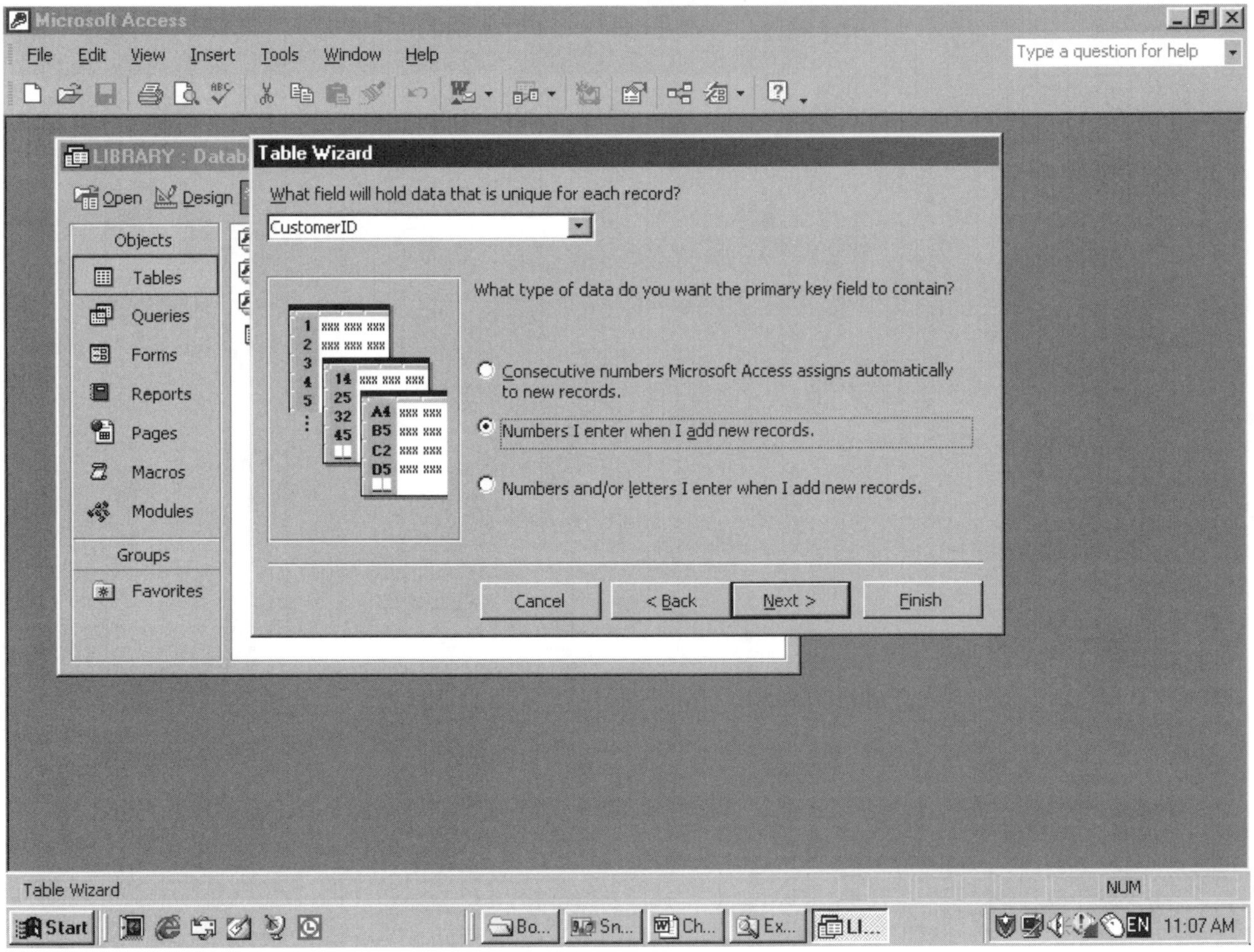

7. Click on **Next**.
8. Access displays a Relationships window. We will cover table relationships in the next section. For now, click **Next**.
9. In this screen, you opt either to modify the design or start entering records. Click **Enter data directly into the table** (see Figure 3.21).

Figure 3.21 Wizard Completion Screen

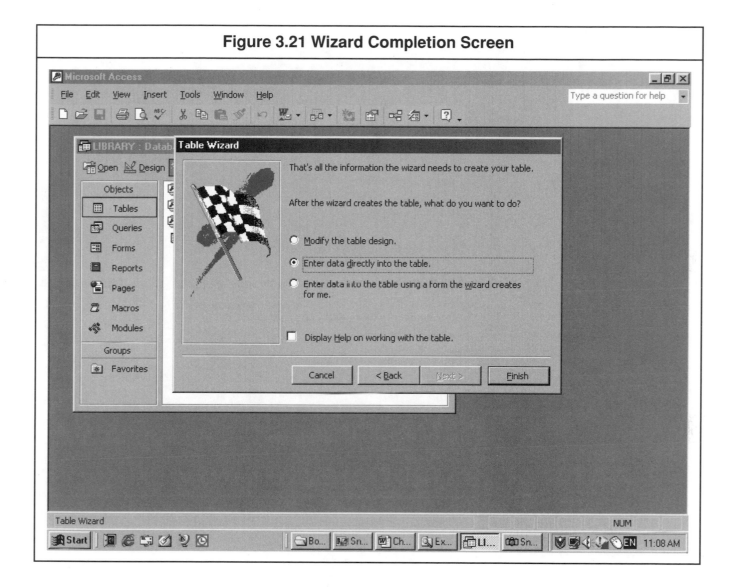

10. Click the **Finish** button.

Now the table you just created is open in datasheet view and is ready for you to enter records. We will cover entering records in the next chapter. For now we will close the table in datasheet view.

11. Click **File** and then **Close** from the menu bar.
12. Exit from Microsoft Access.

4 RECORDS

OBJECTIVES

4.1 ENTERING RECORDS
4.2 DELETING RECORDS
4.3 FINDING RECORDS

In this chapter we are going to work with records. We will add and delete records within the tables we created in the previous chapter. We will also learn how to search for records in these tables.

Records consist of a group of related fields. Examples of records include customers, book inventory, etc. We are going to begin the chapter by entering records into the BOOKS table.

4.1 ENTERING RECORDS

Open Microsoft Access. Select and open the **Books** table from the **LIBRARY.mdb** database (see Figure 4.1). You should see an empty records screen. This is called the *Datasheet View* (see Figure 4.2).

Figure 4.1 Table Selection Screen

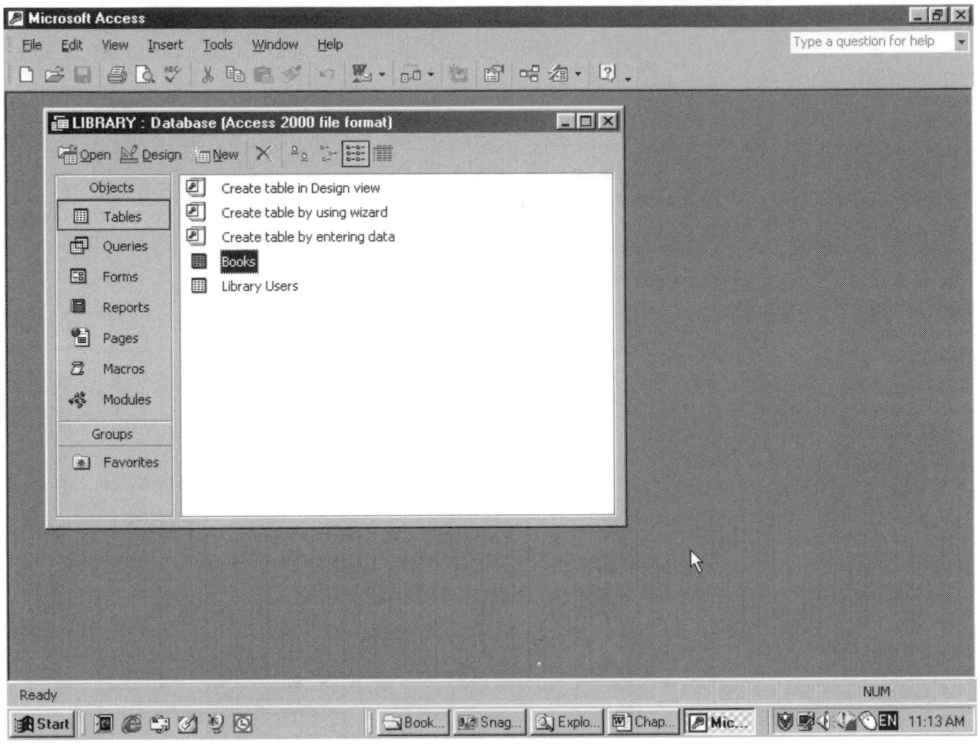

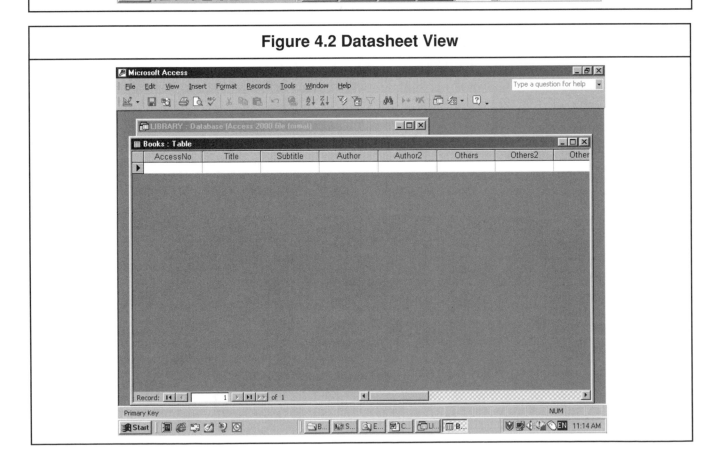

Figure 4.2 Datasheet View

1. When entering data into a table, enter data into the blank space specific to each field name. If you have designed well, you should be able to enter information easily.
2. When you finish entering data in a field, press <Enter> to move to the next blank field.
3. Access always places a blank record at the end of the record list. This record is designated by an asterisk in the column before the first field. The selected record is shown by an arrow head and a field with unsaved data is marked by a pencil.
4. The **Notes** field, a field using the Memo data type, is handled exactly the same as other fields. Enter the data in the field. In many of the fields, you won't be able to see the whole entry, but all of the data is there.
5. Enter the information for the following books in the **Books** table.

LIST OF BOOKS

ACCESSION:	19062
TITLE:	Monet, A Retrospective
AUTHOR2:	Stuckey, Charles F.
PLACE PUB:	New York, NY
PUBLISHER:	Hugh Lauter Levin Assoc. Inc.
YR PUB:	1985
CALL NO:	O 7559.4 MON (oversized)
ISBN:	088363385X
SUBJ:	1. Monet, Claude–1840–1926
	2. Painters–France–Biography
NOTES:	Phys. Desc.: 387P. Ill (Some Colored); 34 CM.

ACCESSION:	26426
TITLE:	Life of Langston Hughes Vol 1
AUTHOR:	Rampersad, Arnold
PLACE PUB:	New York, NY
PUBLISHER:	Oxford Univ. Press
YR PUB:	1986
CALL NO:	818.52 RAM Vol 1
SUBJ:	1. Hughes, Langston–1902–1967–Biography
	2. Poets, American–20th Century–Biography
NOTES:	Phys Desc: V. 1 of 2: Ill, Ports.; 24 CM
	Contents: Vol 1: 1902–1941, I, Too, Sing America

LIST OF BOOKS *(continued)*

ACCESSION:	10970
TITLE:	Dartnell Marketing Manager's Handbook
AUTHOR2:	Britt, Steuart H. 1902–
PLACE PUB:	Chicago, Ill
PUBLISHER:	Dartnell Corp.
YR PUB:	1983
CALL NO:	658.8 DAR
ISBN:	0850131359
SUBJ:	1. Marketing–Management
	2. Marketing–Handbooks, Manuals, Etc.
NOTES:	Phys Desc: 1293 P.: Ill; 23 CM. Series: Dartnell Handbooks Title Var: Marketing Manager's Handbook

ACCESSION:	94630
TITLE:	Medical Detectives
AUTHOR:	Roueche, Berton, 1911–
PLACE PUB:	New York, NY
PUBLISHER:	NY Times Books
YR PUB:	1980
CALL NO:	610.926 ROU
ISBN:	0812909208
SUBJ:	1. Epidemiology–Case Studies
	2. Medicine–Case Studies
NOTES:	Phys Desc: 372 P.: 24 CM.

ACCESSION:	97220
TITLE:	Great Cases of Scotland Yard
AUTHOR2:	Readers Digest Assn.
PLACE PUB:	Pleasantville, NY
PUBLISHER:	Readers Digest Assn.
YR PUB:	1978
CALL NO:	345.421 GRE
ISBN:	0895770539
SUBJ:	1. GT Britain–Metropolitan Police–CID
	2. Crime and Criminals–GT Britain–Case Studies
	3. Criminal Investigation–GT Britain–Case Studies
NOTES:	Phys Desc: 690 P. (5) Leaves of Plates: Ill; 24 CM 1st Edition

ACCESSION:	30679
TITLE:	Seven Gothic Tales

LIST OF BOOKS *(continued)*

AUTHOR:	Dinesen, Isak
PLACE PUB:	New York, NY
PUBLISHER:	Modern Library
YR PUB:	1961
CALL NO:	F FIN
NOTES:	Copyright: 1934
	Phys Desc: 420 P. Ill.; 20 CM
	Contents: The Deluge at Norderney–The Old Chevalier–The Monkey–The Roads Round Pisa–The Supper at Elsinore–The Dreamers–The Poets.

ACCESSION:	293800
TITLE:	Hard Times
AUTHOR:	Dickens, Charles
PLACE PUB:	London, GB
PUBLISHER:	Collins
YR PUB:	1959
CALL NO:	F DIC
NOTES:	Phys Desc: 288 P. Port.
	Series: Collins Classics

ACCESSION:	174548
TITLE:	Big Cats
AUTHOR:	Simon, Seymour
PLACE PUB:	New York, NY
PUBLISHER:	Harper Collins
YR PUB:	1991
CALL NO:	J 599.744 SIM
ISBN:	0060216476
SUBJ:	1. Felidae–Juvenile Literature
	2. Cats
	3. Bluebonnet Book–1992–1993
NOTES:	Phys Desc: 40 P. Col. Ill.; 24X29 CM

ACCESSION:	78MAR1213
TITLE:	East O' The Sun and West O' The Moon
SUBTITLE:	Norwegian Folk Tales
AUTHOR:	Asbjornsen
PLACE PUB:	Garden City, NY
PUBLISHER:	Nelson Doubleday
YR PUB:	1957
NOTES:	Phys Desc: 288 P. Ill.; 22CM.
	Edition: Junior Deluxe Edition

LIST OF BOOKS *(continued)*

ACCESSION: 15763
TITLE: Stinky Cheese Man and Other Fairly Stupid
                Tales
AUTHOR: Scieszka, Jon
AUTHOR2:   Smith, Lane
PLACE PUB: New York, NY
PUBLISHER: Viking
YR PUB: 1992
CALL NO: J F SCI
ISBN: 067084487X
SUBJ: 1. Fairy Tales–United States
                2. Children's Stories, American
                3. Bluebonnet Book–1994–95
NOTES: Phys Desc: 1 V. (Unpaged); Col. Ill.; 28 CM

ACCESSION: 150557
TITLE: Best Books for Children,
                Preschool Through Gr. 6
AUTHOR: Gillespie, John Thomas
AUTHOR2:   Naden, Corrine J.
PLACE PUB: New York, NY
PUBLISHER: R. R. Bowker
YR PUB: 1990
CALL NO: J REF 011.62 GIL
ISBN: 0835226689
SUBJ: 1. Bibliography–Best Books–Children's
                2. Children's Literature–Bibliography
                3. Libraries, Children's–Book List
NOTES: Phys Desc: 1002 P.
                Edition: 4th Edition

ACCESSION: 87927
TITLE: Scholarships, Fellowships, and Loans
SUBTITLE: A Guide to Education–Related Financial Aid
                Programs
PLACE PUB: Detroit, MI
PUBLISHER: Gale Research
YR PUB: 1992
CALL NO: REF 378.3
SUBJ: 1. Scholarships–United States–Directories
                2. Student Loan Funds–United States–Di-
                   rectories
                3. College Costs–United States
NOTES: Edition: 9th Edition, First Gale Edition

Figure 4.3 shows the Datasheet View of the table with records entered. The fields not showing in the screen can be viewed by using the scroll bars at the bottom of the screen. The arrows at the bottom left of the screen are used to move the cursor among the records, one record at a time, or to the beginning or end of the set of records.

Figure 4.3 Datasheet View of Records Entered

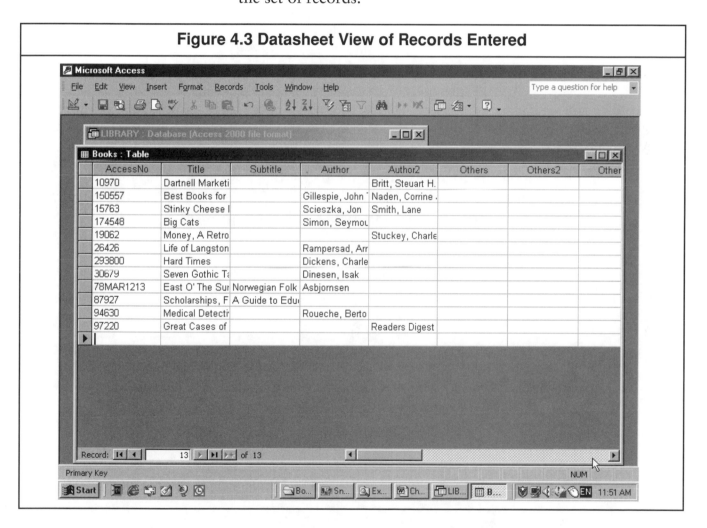

4.2 DELETING RECORDS

After entering these twelve books, you notice the book *East O' The Sun and West O' The Moon* has an accession number that does not follow the pattern of the accession numbers in your library and actually belongs to another library. Since the **Books** table is already in Datasheet View, you are now ready to edit the table of records.

You only have a few records entered at this point, so it will be easy to just browse through the records until you find the one you want. The record you are going to delete contains the information about the book *East O' The Sun and West O' The Moon*. Delete this record by following these steps:

1. Click on this record
2. Click on **Edit** in the menu list. Click on **Select Record** to highlight it (see Figure 4.4).

Figure 4.4 Edit Selected Records

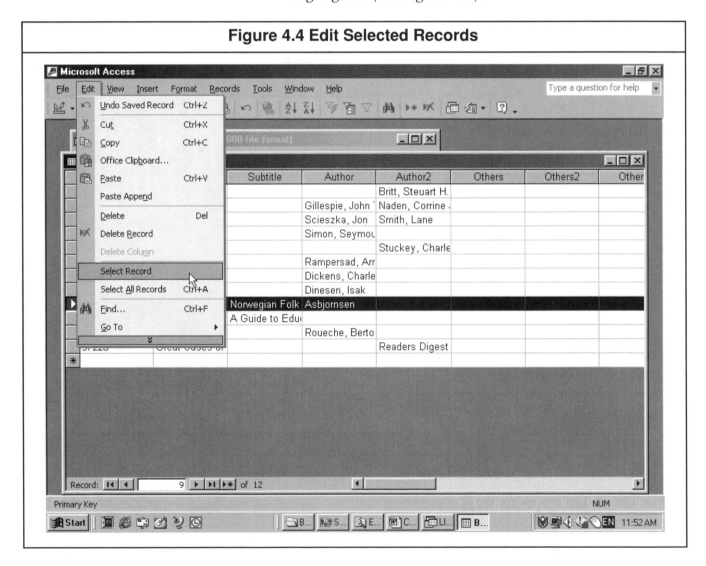

3. Press the <Delete> key on your keyboard.

Access displays a message screen asking you to confirm that you want to delete this record of group of records.

4. Click **OK**.

Notice that the record immediately disappears (see Figure 4.5).

Figure 4.5 Deleted Record Datasheet View

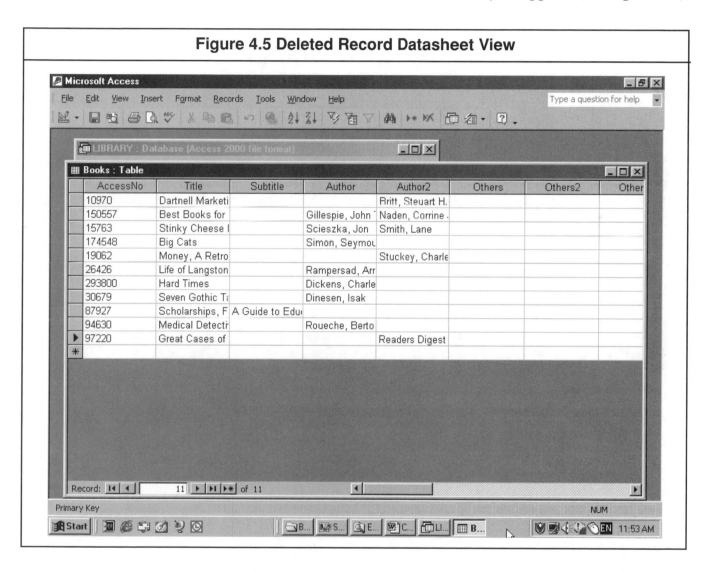

4.3 FINDING RECORDS

Later in this manual, you will be working with ways to manipulate the checkout or circulation records in your library. Use the **Find** feature on the Table Datasheet toolbar to locate book records and enter user numbers in the UserNo field, "Y" in the Checkout field, and dates in the DateCheck field.

1. Click in the **AccessNo** field in the first record to indicate that this is where you want Access to search for the indicated information.
2. Click on the **Find Records** dialog box (see Figure 4.6).

Figure 4.6 Find Records Dialog Box

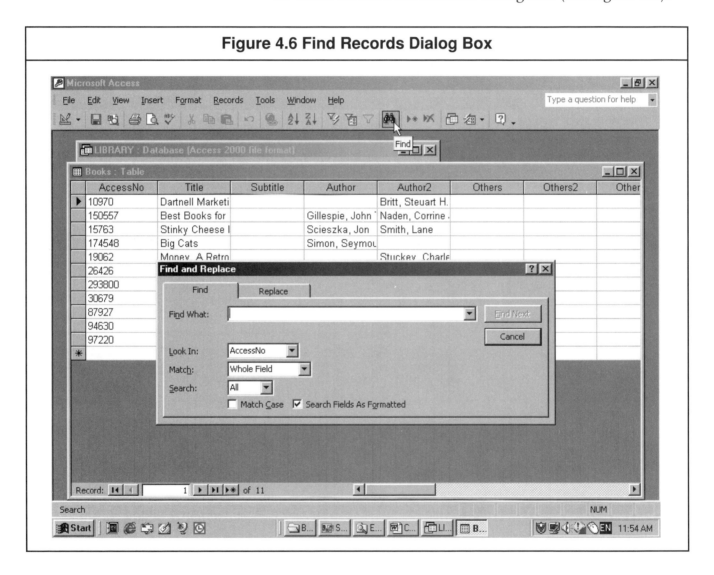

3. Type "150557" in the **Find What** box (without the parenthesis).
4. In **Match** select **Whole Field** if it is not already selected.
5. Select **All** from the **Search** box if it is not already selected.
6. Click on the **Find Next** button. Access immediately locates the record requested, and highlights the **AccessNO** for record number 150557 (see Figure 4.7).

Figure 4.7 Find Records

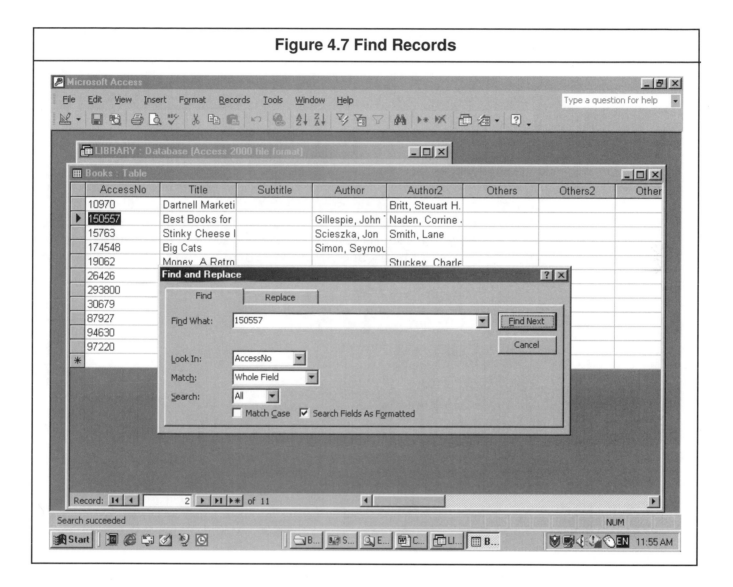

7. Close the **Find Records** dialog box.
8. Scroll across and enter the selected record to the **Checkout** field. Click in the **Checkout** box to place a check mark in the selected box.
9. Enter "35986" in the **UserNo** field.
10. Enter "4/03/95" in the **DateDue** field.

Repeat steps 1 through 10 to find the following records and enter the following information (remember to click in the **Checkout** box for each record listed below):

ACCESSNO	USERNO	DATEDUE
30679	74624	03/30/95
97220	46873	03/27/95
10970	87234	03/31/95
19062	74624	01/24/95

11. Close the **Books** table.

This chapter has covered entering records, deleting records, and finding records using Access. You are now prepared to do further manipulations of your data such as sorting records, filtering, selection criteria, and complicated sorts. These procedures can simplify library operations by providing the tools to manage and display the data in the records in a variety of ways. The next chapter will cover sorting your records, including filtering, selection criteria, and complicated sorts.

5 SORTING AND FILTERING

OBJECTIVES

5.1   SORTING RECORDS
5.2   FILTERING
5.3   SELECTION CRITERIA
5.4   COMPLICATED SORT

Sorting and filtering are two different methods of putting records in a particular order. Each method has its advantages and disadvantages. Sorting allows you only to sort all the data in a particular table. Filtering allows you to exclude information in the table. Both methods allow only temporary changes.

5.1 SORTING RECORDS

Before we begin with the sort function, we will add records to the **Library Users** table. Open the **Library Users** table (see Chapter 3, "Tables," for instructions). Enter the following records in the **Library Users** table:

CUSTOMER ID:	39876
FIRSTNAME:	William
LASTNAME:	Burton
ADDRESS:	692 Redbird Ave #2
CITY:	Manchester
STATE:	KY
POSTAL CODE:	40477
CUSTOMER ID:	35986
FIRSTNAME:	Elizabeth
LASTNAME:	Burton
ADDRESS:	692 Redbird Ave #2
CITY:	Manchester
STATE:	KY
POSTAL CODE:	40477
CUSTOMER ID:	74624
FIRSTNAME:	Bonnie
LASTNAME:	Burton

ADDRESS:	692 Redbird Ave #2
CITY:	Manchester
STATE:	KY
POSTAL CODE:	40477
CUSTOMER ID:	46873
FIRSTNAME:	Thelma
LASTNAME:	Thompson
ADDRESS:	2515 Magnolia Ct.
CITY:	Coalmine
STATE:	KY
POSTAL CODE:	40798
CUSTOMER ID:	56734
FIRSTNAME:	Trace
LASTNAME:	Crow
ADDRESS:	249 Moonbeem Dr.
CITY:	Coalmine
STATE:	KY
POSTAL CODE:	40798
CUSTOMER ID:	87905
FIRSTNAME:	Herman
LASTNAME:	Helminth
ADDRESS:	5629 Hunsdale St.
CITY:	Corbin
STATE:	KY
POSTAL CODE:	40879
CUSTOMER ID:	87234
FIRSTNAME:	Blanche
LASTNAME:	White
ADDRESS:	984 Blanco Ln.
CITY:	Corbin
STATE:	KY
POSTAL CODE:	40879
CUSTOMER ID:	56498
FIRSTNAME:	Bobbie
LASTNAME:	Crow
ADDRESS:	456 Mainstay St.
CITY:	Danville
STATE:	KY
POSTAL CODE:	79823

There are several reasons why a library would want a list of library users sorted according to where they live. For example, the library might be considering a new location for a branch and the management of the library might want to consider only those areas that have current library users. Or perhaps the library is planning special events to be held in different user areas.

To sort the records in the **Library Users** table by **Postal Code,** follow the directions below (the table should still be open since we just added records to it):

1. Move the cursor to the top of the **Postal Code** field. The cursor should change to a down pointing arrow. Click the field name **Postal Code,** which will select the entire field (see Figure 5.1).

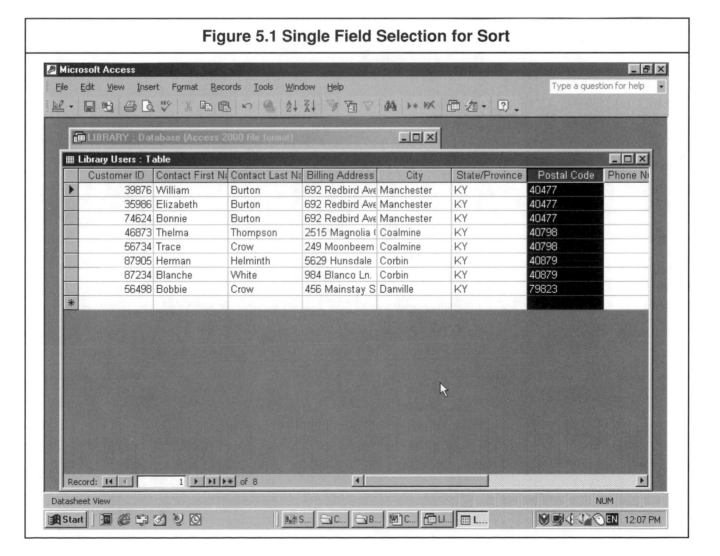

Figure 5.1 Single Field Selection for Sort

2. Click the Sort Ascending button on the Table Datasheet toolbar. The records are now arranged in numerical order according to their ZIP code (see Figure 5.2).

Figure 5.2 Sorted Records

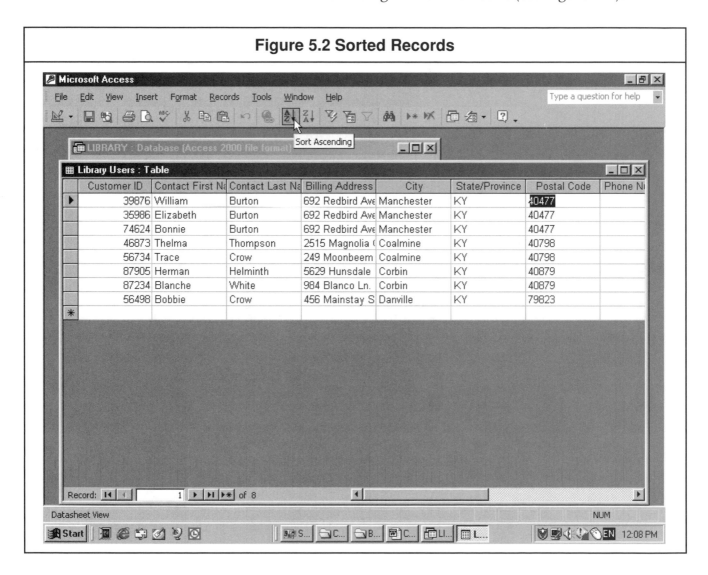

The sort shows Postal Codes in numerical order. Notice that the Postal Codes with the same number are not sorted in any particular order such as alphabetically by first name.

Now suppose we want to sort the records by last name and then by first name. Anytime a sort is done in an Access table, it is performed from the left to the right. For example, if we wanted to sort by last name and then by first name, we would have to move the **Last Name** field to the left of the **First Name** field.

3. Click on the column heading for the **Last Name** field so that the entire column is highlighted, and then release the mouse button. Then click on the **Last Name** column and drag the column to the left of the **First Name** column heading. You should see a vertical placement bar that shows where the **Last Name** column will now be placed (see Figure 5.3).

Figure 5.3 Moving Fields Within a Table

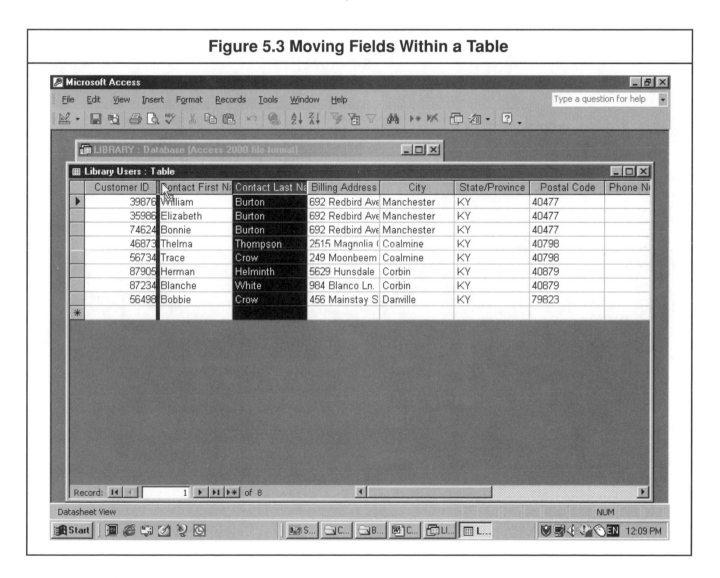

4. Click on the **First Name** column heading and move the mouse over to the **Last Name** column heading (without releasing the mouse button). You now have both columns selected and you are ready to sort (see Figure 5.4).

Figure 5.4 Multiple Field Selection for Sort

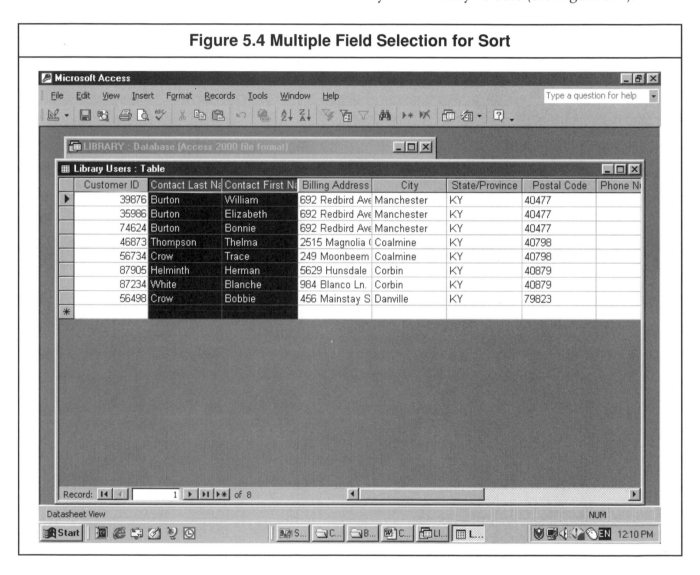

5. Click **Records,** then **Sort,** then **Sort Ascending** (see Figure 5.5).

Figure 5.5 Sorting on Multiple Fields

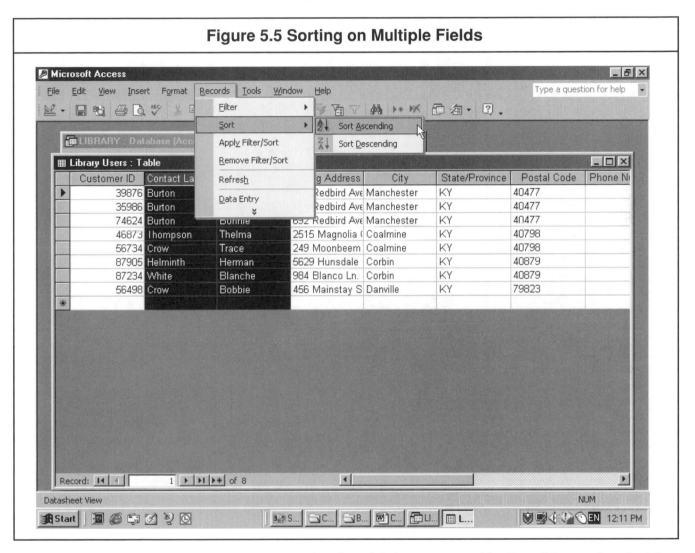

6. Notice the table is now sorted by **Last Name,** then by **First Name** (see Figure 5.6).

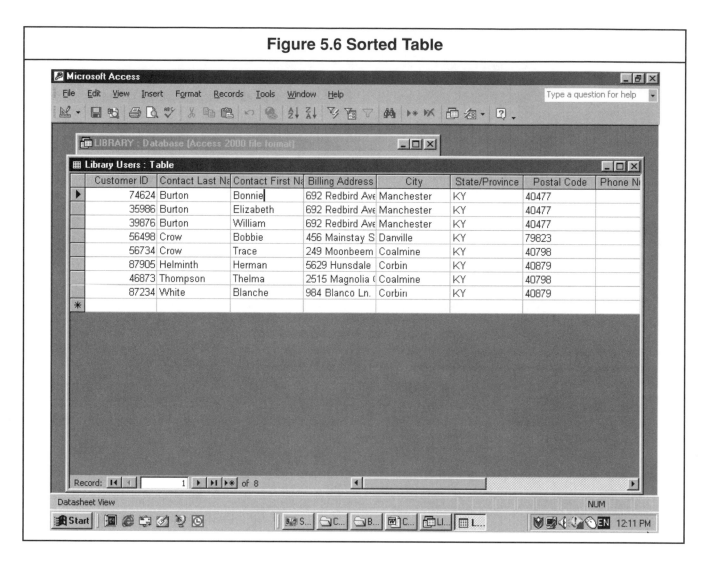

Figure 5.6 Sorted Table

Close the **Library Users** table.

5.2 FILTERING

Filtering allows you to sort the data and view only the desired records. For example, this function would be useful if the library wanted to see exactly how many users have checked out books. Keep in mind that filtering is only temporary and cannot be saved with the table. To filter the records so only the users that have checked out books are shown, follow the steps below.

1. Open the **Books** table.

Locate the **Checkout** field. Since this is a yes/no field we cannot click in this field to select a value because it will change the value of yes or no for a particular record. Since we are looking for library users who have checked out books, however, we can right click in the **Checkout** field for any record where a user has checked out a book.

2. Right click in the first record. Checkout should have a value of yes which means that this box has a check mark (see Figure 5.7).

Figure 5.7 Filtering Records Based on a Single Field Value

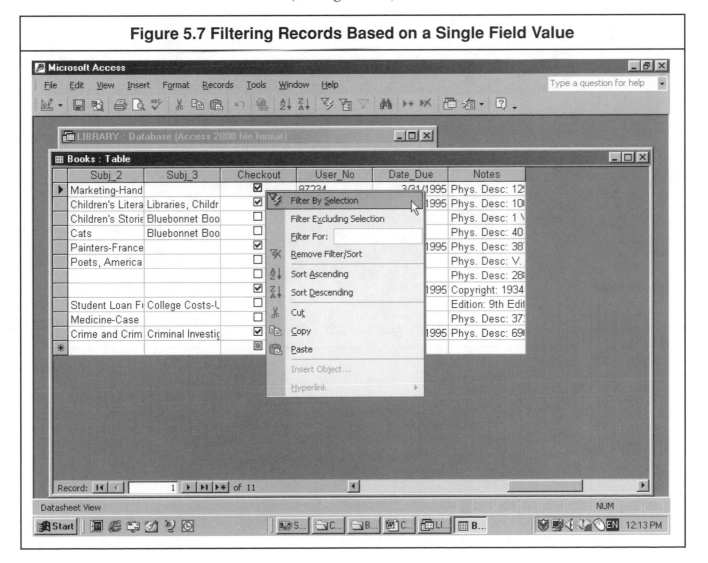

3. Click **Filter By Selection** (see Figure 5.8).

Figure 5.8 Filtered Records

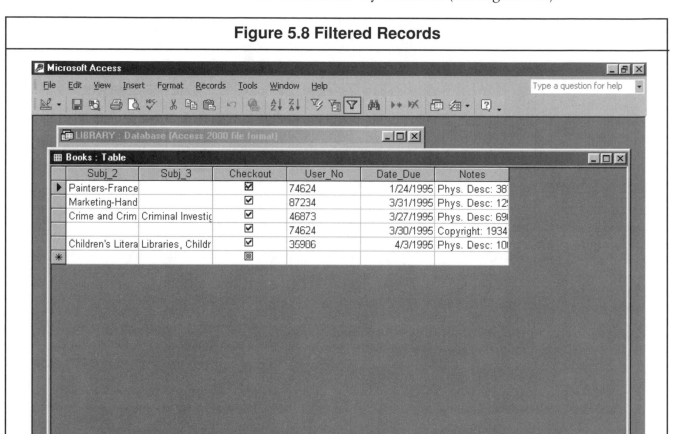

4. To show all of the records again, click the **Remove Filter** button on the **Table Datasheet** toolbar (see Figure 5.9).

Figure 5.9 Remove Filter

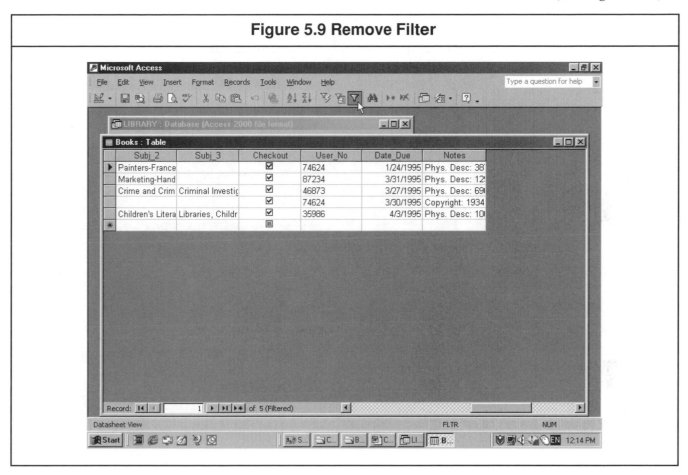

5. Close the **Books** table.

Now that we have removed the filter, all of the records should appear in the table. We are now ready to perform an advanced filter using selection criteria.

5.3 SELECTION CRITERIA

Understanding the filter criteria will help the user to create a filter containing only the required information. You can sort data by a value or a range of values. Using the chart below will assist in determining how to enter the criteria.

INPUTS	DESCRIPTION
=	Equal to
<>	Not equal to
>	Greater than
<	Less than
>=	Greater than or equal to
<=	Less than or equal to
Between...And	Between two specified values
Is Null	Doesn't contain data
Like	Matches a pattern containing wildcard characters

Using the table as a guide for the criteria of the filter, you can obtain exactly the information you require. For example, if you want only the people who checked out books on March 25, 1996, in the criteria field, you would type "=3/25/1996" (without the parenthesis).

5.4 COMPLICATED SORT

This sort will demonstrate how to utilize sorting criteria while sorting. Here we want to show only those records who live in Manchester and have User numbers greater than 40000.

1. Open the **Library Users** table (see 5.10).

Figure 5.10 Library Users Table

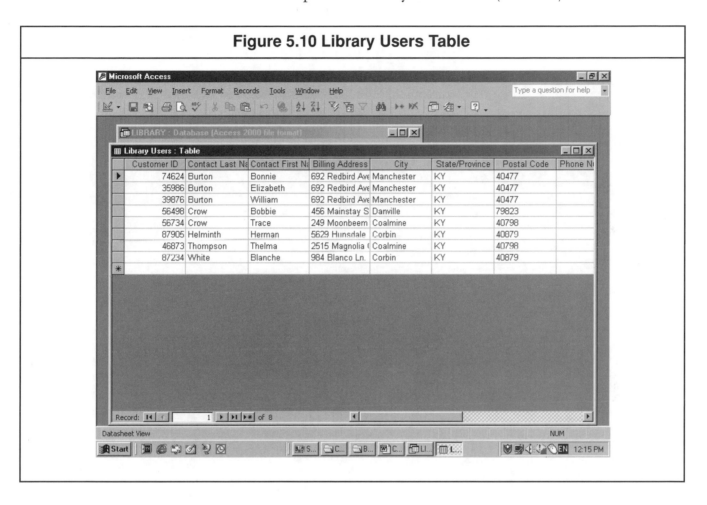

2. Click **Records**, then **Filter**, then **Advanced Filter/Sort** (see Figure 5.11).

Figure 5.11 Advanced Filter/Sort

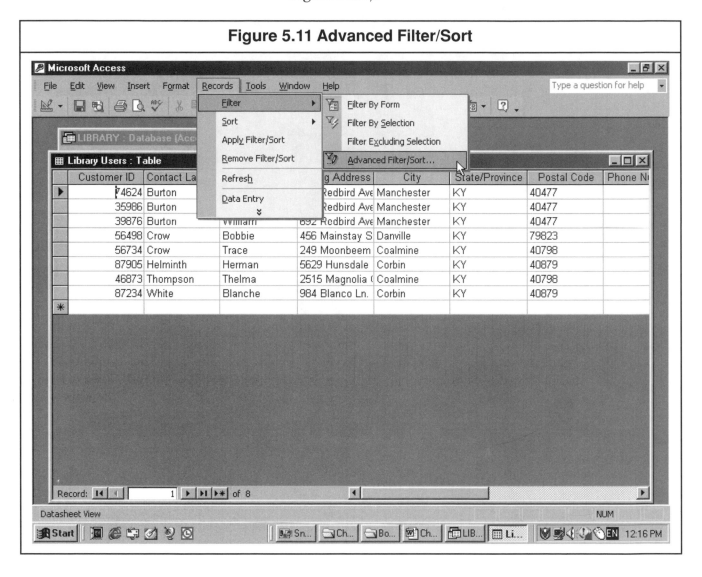

3. You should now see the Advanced Filter/Sort window (see Figure 5.12).

Figure 5.12 Advanced Filter/Sort Window

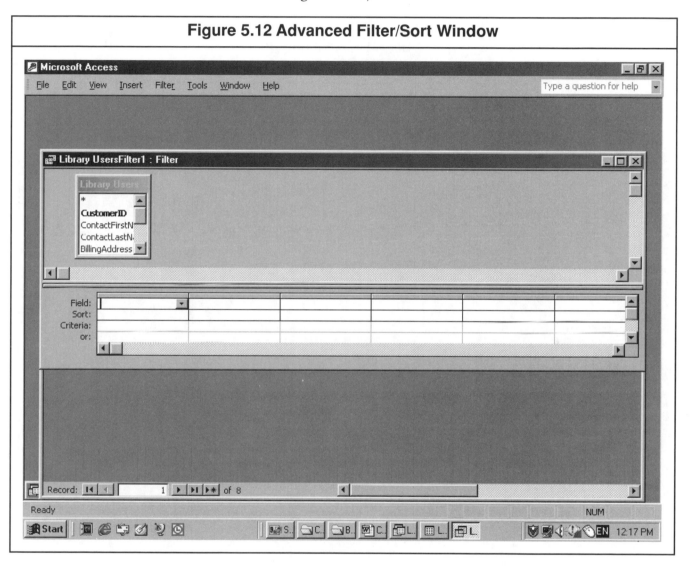

4. Double click on **CustomerID** in the **Library Users** field list. **CustomerID** will appear in the selected fields list. Now double click on **FirstName, LastName,** and **City.** You may have to scroll to see these fields. You have selected the fields to be used in our sort (see Figure 5.13).

Figure 5.13 Selected Fields to be Used in Sort

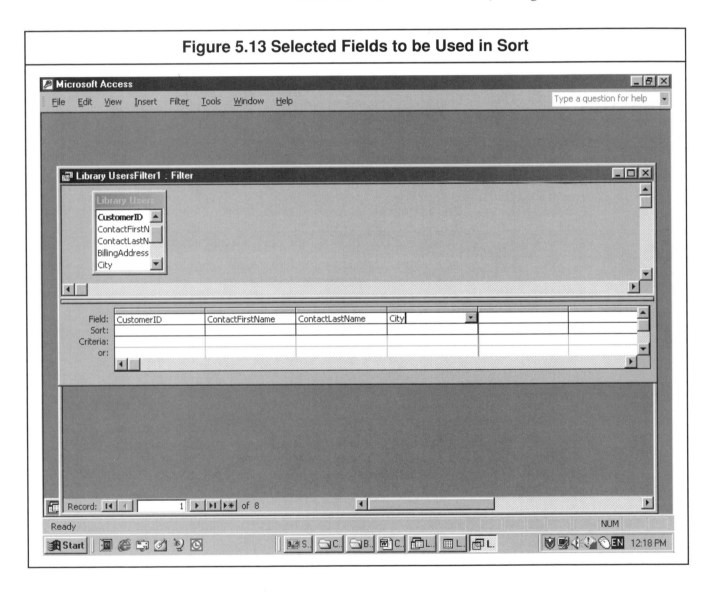

5. To create the sort with the criteria of only those individuals in Manchester, click **Criteria** under **City**, then type "Manchester" (without the parenthesis).
6. In order to include only those people in Manchester with **CustomerID** numbers greater than 40000, click **Criteria** under **CustomerID** and type ">40000" (without the parenthesis) (see Figure 5.14).

Figure 5.14 Criteria for Multiple Field Sort

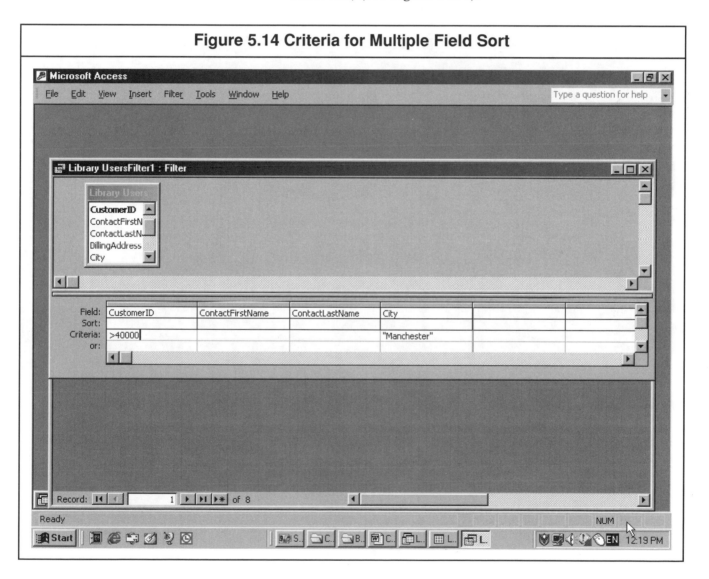

7. Click on the **Apply Filter** (see Figure 5.15).

Figure 5.15 Apply Filter

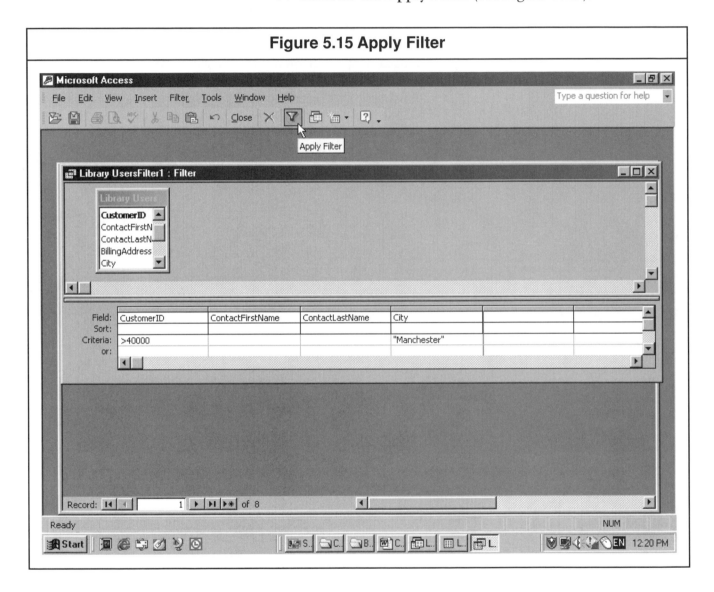

This sort shows only those individuals in Manchester whose CustomerID numbers are greater than 40000. There was only one customer meeting these criteria (see Figure 5.16).

Figure 5.16 Results of Sort

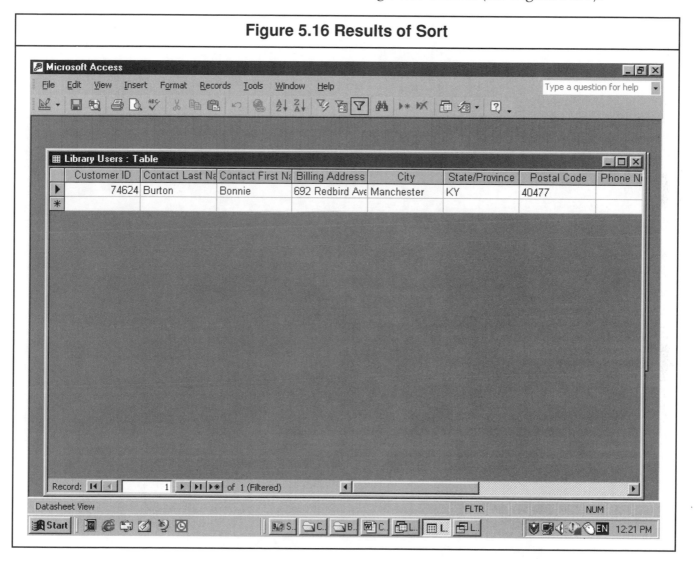

Filtering is used when the selection is needed temporarily. When more permanent data manipulations are needed, queries (discussed in Chapter 6) offer yet another way to extract information from your database.

Sorting can accomplish many different things. Every field in the database can be sorted for ease of use. One of the primary purposes of database management systems is to retrieve information in ways that are the most useful to the users of the system. In the next chapter we will discuss how to set up a query to retrieve information.

6 QUERIES

OBJECTIVES

6.1 CREATE A QUERY
6.2 A SIMPLE QUERY
6.3 COMPLEX QUERY
6.4 MODIFYING AND RENAMING A QUERY

In Chapter 4 we used the Find command to search for a single record. In Chapter 6 we will use a query to search for a single record or multiple records that meet a single criterion or multiple criteria. A query allows you to display a group of records that meet the specified search parameters and also certain fields within those records.

The query function compares each record to the conditions specified in the query. When a query has been designed for a specific purpose, such as an author search, you can save it and use it again for other author searches. You can also use a query to create a report. A query can be used as a one time gathering of information for an individual report, or a query can be used regularly for continual reports.

In previous chapters, you worked with tables and forms to locate specified records. Queries allow you to work with one table or multiple tables to retrieve the necessary records and their respective information. In this chapter we will create Select Queries to retrieve information about library users and library books.

6.1 CREATE A QUERY

Create a new query the same way you would create any other item, for example a table.

1. Open Access.

2. Open the **LIBRARY.mdb** database (see Figure 6.1).

Figure 6.1 The LIBRARY.mdb Database

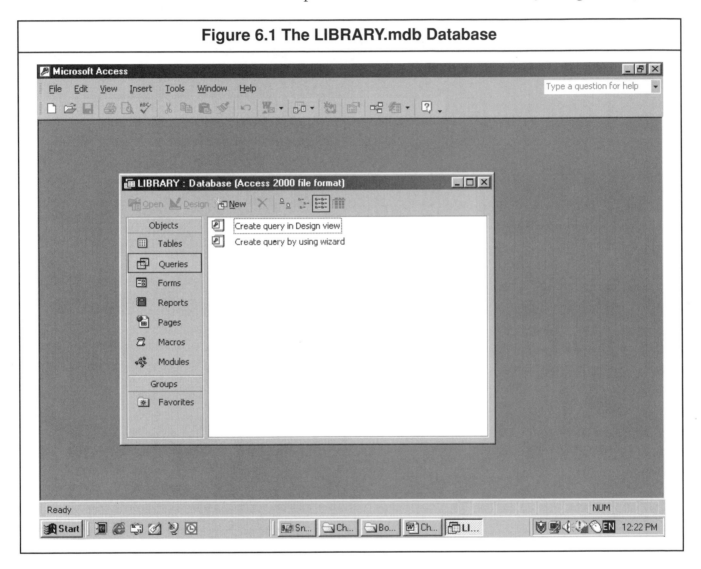

3. Click **Queries** under the Objects menu. There should not be any existing queries in the query display window.
4. Click **New**. The **New Query** window now displays (see Figure 6.2).

Figure 6.2 New Query Window

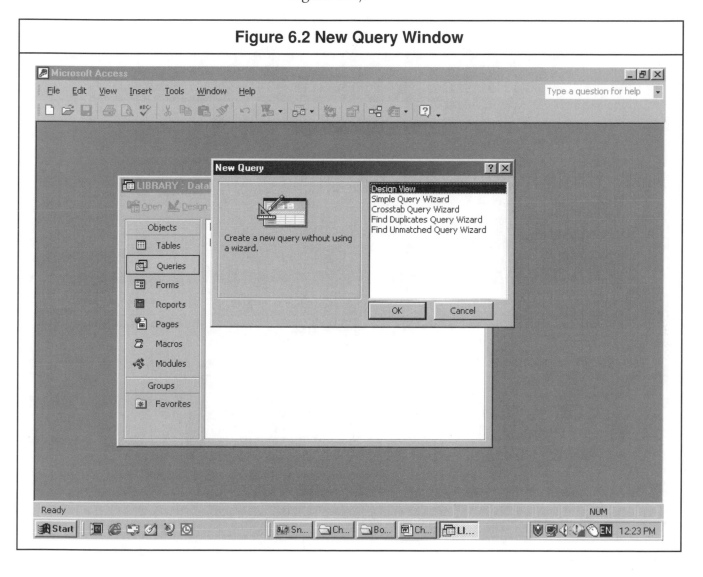

5. Select **Design View** if it is not already selected. Click on the **OK** button and the **Select Query** window should appear (see Figure 6.3).

Figure 6.3 Select Query Window

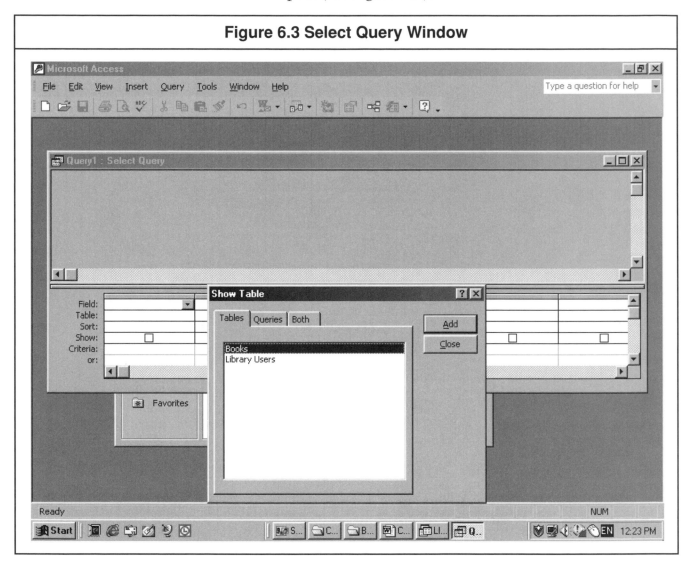

You are asked which table you want to include in the query.

6. Double click on the **Library Users** table.
7. Click the **Close** button on the **Show Tables** window. You should now have the Select Query design grid open with the **Library Users** table fields displayed (see Figure 6.4).

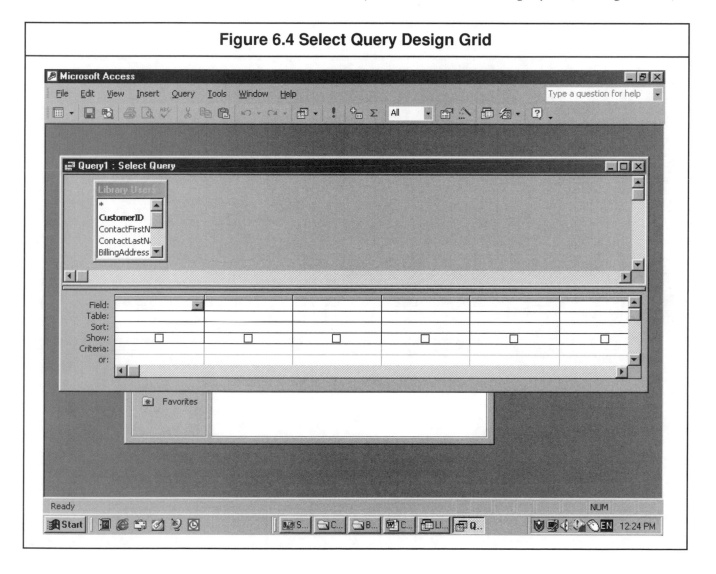

Figure 6.4 Select Query Design Grid

Now we can select which field we want to use in our query. We can also specify search parameters to use in our search.

8. Double click the **ContactLastName** field in the table field list. The **ContactLastName** field now appears in the field list in the grid below (see Figure 6.5).

Figure 6.5 Selected Field in Field List

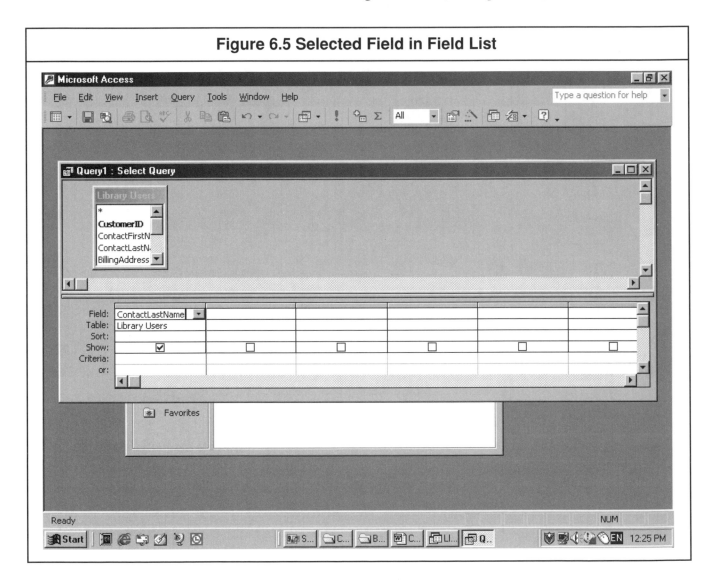

9. Double click the following fields in the table field list to add them to the field list in the grid: **ContactFirstName**, **BillingAddress**, **City**, and **StateorProvince** (see Figure 6.6).

Figure 6.6 Multiple Fields in Field List

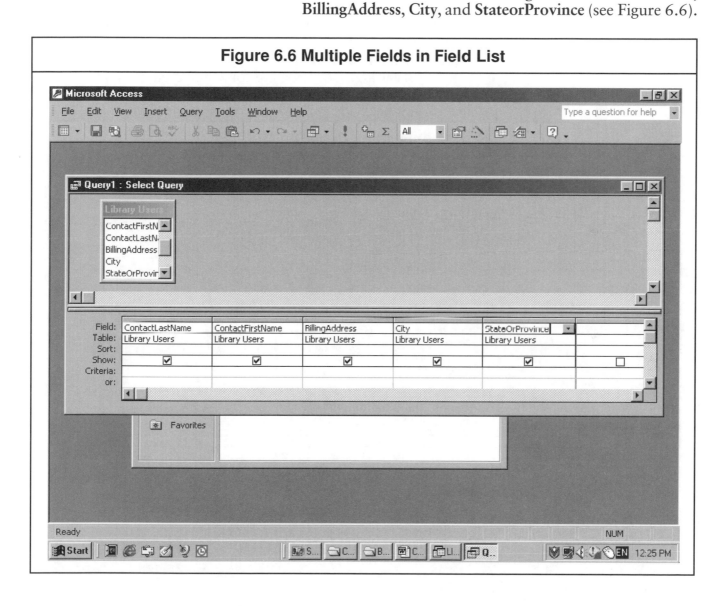

We can also sort the records that are returned from our query. In this example we are going to sort by last name and then by first name. We will also create a search condition to return only those records where the user lives in Manchester.

10. Click on the **Sort** box below **ContactLastName** and select **Ascending**. Do the same for **ContactFirstName** (see Figure 6.7).

Figure 6.7 Sort in Ascending Order on Multiple Fields

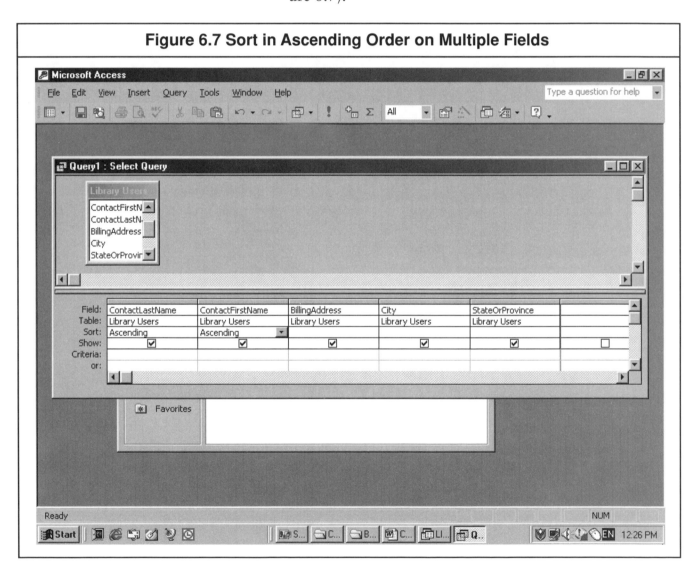

11. Click on the **Criteria** box under **City.** Type "**Manchester**" with or without the parenthesis (see Figure 6.8).

Figure 6.8 Criteria Specified

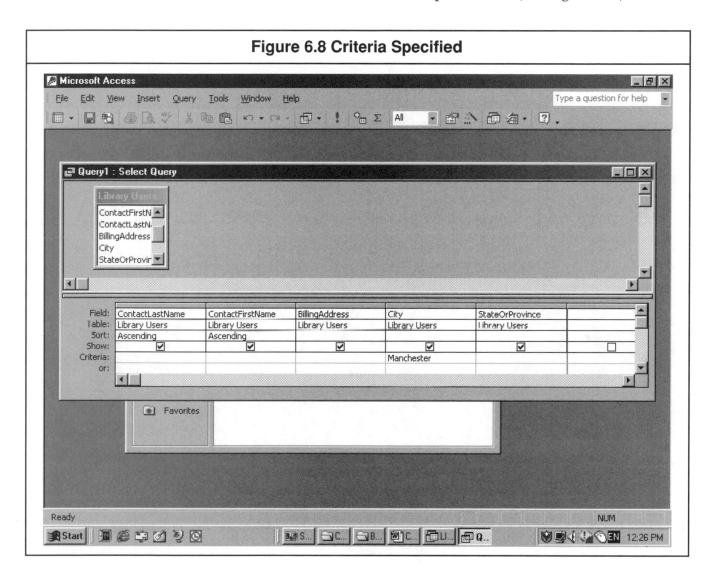

Now we are ready to run the query and see the results of the search on the selected table.

12. Click the **Run** button on the Query Design toolbar. Your search should have returned three records (see Figure 6.9).

Figure 6.9 Results of Query

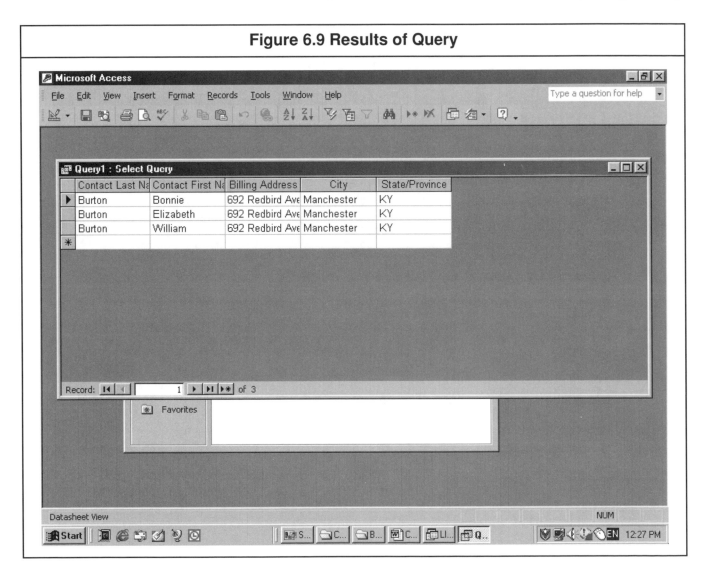

13. Click **File** on the menu bar, then click **Save As.** Name the query **Manchester** (see Figure 6.10).

Figure 6.10 Saving the Query

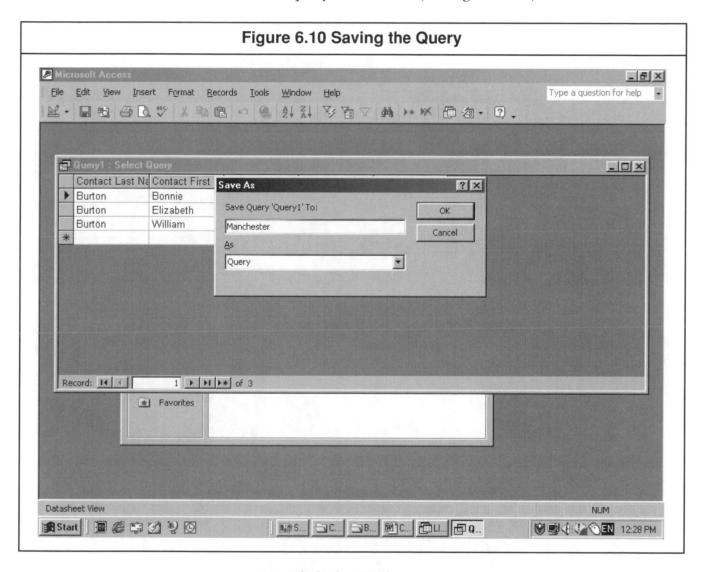

14. Click the **OK** button.
15. Close the query by clicking on **File** and then **Close.** This takes you back to the Database window.

6.2 A SIMPLE QUERY

1. Make sure the **LIBRARY.mdb** database is still open and the **Queries** object button is selected.
2. Click **New**, then **Design View** (see Figures 6.11 and 6.12).

Figure 6.11 Create Query

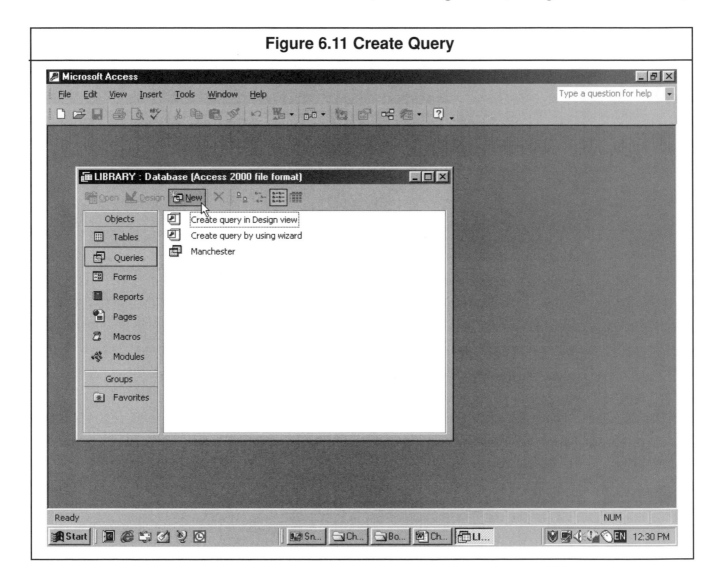

Figure 6.12 New Query

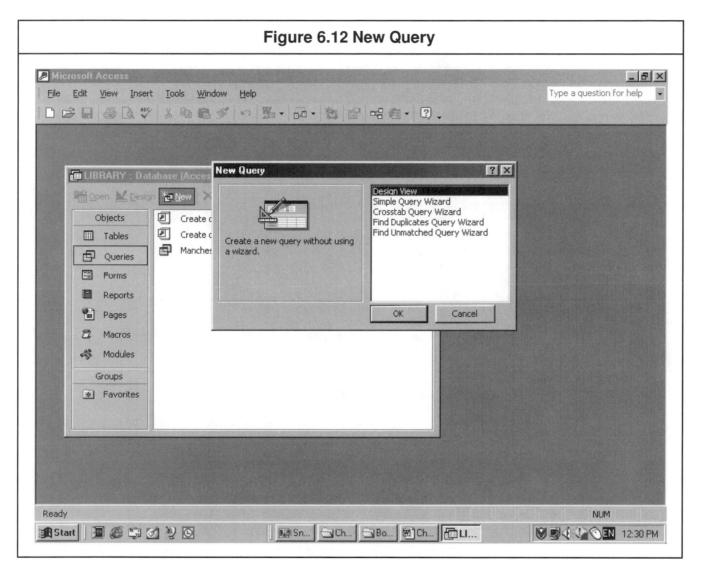

3. Click the **OK** button.

4. Click the **Books** table, then click the **Add** button (see Figure 6.13).

Figure 6.13 Query Table Select

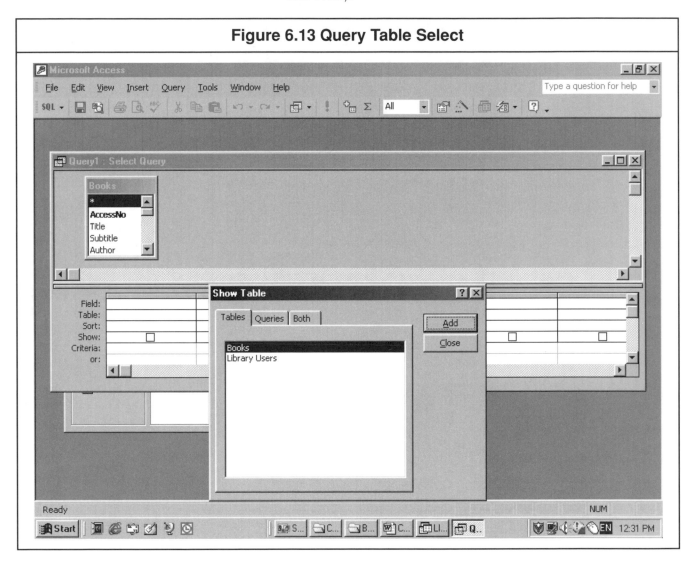

---

5. Click the **Close** button to close the Show Table box.

6. Double click the following fields in the field list: **Title,
Author, CallNo,** and **Checkout.** Under **Checkout** enter
"Yes" in the Criteria box (see Figure 6.14).

Figure 6.14 Select Query

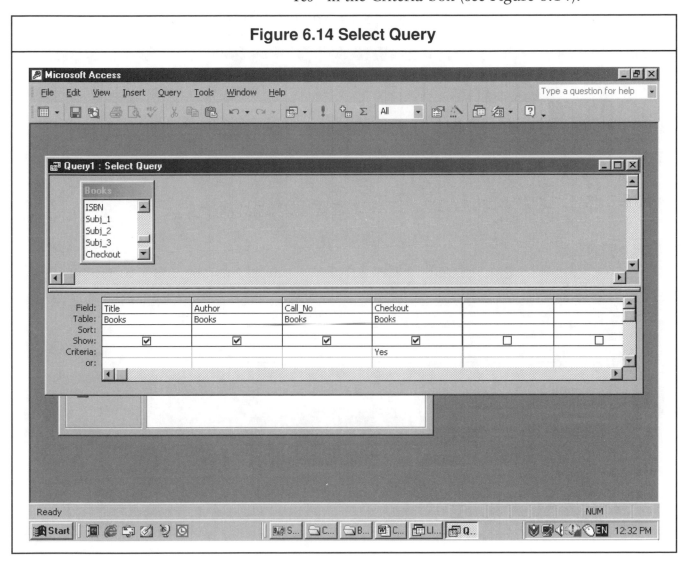

7. Under **Title,** click on **Sort,** and select **Ascending** (see Figure 6.15).

Figure 6.15 Ascending Sort

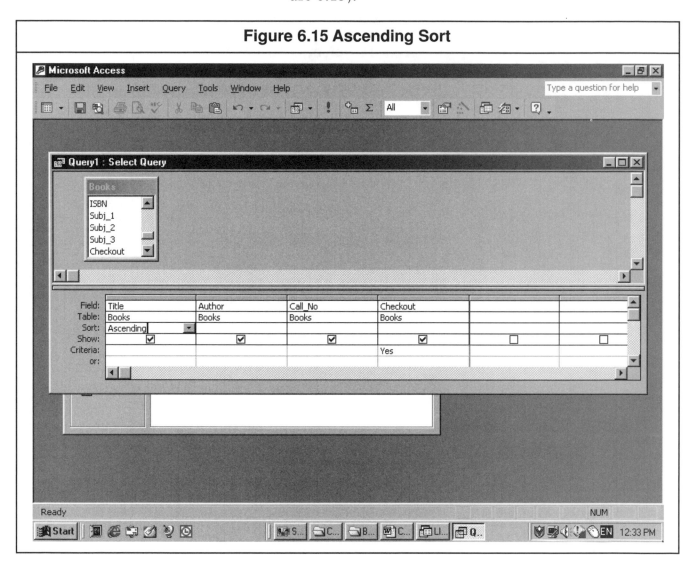

8. Click the **Run** button to display the results of the query (see Figure 6.16).

Figure 6.16 Query Results

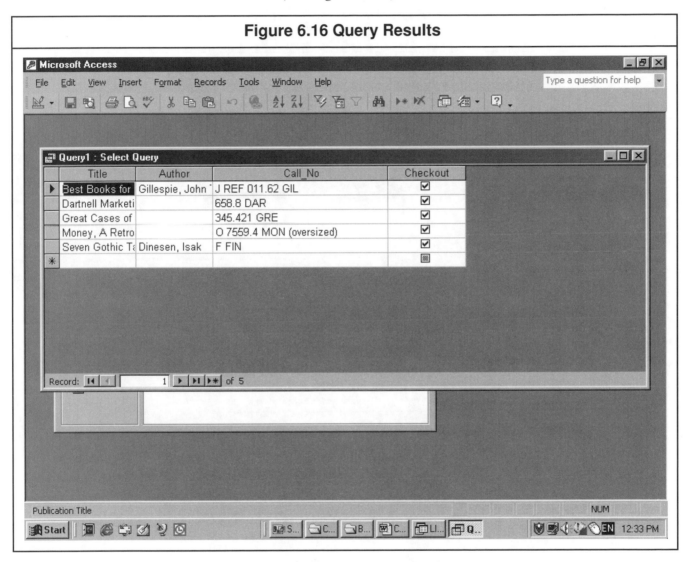

9. Click the **Design** button, and add an additional condition to the query.

10. Double click on **DateDue** from the field list. Under
    DateDue enter "1/24/95" in the criteria box. This will dis-
    play only those books that are due on that particular date
    (see Figure 6.17).

Figure 6.17 Updated Query

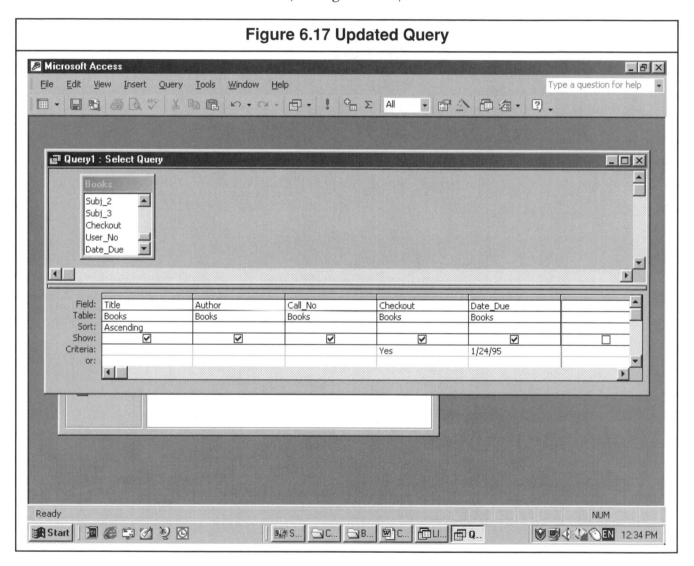

11. Run the query. There should only be one book with a due date of 1/24/95 (see Figure 6.18).

Figure 6.18 Due Date Query Results

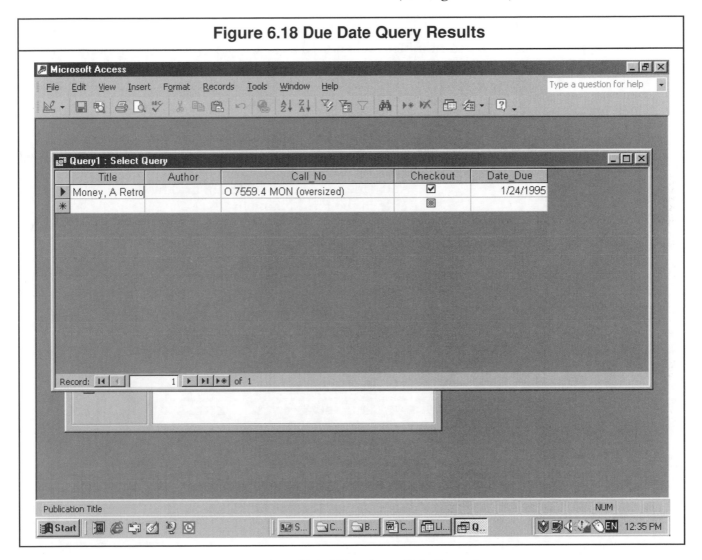

12. Click **File**, then click **Save As**.
13. Type "OverDue" as the file name, then click the **OK** button.
14. Close the query.

6.3 COMPLEX QUERY

We usually think of logical or mathematical concepts as applying to numbers. When used as a comparison (or relational) operator, however, they also can be used with character fields. Ascending order is A through Z, so B is greater than A. The following is an example of B being greater than A.

1. Create a new query (click **Queries, New,** and **OK**).
2. Click on the **Books** table, click **Add** and close the **Show Table** window.
3. Add Title to the Query Design grid by double-clicking on **Title** in the **Field Name** list.
4. Enter "<B" (without parenthesis) in the criteria field for Title box (see Figure 6.19).

Figure 6.19 Entering Criteria

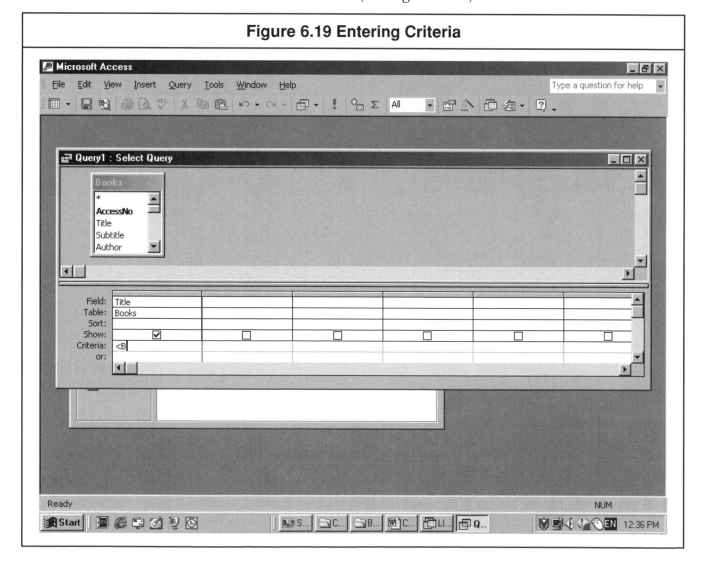

5. Click the **Run** button to display the query. Since there are no books with the title beginning with A, the query was empty (see Figure 6.20).

Figure 6.20 Query Results

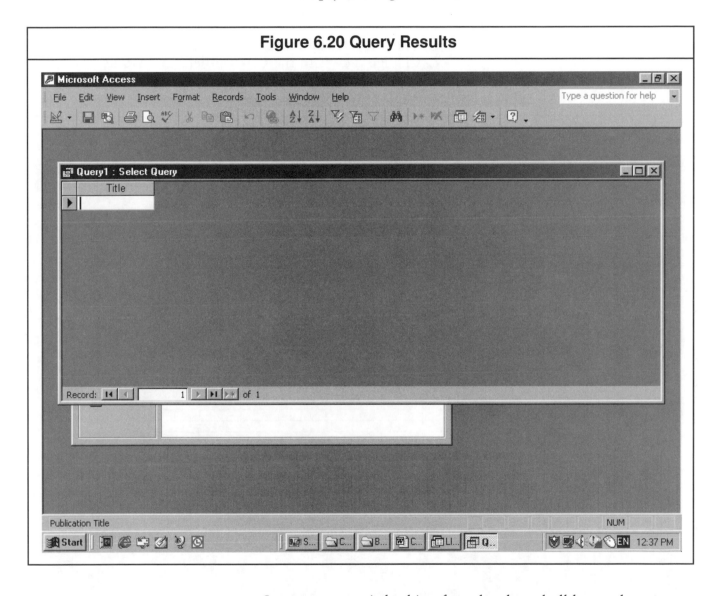

Suppose a user is looking for a book and all he or she remembers is that it is about Monet's paintings. He or she knows that the title contains the word "Monet." He or she can search the table of books by creating a search condition that will find only those books with "Monet" in the title. Since the user is not certain if Monet is the first word in the title, the last word, or any other word, he or she will have to use a wildcard character in the search.

The asterisk wildcard character allows you to search for records when you are not sure of the exact spelling of the specific data of a particular field. The asterisk wildcard character represents any letter, number, symbol, space, or nothing at all.

6. Click the **Design** button.
7. Change the **<B** in the Criteria field to ***Monet*** (see Figure 6.21).

Figure 6.21 Query Results Using Wildcard Character

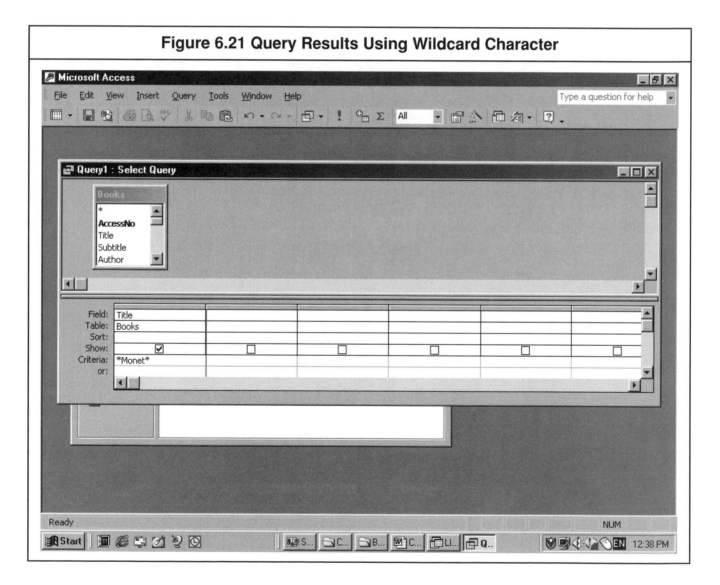

8. To complete the query, add the following fields: **Publisher,** **CallNo,** and **ISBN** (see Figure 6.22).

Figure 6.22 Query with Wildcard Character

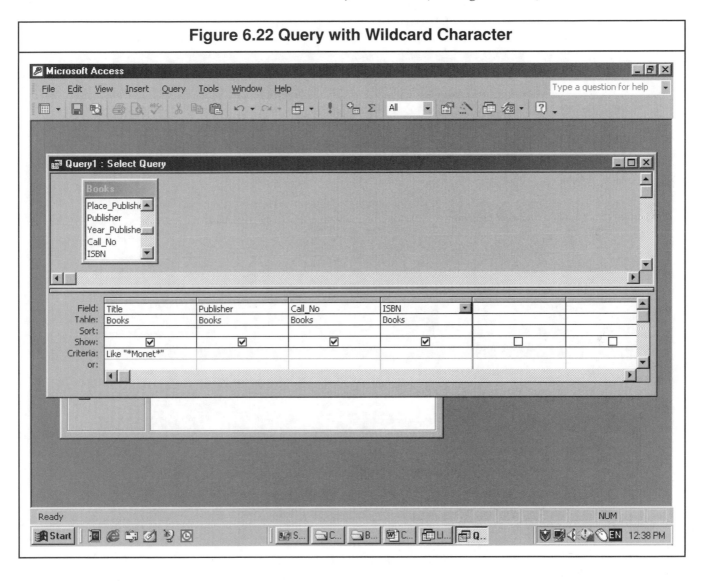

9. Click **Run** to execute the query (see Figure 6.23).

Figure 6.23 Query Results

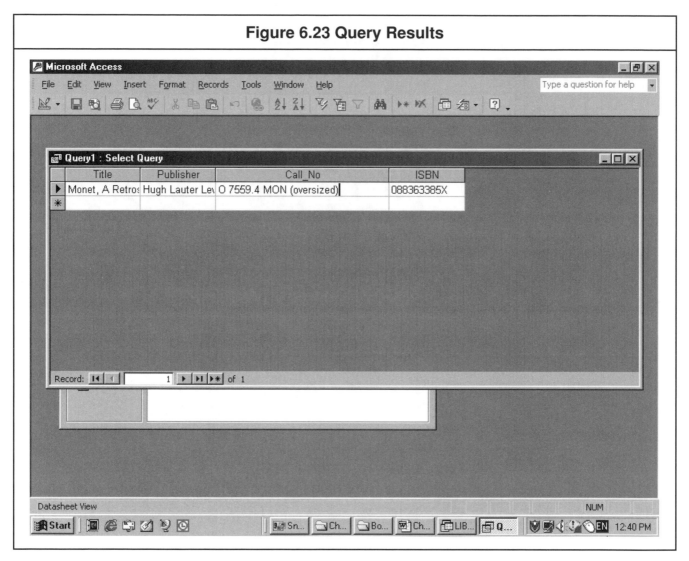

10. Close the query and save it with the file name **Monet,** and then return to the database window.

6.4 MODIFYING AND RENAMING A QUERY

Suppose, after a query has been saved, you decide that the results of the query are not what you want. You can quickly modify a query and save it with a different query name. Let's modify the query for overdue books and have the modified query search for books currently in the library.

1. Open the query **Overdue** in **Design** view.
2. Delete the field **DateDue** from the query design grid. To delete a field, highlight the field by clicking at the top of the field; when the mouse pointer changes to the down arrow, click the mouse button to select the field, then press the <Delete> key on the keyboard (see Figure 6.24).

Figure 6.24 Delete Field from Query

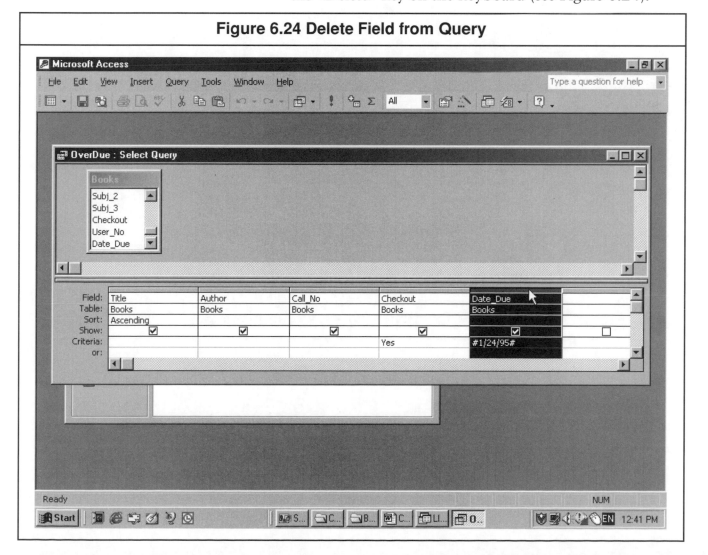

3. Add the **ISBN** field by double-clicking the field name in the field list.
4. To change from books checked out of the library to books in the library, click in the criteria field of **Checkout** and type **No** (see Figure 6.25).

Figure 6.25 Modified Query

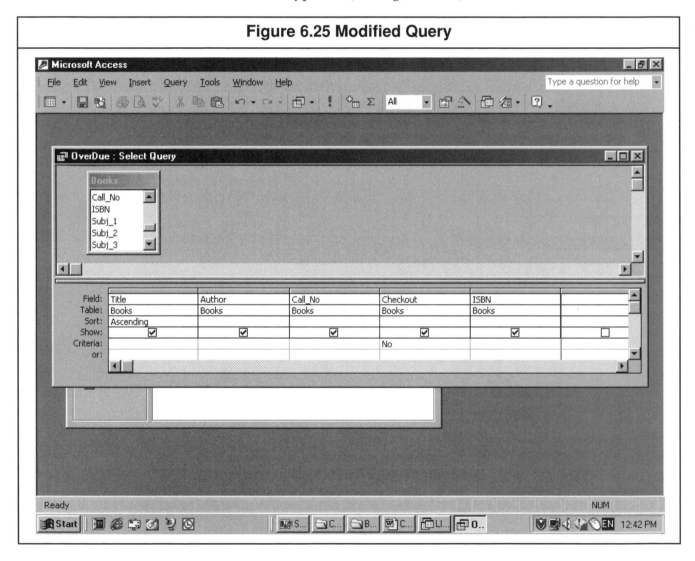

5. Run the Query.
6. Click **File, Save As,** and name the query **In Library** (see Figure 6.26).

Figure 6.26 Save Query

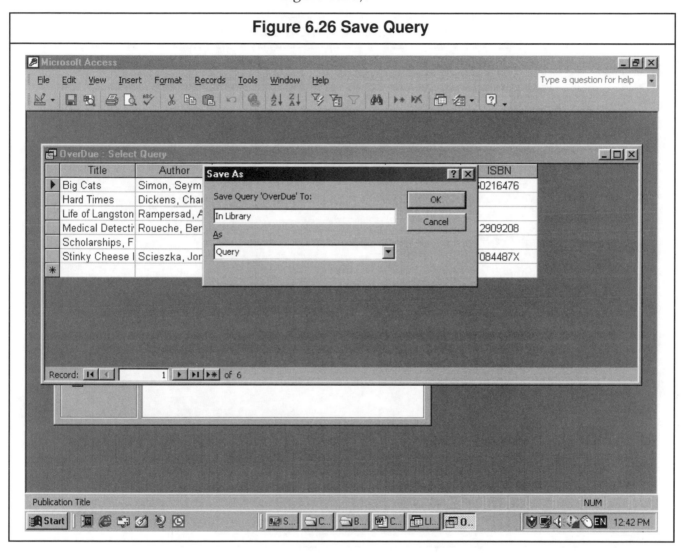

7. Click **OK,** then close the query window and return to the database window.

8. Now let's change the name of the query we just saved from **In Library** to **Books In**. Right click the **In Library** query and left click on **Rename** (see Figure 6.27).

Figure 6.27 Rename a Query

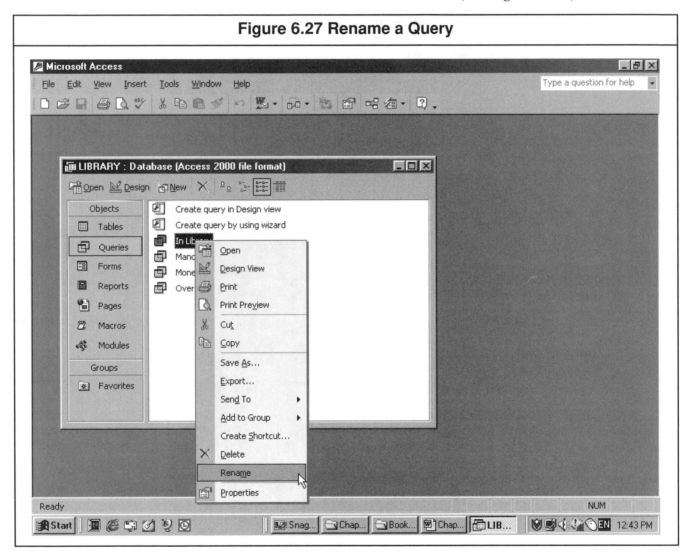

9. Type **Books In** for the new query name. Then press the <Enter> key. Now the query has successfully been renamed.

7 FORMS

A form is an object used to update, delete, view, and print records from a table. In Access, you can design your own forms or you can use form wizards to automatically create them for you.

It is good practice for users to modify table records using forms. You don't want the user to be able to directly access the table. When the user directly accesses the table, they can accidentally change the table structure or even delete all of the records in the table. Therefore, we use forms to allow the user the same useful functionality as if they were directly accessing the table.

In this chapter we will create forms using two types of methods: form wizard and form design. We will then use forms to add, update, and delete records. Finally, we will create a form with a main form and a subform.

7.1 CREATE A FORM USING FORM WIZARD

Make sure the Library database is open and the Database Window is displayed. Now we can create a form using the form wizard.

1. Click the **New Object** button.
2. Click **Form** (see Figure 7.1).

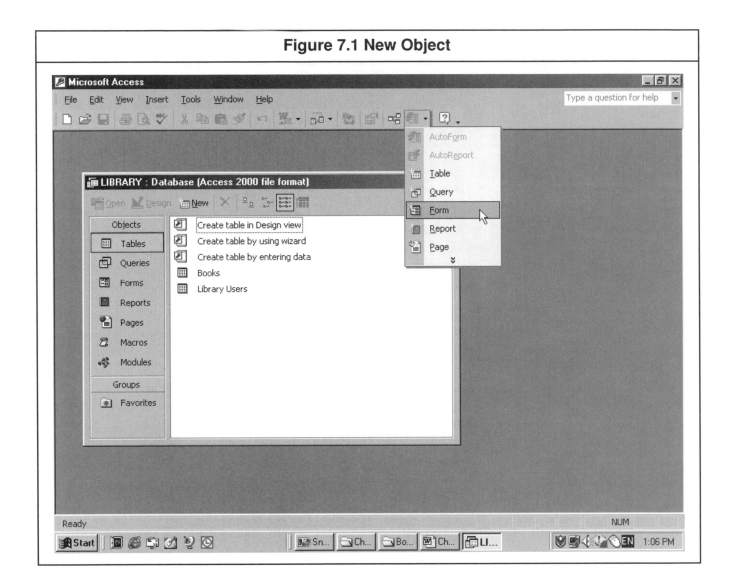

Figure 7.1 New Object

The New Form window is displayed.

3. Click **Form Wizard.**
4. Select **Library Users** from the **Choose the table or query where the object's data comes from** list (see Figure 7.2).

Figure 7.2 New Form

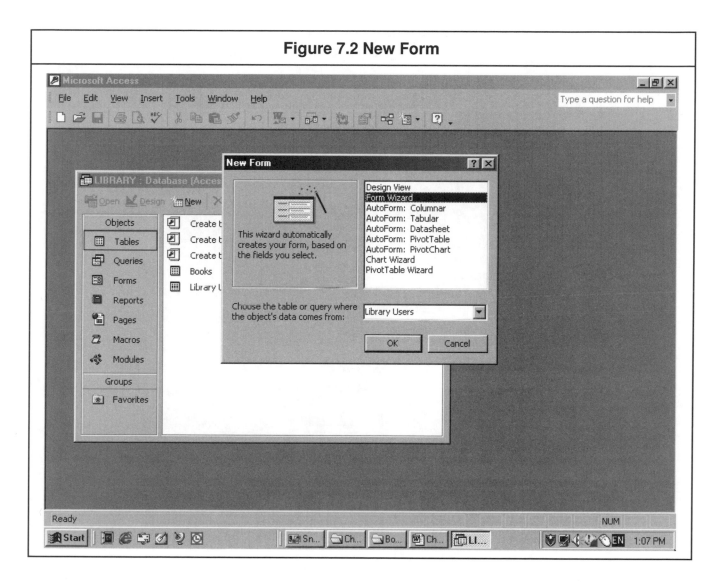

5. Click **OK**.

We can now select the fields that we want to be displayed in our form. In this form, we want to display all of the fields in the Library Users table.

6. Click the **Select All** button to add all of the available fields to the selected fields list (see Figure 7.3).

Figure 7.3 Selected Fields

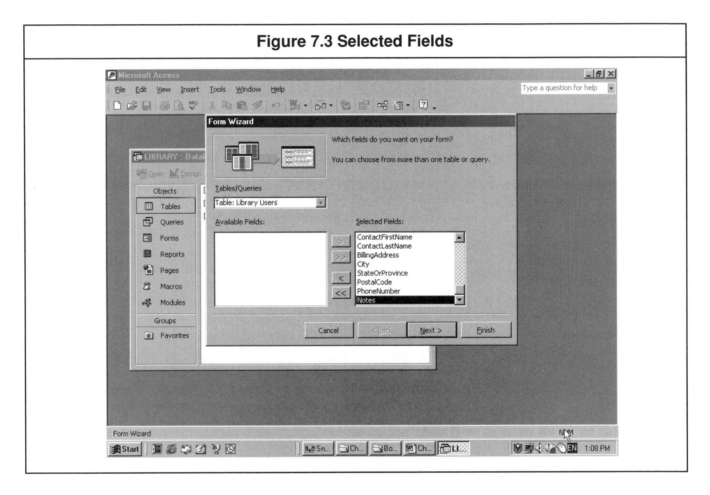

7. Click **Next**.

8. Make sure **Columnar** is selected and then click **Next** (see Figure 7.4).

Figure 7.4 Form Layout

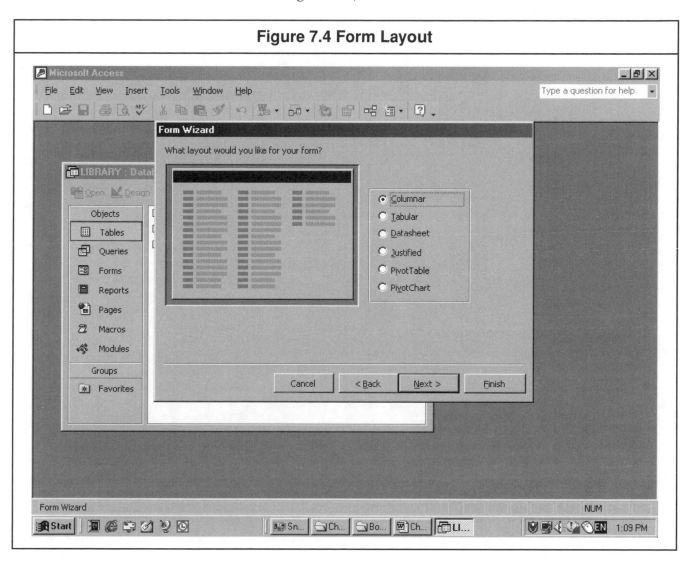

9. Make sure **Standard** is selected and then click **Next** (see Figure 7.5).

Figure 7.5 Form Style

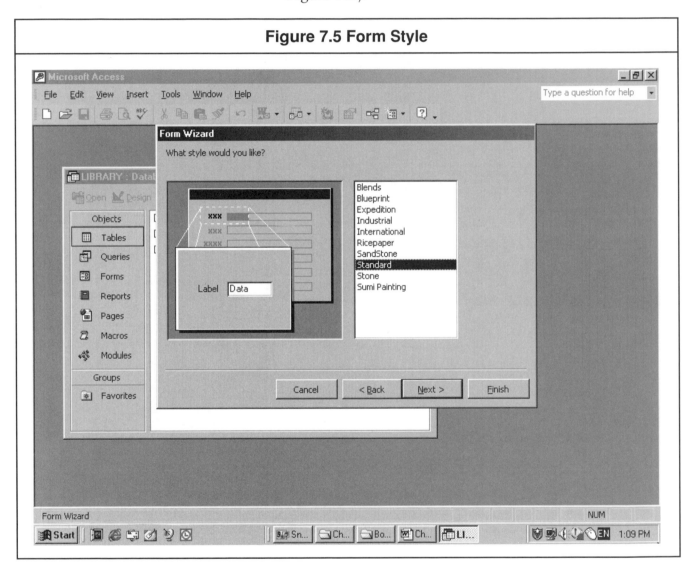

10. Change the title of the form to **Library Users** (if necessary).
11. Make sure the **Open the form to view or enter information** option is selected (see Figure 7.6).

Figure 7.6 Final Form Wizard Dialog Box

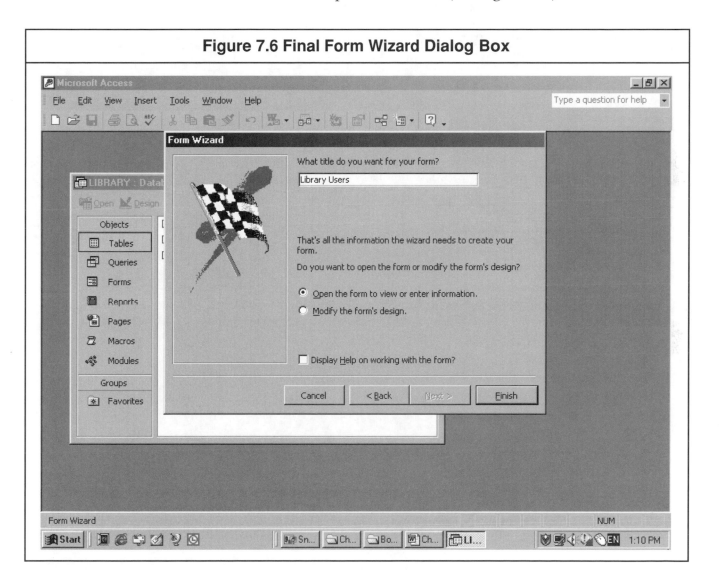

12. Click **Finish** and the form will appear on your screen (see Figure 7.7).

Figure 7.7 Form Created With Form Wizard

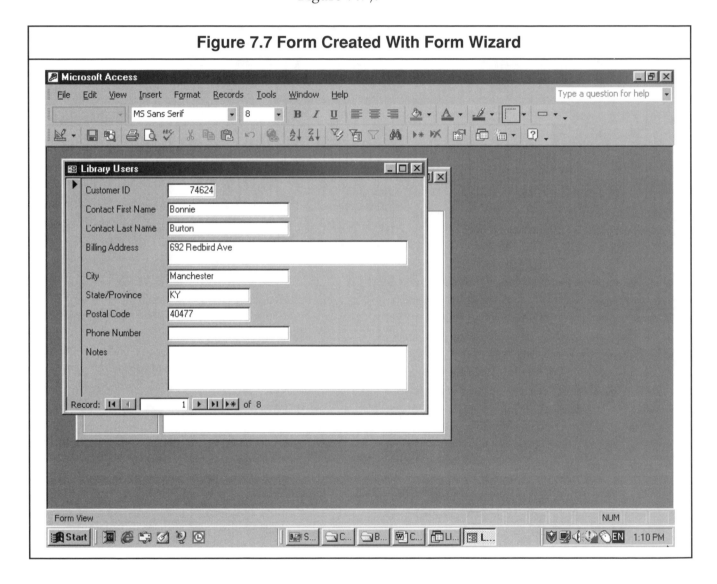

13. Scroll through the records using the **Next Record** navigation button until you reach the last record (record 8).
14. Click the **First Record** button to quickly navigate to the first record in the table.
15. Close the form and this returns you to the database window.

7.2 CREATE A FORM USING FORM DESIGN

1. Click **Forms** in the **Objects** list.
2. Click **New**.
3. Click **Design View** (if necessary).
4. Select **Books** from the **Choose the table or query where the object's data comes from** list (see Figure 7.8).

Figure 7.8 New Form Window

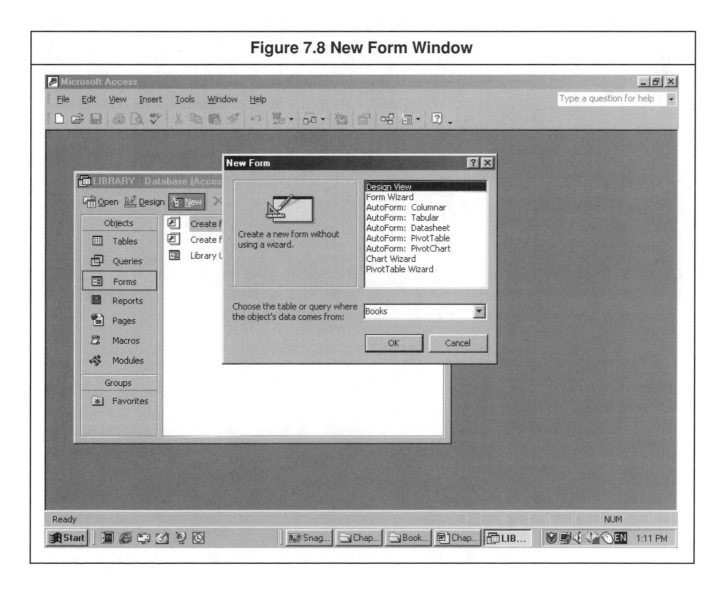

5. Click **OK** (see Figure 7.9).

Figure 7.9 Form Design View

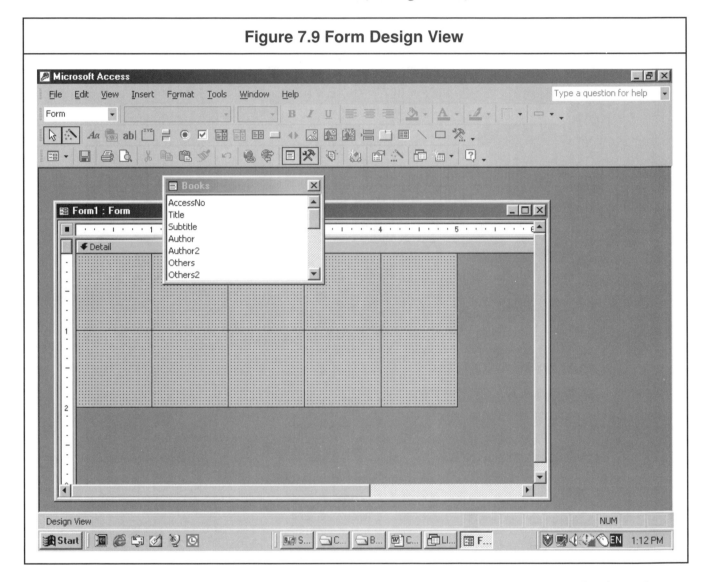

This opens the form in Design View. We see the form layout grid and the field list. Here we can select the fields that we want to appear in our form. We can also arrange the fields on the form as we choose. The fields' attributes can also be modified. For example, we can change the size of a field text box or the font size of the contents of the field.

When creating a form in Design View, we have to manually add the fields to the form. We do this by clicking and dragging the field(s) from the table field list to the form layout grid. In our example, we want to add all of the fields to the form. First, we will add a single field, then we will add the remaining fields. Before we begin adding fields, we need to maximize our form and then move the field list to the side of the form so it will not be in the way.

> 6. Click the **Maximize** button on the form to maximize the form layout grid (see Figure 7.10).

Figure 7.10 Maximized Form Layout Grid

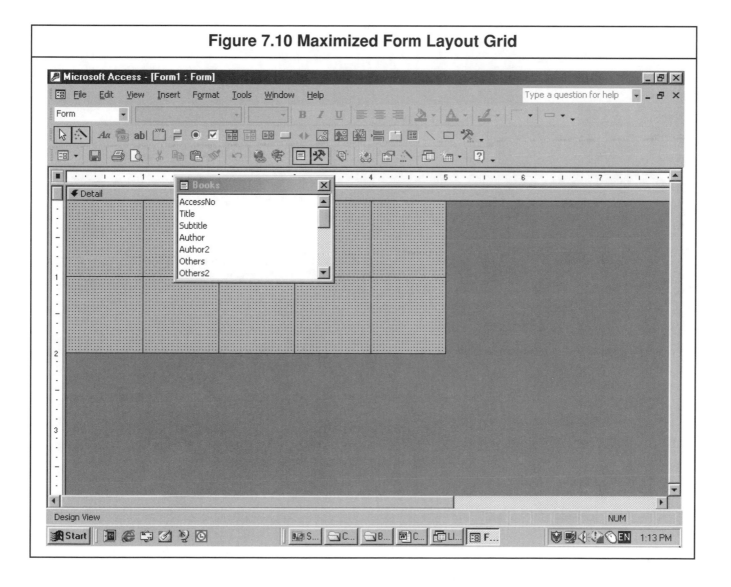

7. Click the field list **Title Bar** labeled **Books** and, while holding down the left mouse button, drag the field list to the right of the screen (see Figure 7.11).

Figure 7.11 Form Layout Grid

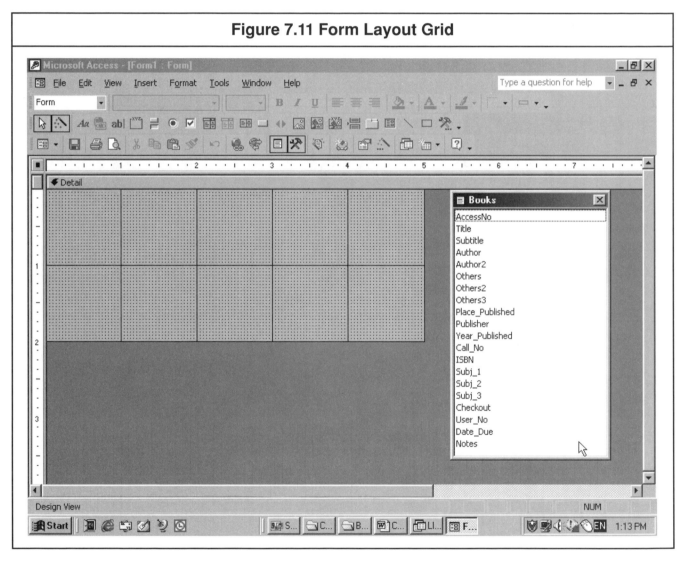

8. Click **AccessNo** in the field list.

9. Drag the **AccessNo** field (hold down the left mouse button and drag) to the form layout grid to the location that is 1/4 inch from the top of the grid and one inch from the left (see Figure 7.12).

Figure 7.12 Field Added to Form

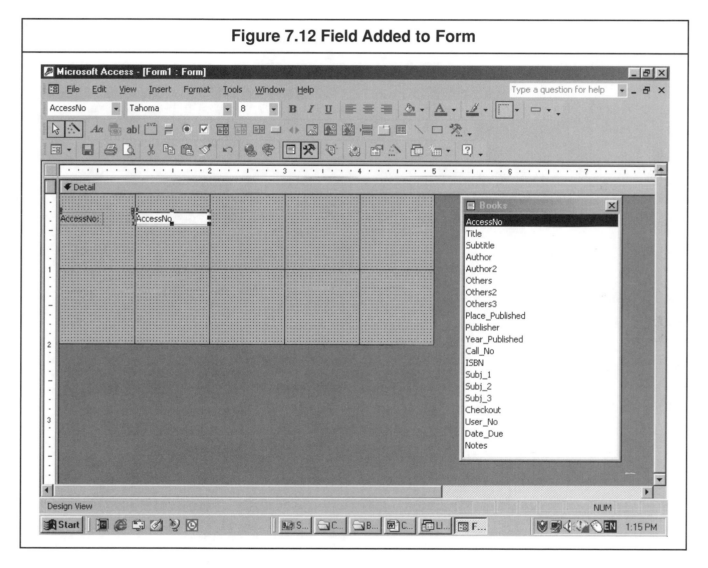

Before we add the remaining fields to the form, we will increase the size of the form.

10. Click the lower right edge of the form (your mouse pointer will change) and drag down and to the right. The width of the form should be 6 inches and the height should be 3.5 inches (see Figure 7.13).

Figure 7.13 Resized Form Layout Grid

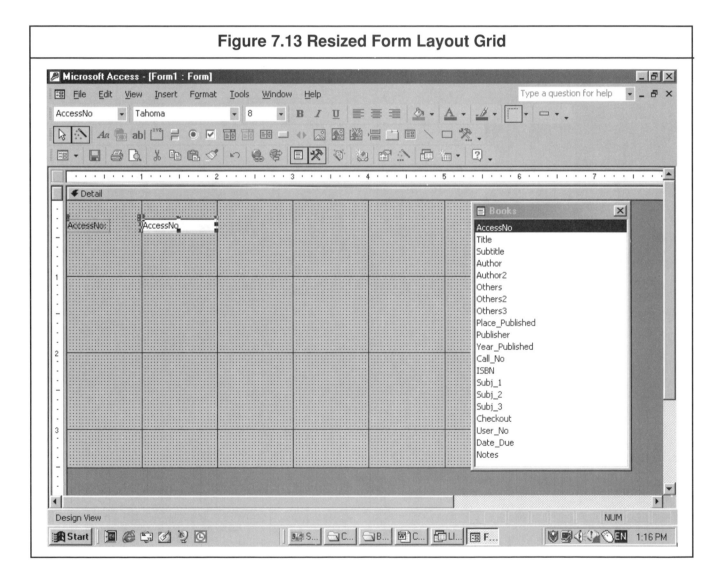

11. Add the following fields to the form layout grid and position them accordingly (see Figure 7.14).

Figure 7.14 Form With Multiple Fields

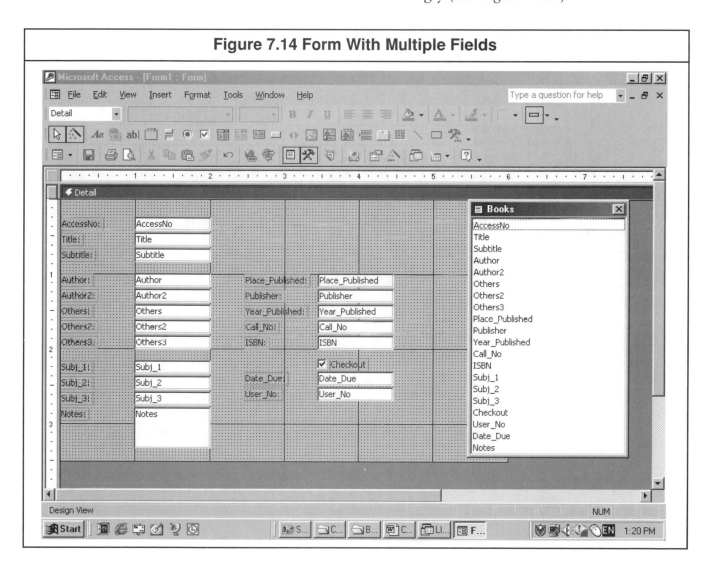

12. Close the **Books** field list.
13. Increase the width of the form to seven inches.

14. Rearrange and change the sizes of the fields (see Figure 7.15).

Figure 7.15 Redesigned Form Layout Grid

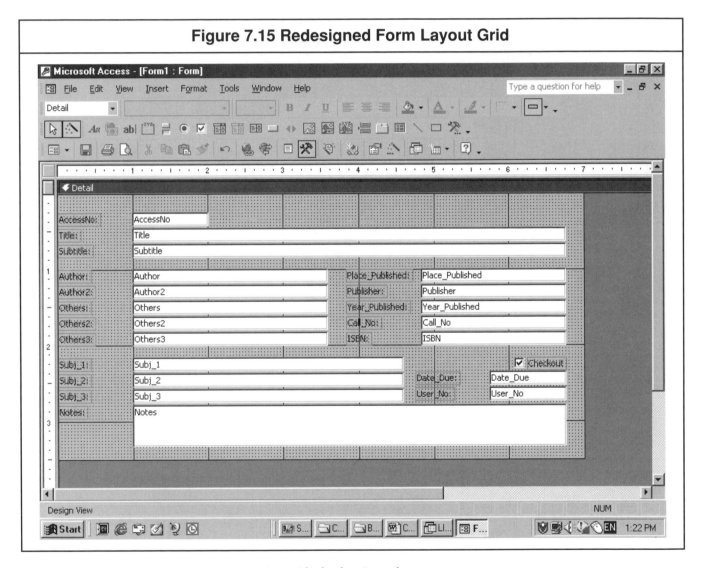

15. Click the **Save** button.
16. Name the form **Books**.
17. Click **OK**.

18. Click the **Form View** button (see Figure 7.16).

Figure 7.16 Form View

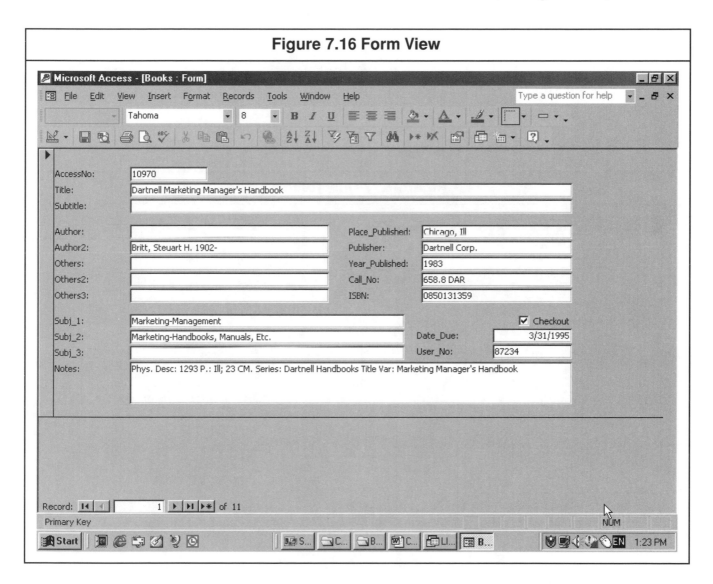

---

19. Navigate through the records.
20. Close the **Books** form and this returns you to the database window.

7.3 MODIFYING TABLE RECORDS USING FORMS

In this section we are going to add, update, and delete records from the **Library Users** table using the **Library Users** form.

1. Open the **Library Users** form.
2. Click the **New Record** button (see Figure 7.17).

Figure 7.17 New Record

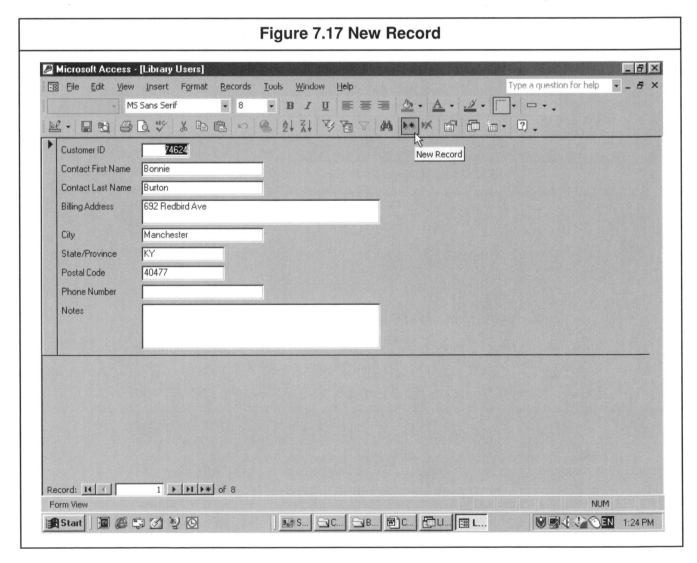

3. Add the following library user to the table (see Figure 7.18):

CustomerID	46587
First Name	Tom
Last Name	Wilson
Address	29 University Drive
City	Pineville
State	KY
Zip	40977

Figure 7.18 New Record Added

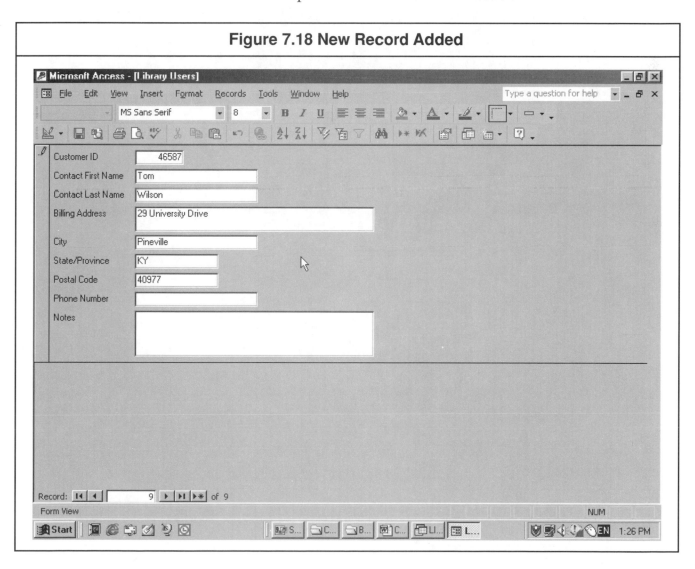

4. Update record number three for Thelma Thompson accordingly (see Figure 7.19).

Last Name	Mills
Address	123 Perry Lane
City	Danville
Zip	40569

Figure 7.19 Update Record

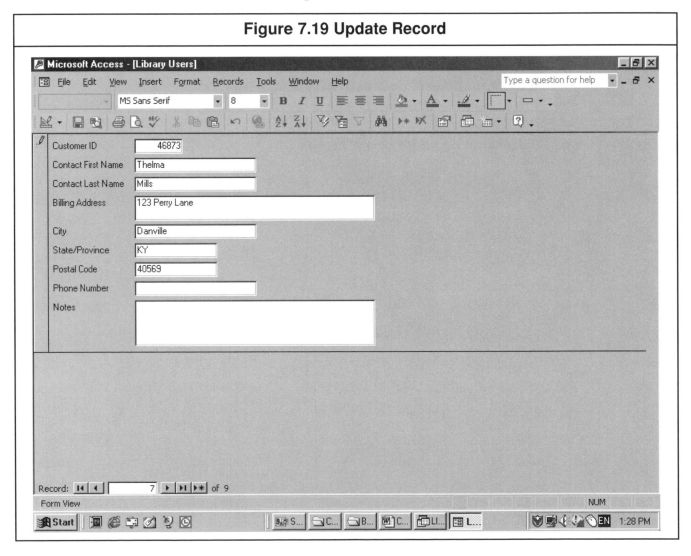

5. Navigate to record number five for Trace Crow.

6. Delete this record by clicking on the **Delete Record** button (see Figure 7.20).

Figure 7.20 Delete Record

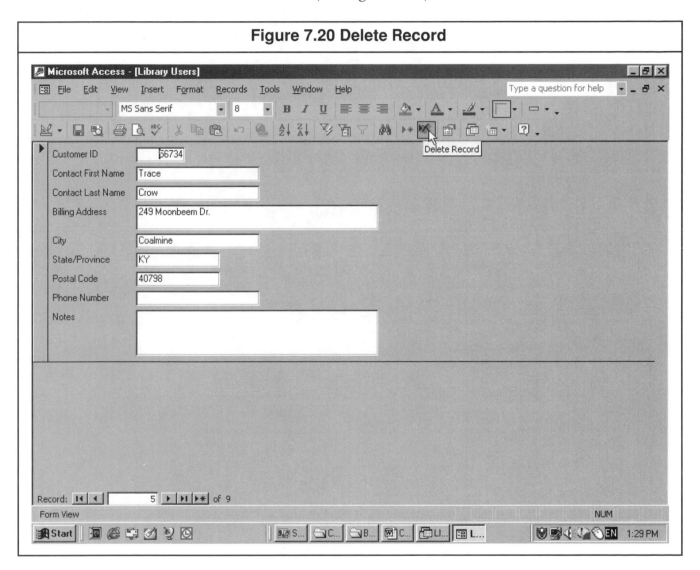

7. Close the **Library Users** form and this will return you to the database window.

7.4 FORM WITH SUBFORM

As a librarian you may find it useful to look up each library user and determine which books they have checked out. We can create a form with a subform that will allow you to quickly and easily accomplish this. Each library user can be viewed as well as the books, if any, that each user currently has checked out.

1. Click the **Tables** object.
2. Click the **New Object** button.
3. Select **Form** (see Figure 7.21).

Figure 7.21 New Form

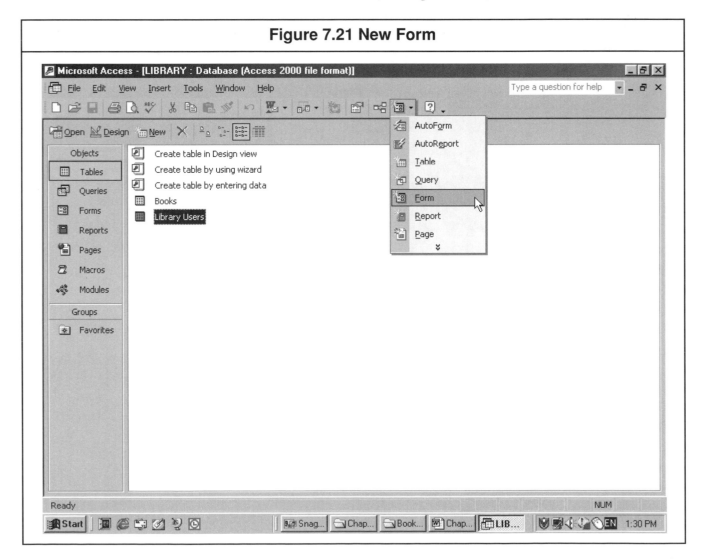

4. Select **Form Wizard** from the **New Form** window.
5. Select **Library Users** from the **Choose table or query where the object's data comes from** list (see Figure 7.22).

Figure 7.22 New Form

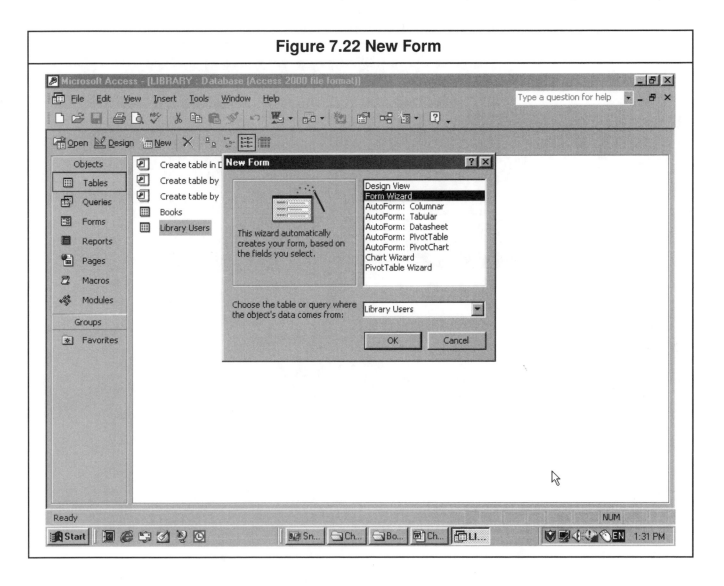

6. Click **OK**.
7. Click the **Select All** button to add all of the available fields to the selected fields list.

8. Select **Table: Books** from the **Tables/Queries** list (see Figure 7.23).

Figure 7.23 Multiple Table Select

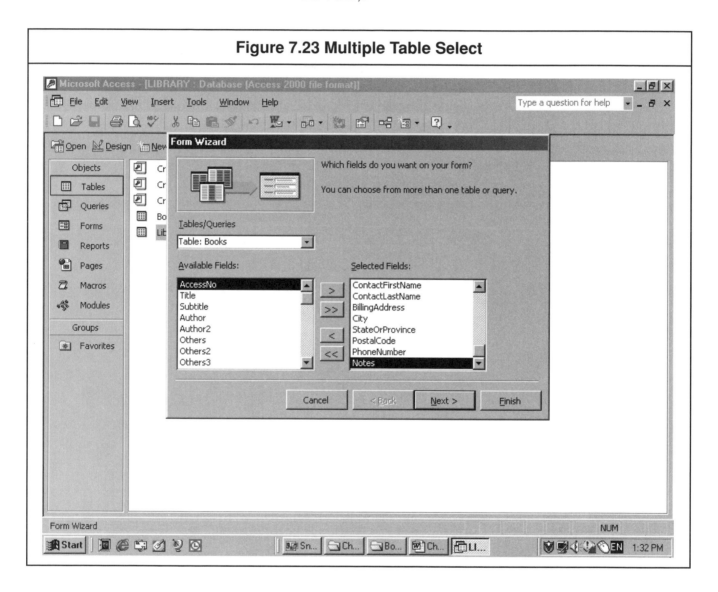

9. Click the **Select All** button to add all of the available fields to the selected fields.

10. Click the **Select All** button to add all of the available fields to the selected fields list (see Figure 7.24).

Figure 7.24 All Fields Selected

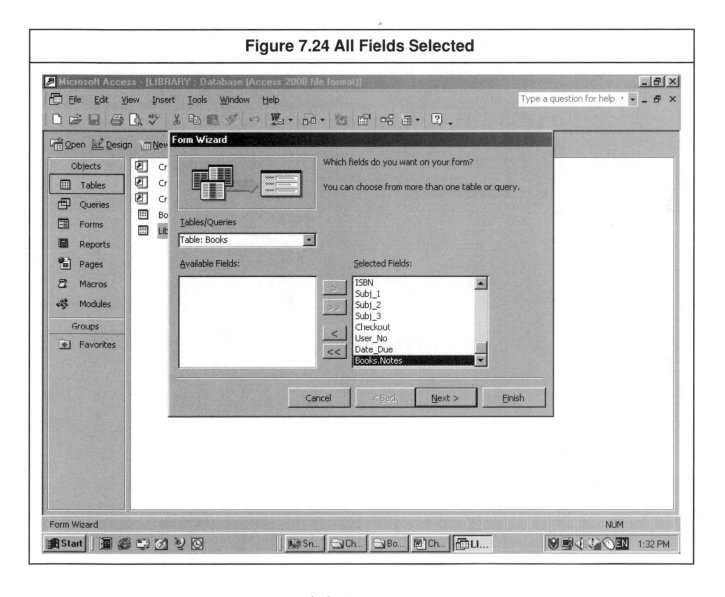

11. Click **Next**.

12. Click **Form with subform(s)** if it is not already selected (see Figure 7.25).

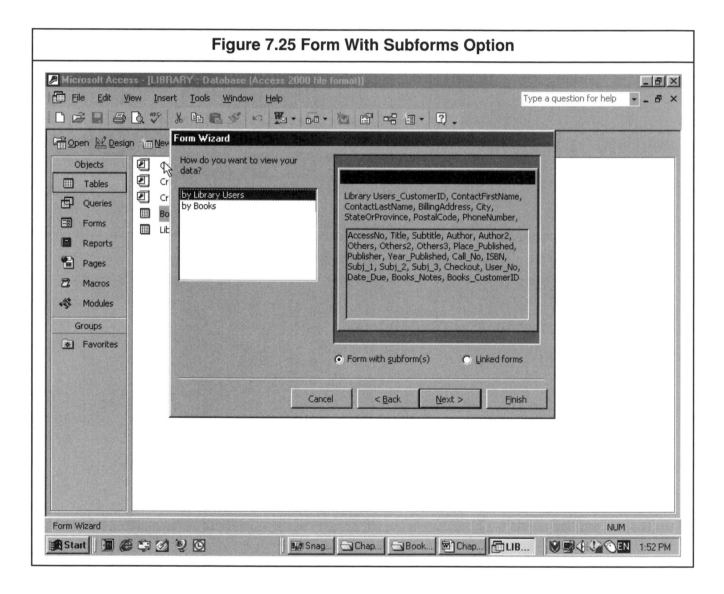

Figure 7.25 Form With Subforms Option

13. Click **Next**.
14. Click **Datasheet** if it is not already selected.
15. Click **Next**.
16. Click **Standard** if it is not already selected.

17. Click **Next** to open the last screen of the Form Wizard (see Figure 7.26).

Figure 7.26 Form Wizard Screen

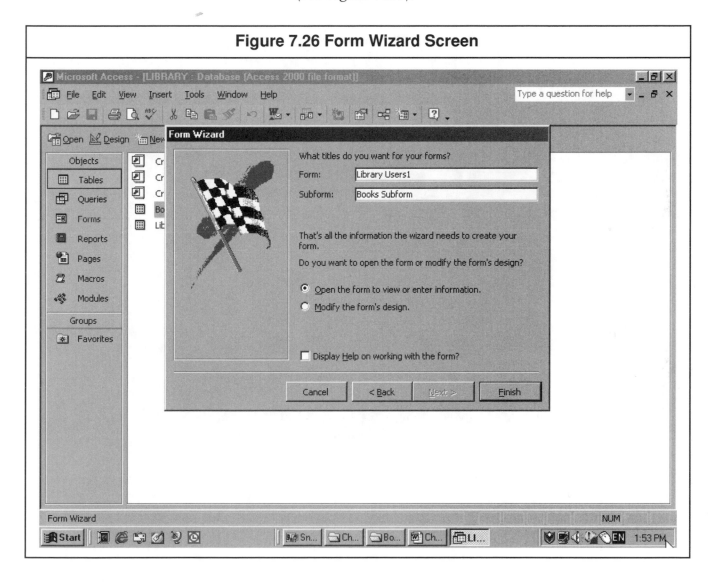

18. Click **Finish** to create the form and it will open in Form View (see Figure 7.27).

Figure 7.27 Form With Subform

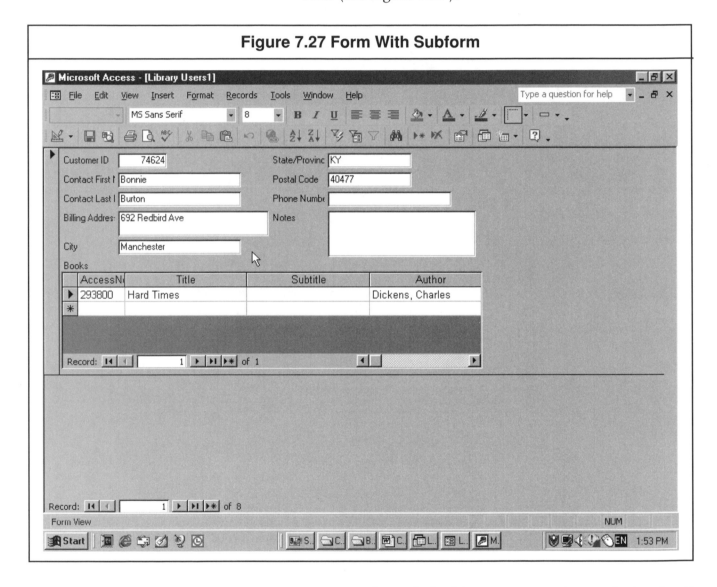

19. Navigate through the library users and view the books, if any, that each library user has checked out.
20. Close the form and this takes you back to the database window.
21. Click on the **Forms** object. Two forms were created when you created the last form: Library Users1 and Books Subform.
22. Close the database.
23. Exit Access.

8 DATABASE STRUCTURE

OBJECTIVES

8.1 RELATIONSHIPS
8.2 RELATED TABLES
8.3 QUERY WITH TABLE DEFINED RELATIONSHIP
8.4 DATABASE DESIGN ANALOGY

You now know how to create queries to retrieve information from tables. Suppose, however, that you need to retrieve information from several tables at once. To do this you must create relationships between the tables from which you want to simultaneously retrieve data. Once the relationships are created between the tables, you can use two or more tables in a query to retrieve the information that you need. Creating these relationships between tables allows you to create a relational database.

Relational databases combine information in different tables by linking the tables using a common field that is found in each table. We will create a list of users who have overdue books using this method.

Assume we have a list of the books in the library in one table, and a list of the library users in another table. If we considered only the information we are gathering and not how we plan to use it, we would probably duplicate information that we enter into the database. Without planning, for example, we might have created the tables so that every time a book was checked out, the user's name would have to be typed in, which is a waste of valuable resources, disk storage space, and staff time.

Data Normalization is the process of organizing your data structure to preclude entering more information than necessary or to avoid data redundancy. To link the **Books** table with the **Library Users** table to find out who has checked out which books, we need to link the tables using a common field. In our example, we will use the CustomerID in both tables to link the tables together.

Note
When deciding which field should be used in linking, you must choose carefully. Never use a field that changes or might be confused with another field. For example, LastName might be a logical choice, but names can change, and more than one person can have the same last name. Social Security numbers are specific to each person, but some people don't have Social Security numbers.

For our library book example, we need an identifier that identifies each book in the library and that is unique to each book. Every book in the library has an assigned number called the accession number. The sole purpose of the accession number is to identify one specific copy of a title; therefore, the unique identifier to use for linking tables could be the accession number.

8.1 RELATIONSHIPS

There are three different kinds of relationships in relational database design.

- One-to-one relationship: This is a unique link between two items, not shared by any other relation. The relationship between each user and the user number, or between each book and its accession number, is unique. An example would be that one customer may check out only one book. One-to-one, one book per customer. This type of relationship is not very common. It is used mainly to separate tables with many fields, or to secure part of the data stored in particular fields within a table.
- One-to-many relationship: This is a link to one item that may be shared by many items in the same way. The relation of the user to the books is one-to-many. This is because the user may check out several books. But those books can currently only be checked out by one person. This type of relationship is most common. Most tables are linked with a one-to-many relationship.
- Many-to-many relationship: This is a link between two tables where related records in either table can have related records in the other linked table. Tracking library circulation over time, we find that each user can check out many books, and that each book may have been checked out by many users. This type of relationship is not very common. A many-to-many relationship is really just two one-to-one relationships with a third table that is created to allow the many-to-many relationship.

8.2 RELATED TABLES

For the relation between the two tables to work correctly, each user must have a unique identifier. Also, each book checked out must have the user's identifier entered in its record—otherwise, the tables won't link correctly.

The first step is to make sure that we link the two tables using a primary key and a foreign key. A primary key is a unique identifier of each record in a table. A foreign key refers to the primary key field in another table. The foreign key is used to specify the type of relationship between the tables.

The **Library Users** table has **CustomerID** defined as the primary key. We need to add the **CustomerID** field to the **Books** table as a foreign key. Also, we must define the data type for the foreign key so it is the same as the data type of the primary key.

1. Open the **Books** table in **Design** view.
2. Scroll to the end of the field name list and click in the blank field name after the **Notes** field.
3. Enter **CustomerID** as the field name and **Number** as the data type.
4. Change the field size from **Decimal** to **Long Integer** (see Figure 8.1).

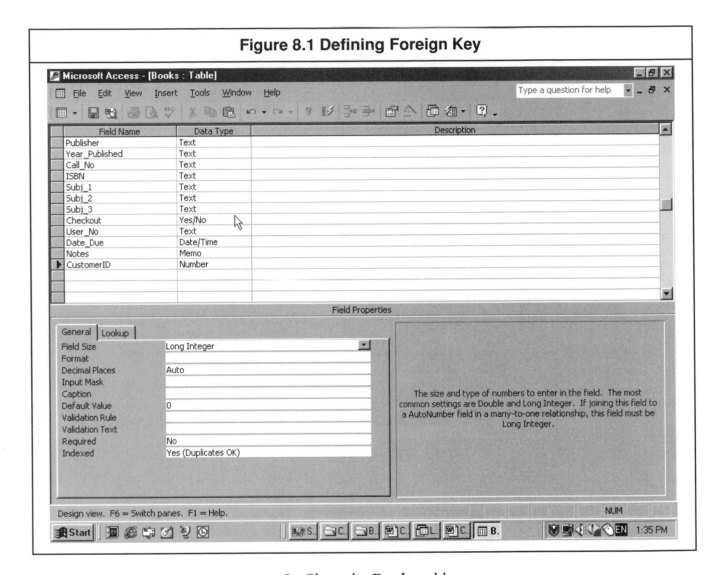

Figure 8.1 Defining Foreign Key

5. Close the **Books** table.
6. Click **Yes** to save changes.
7. Click **Tools** on the menu bar.

8. Then click **Relationships**. This opens the **Relationship** window (see Figure 8.2).

Figure 8.2 Relationships Window

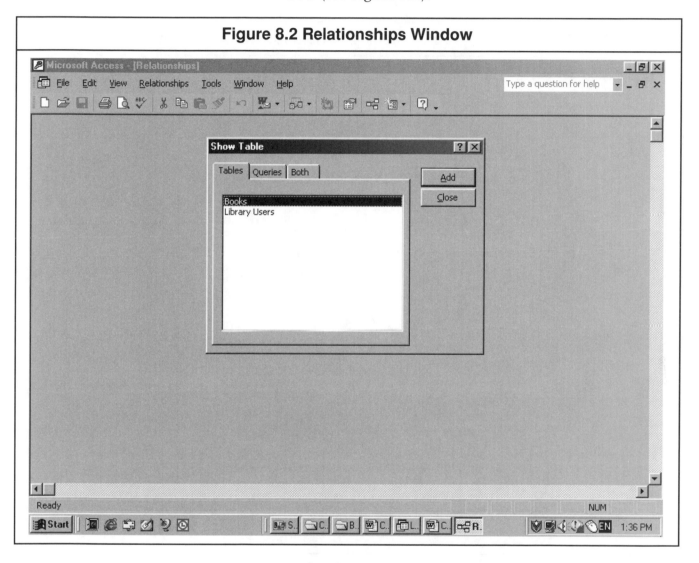

9. In the **Show Table** window, **Books** should be highlighted. Click the **Add** button.
10. Click **Library Users** in the **Show Table** window. Click the **Add** button.

11. Close the **Show Table** window. Now we can create a table relationship (see Figure 8.3).

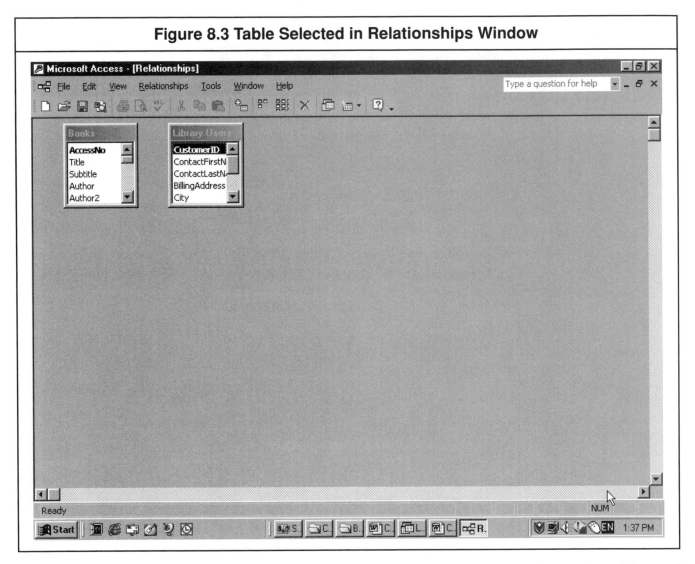

Figure 8.3 Table Selected in Relationships Window

12. Scroll through the field names in the **Books** table until you see the **CustomerID** field.
13. Left click on the **CustomerID** field in the **Books** table field list and drag over to the **CustomerID** field in the **Library Users** table field list. The **Edit Relationships** window opens (see Figure 8.4).

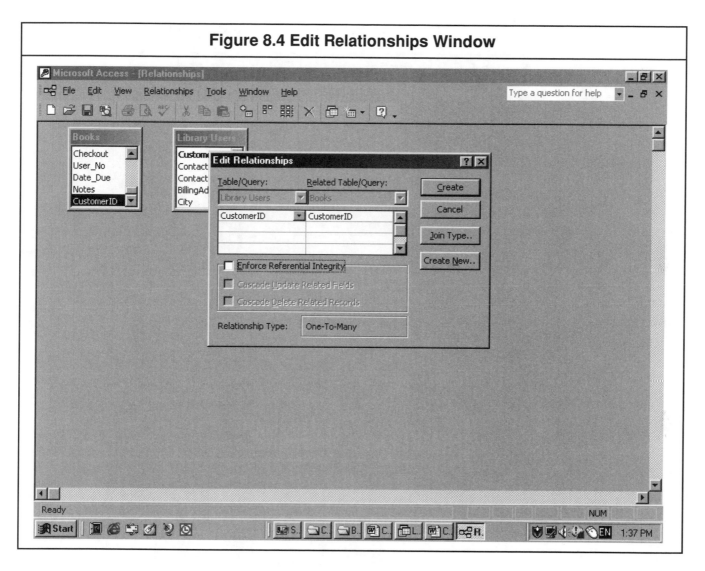

Figure 8.4 Edit Relationships Window

Notice that both tables are listed at the top of this window and that the **CustomerID** field appears as the field to link the tables. Also notice at the bottom of the window that a **One-To-Many** relationship is the type of relationship that Access recognizes between these two tables. This is based on the primary key and foreign key definitions in these tables.

14. Click **Enforce Referential Integrity**.
15. Click **Cascade Update Related Fields**.

16. Click **Cascade Delete Related Fields** (see Figure 8.5).

Figure 8.5 Referential Integrity Rules Enforced

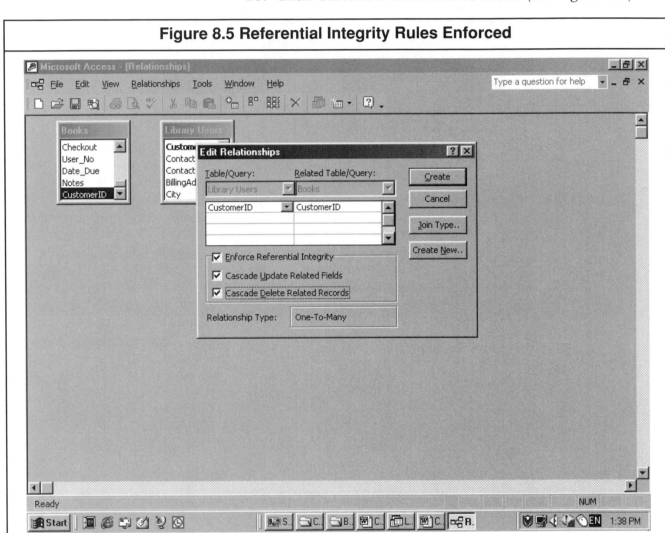

17. Click the **Create** button (see Figure 8.6).

Figure 8.6 Table Relationship Defined

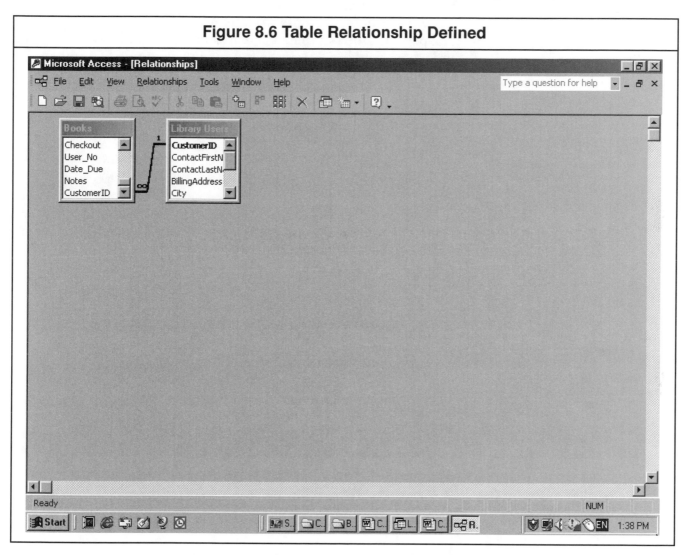

Notice the line connecting the two tables. The line begins and ends with the **CustomerID** fields in each table. The line connecting the **Library Users** table shows a "1" which means this is the one part of the one-to-many relationship. The line connecting the **Books** table shows an infinity symbol, which means this is the many part of the one-to-many relationship.

18. Close the **Relationships** window.
19. Click **Yes** to save changes.

We have created the foreign key field in the **Books** table and we have created the relationship between the tables. As library users check out books, we need to enter their **CustomerID** in the **Books** table. Later we will use forms to update tables. For now we will just enter the data directly into the table.

Open the **Books** table. The **CustomerID** field is located at the end of the field list. Enter the following **CustomerID** numbers for the following books:

Big Cats	35986
Monet, A Retrospective	46873
Hard Times	74624
Medical Detectives	35986
Great Cases of Scotland Yard	87905

Now we will create a query using fields from both tables. When you create the query, you will see the table relationship once you add the tables to the query.

8.3 QUERY WITH TABLE DEFINED RELATIONSHIP

1. Click the **Queries** object button.
2. Click the **New** button.
3. Click **OK** to accept Design View.
4. Add both tables to the query.

5. Close the **Show Table** window (see Figure 8.7).

Figure 8.7 Query With Defined Table Relationship

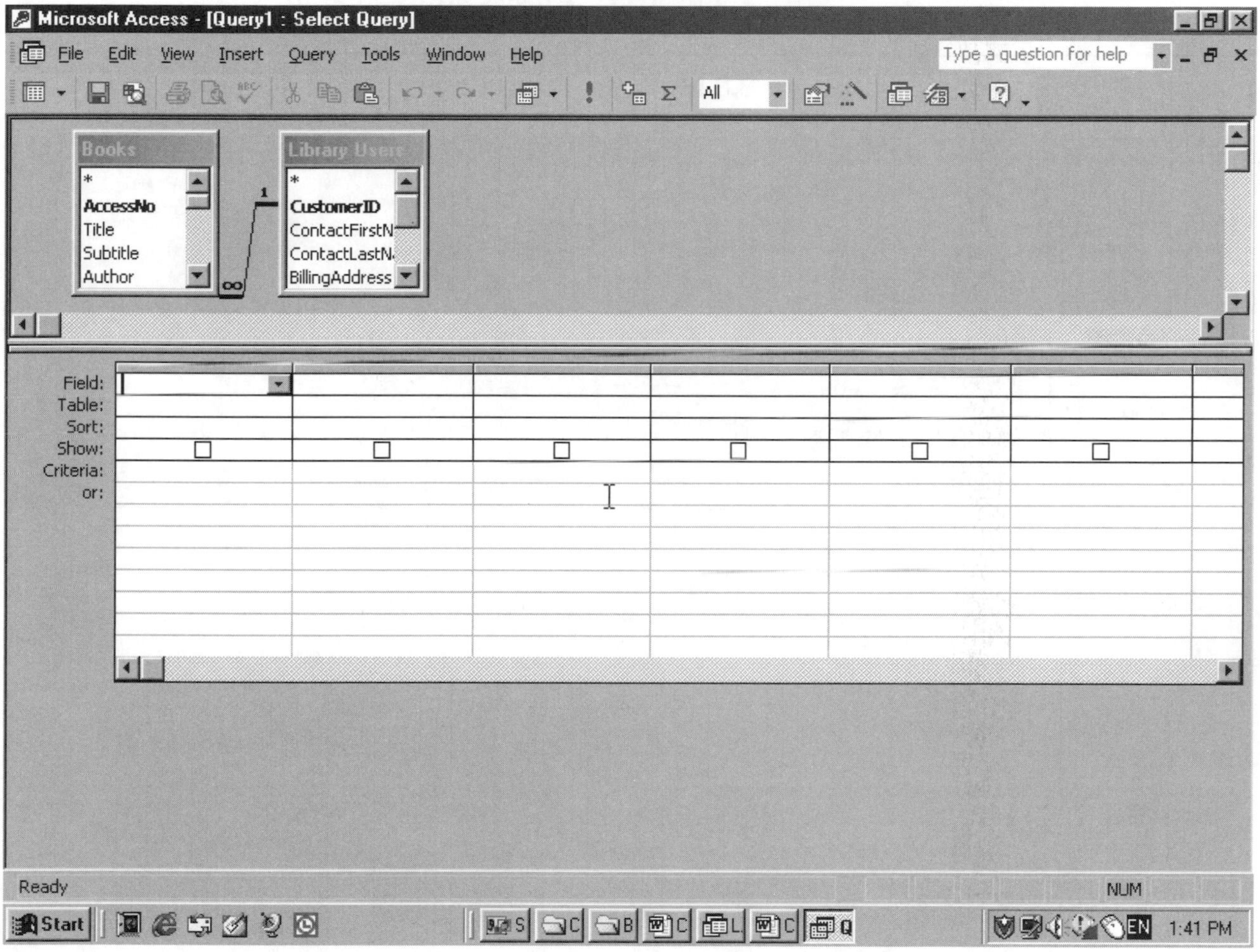

6. Add the following fields to the query design grid: From the Library Users table—**ContactFirstName, Contact LastName, BillingAddress, City, State, StateOrProvince,** and **PostalCode.** From the **Books** table—**AccessNo, Title, CallNo,** and **CheckOut** (see Figure 8.8).

Figure 8.8 Multiple Table Query

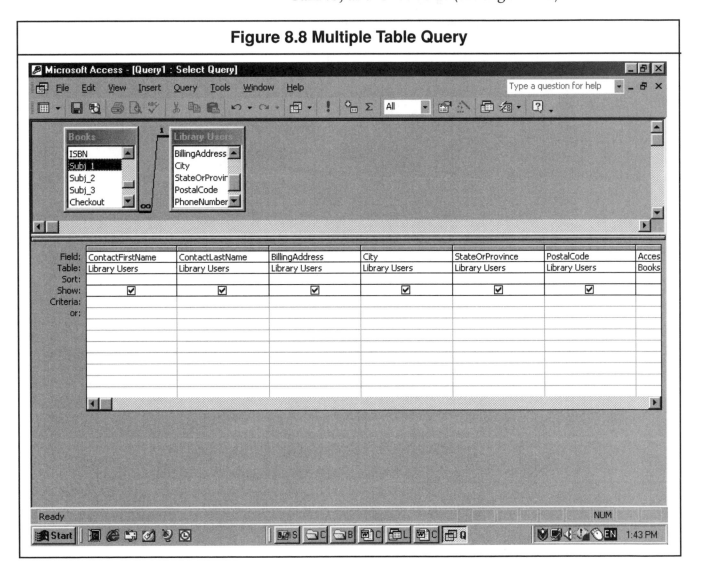

7. Click the **Run** button (see Figure 8.9).

Figure 8.9 Query Results

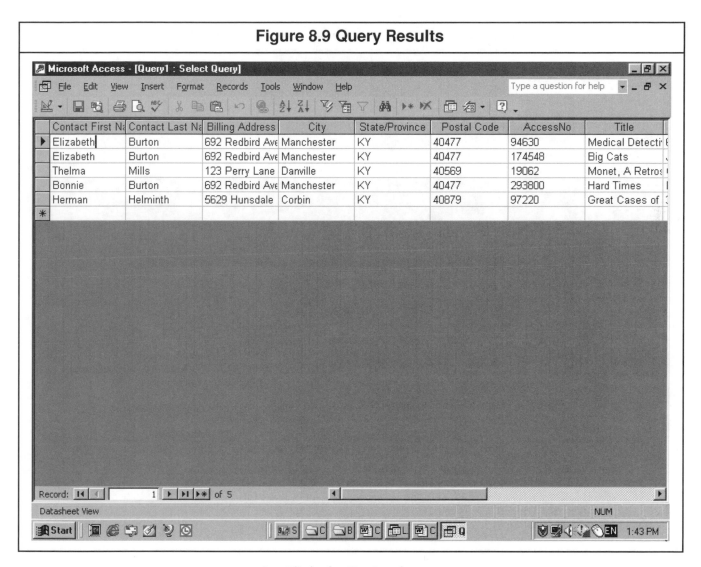

8. Click the **Design** button.
9. Enter "Yes" in the **Criteria** field for **CheckOut**.

10. Run the query (see Figure 8.10).

Figure 8.10 Results with Books Checked Out

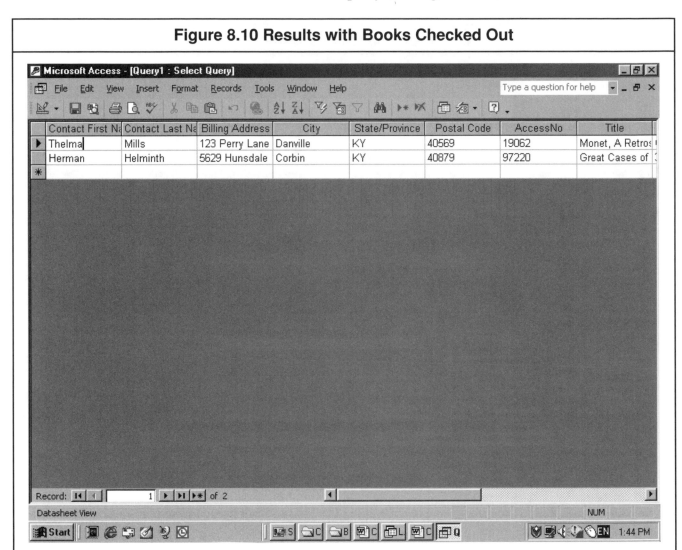

11. Save the query as **Books Checked Out**.
12. Close the query.

This query allowed us to retrieve data from two related tables simultaneously. This is the basis for a relational database. We can relate the data that is stored in separate tables. Then we can retrieve the data that is necessary for queries, forms, and reports.

DATABASE DESIGN ANALOGY

Designing a database requires defining all of the pieces of data, how the data will be stored in tables, the relationships between those tables, and how the data will be used to create informative output such as reports. It is good practice to know all of the different pieces of data that will be used in the database and the necessary relationships between that data before you begin creating the database. If you fail to plan your database design carefully, you could end up having to redesign tables, which means that you will find yourself having to also redefine other objects that are related to those tables such as queries, forms, and reports. The best approach is to understand exactly what you want the database to do and how it should be designed to meet your objectives.

Think of designing a database as being like building a house. Before you build a house you must have a set of blueprints. This allows you to know exactly what material is needed and how those materials are used to create the design that you have in mind. Also, you will find that the stability of the house rests on its foundation. If you don't have a solid foundation, then the house will not be suitable to live in.

Designing a database works much the same way. You need to understand everything that will go into the database. Examples include queries, forms, and reports. Think of the foundation of the database as being the tables. Without a full understanding of how the tables should be designed, your database will not function as you would have hoped. Many times databases are created without proper planning and they never perform as they were expected.

9 ADVANCED QUERIES

OBJECTIVES

9.1   FIND DUPLICATES QUERY WIZARD
9.2   FIND UNMATCHED QUERY WIZARD
9.3   CROSSTAB QUERY
9.4   PARAMETER QUERY

In this chapter we are going to create four types of advanced queries. First we will create a Find Duplicates Query to find all instances where we may have the same library user entered twice in the **Library Users** table.

Then we will create a Find Unmatched Query to find those individuals who do not currently have library books checked out. Next we will create a Crosstab Query to find where our library users live. Last we will create a Parameter Query to search for a particular book in the **Books** table.

In order to see how the Find Duplicates Query works, we will need to enter a library user with the same name as an existing library user. We will open the **Library Users** form and enter a new record for the new library user.

9.1 FIND DUPLICATES QUERY WIZARD

1. Click the **Forms** object.
2. Double click the **Library Users** form.
3. Click the **Add Record** button.
4. Enter the following record:

Customer ID	32379
First Name	Tom
Last Name	Wilson
Billing Address	100 Francis Drive
City	Richmond
State	KY
Postal Code	40475

5. Close the **Library Users** form.
6. Click the **Queries** object button.
7. Click the **New** button.

8. Select **Find Duplicates Query Wizard** (see Figure 9.1).

Figure 9.1 Find Duplicates Query Wizard

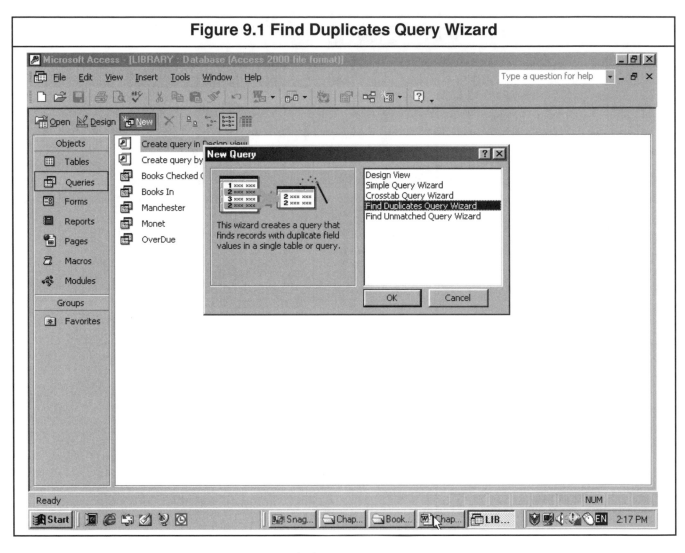

9. Click **OK**.

10. Click **Table: Library Users** (see Figure 9.2).

Figure 9.2 Select Table

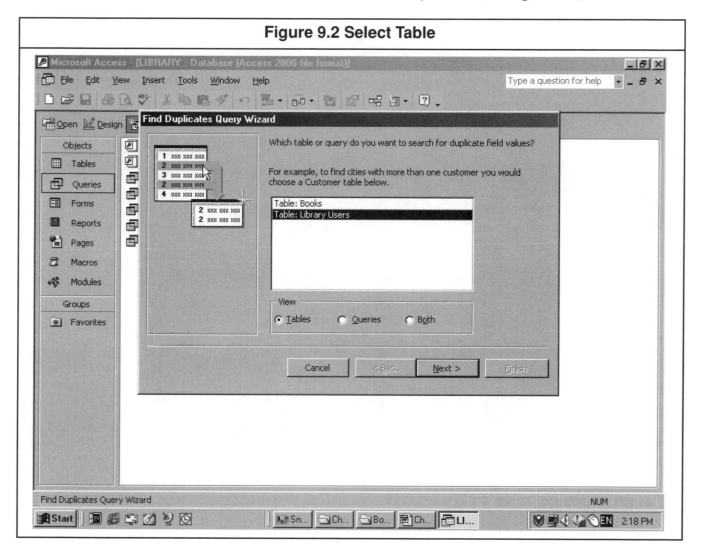

11. Click to add **First Name** and **Last Name** to the Duplicate-value fields list. These are the fields that will be searched within the **Library Users** table for duplicate values (see Figure 9.3).

Figure 9.3 Selected Duplicate-value Fields

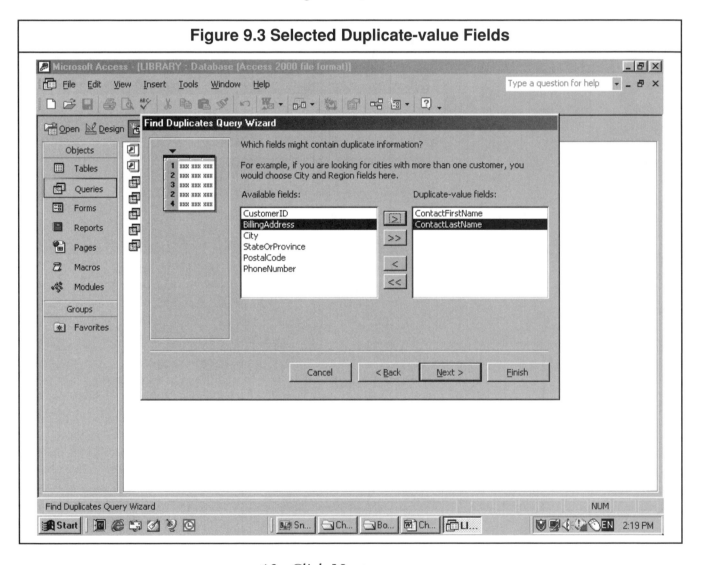

12. Click **Next**.

13. Click to add all of the remaining fields to the Additional Query Fields list. These additional fields will appear in the query results (see Figure 9.4).

Figure 9.4 Additional Query Fields

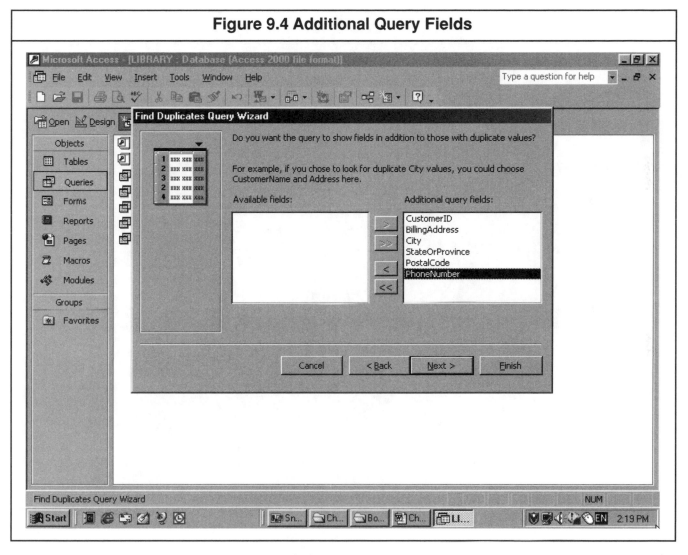

14. Click **Next.**

15. Accept the name **Find** duplicates for **Library Users**. Make sure **View the Results** is selected. Click **Finish** (see Figure 9.5).

Figure 9.5 Results of Find Duplicates Query

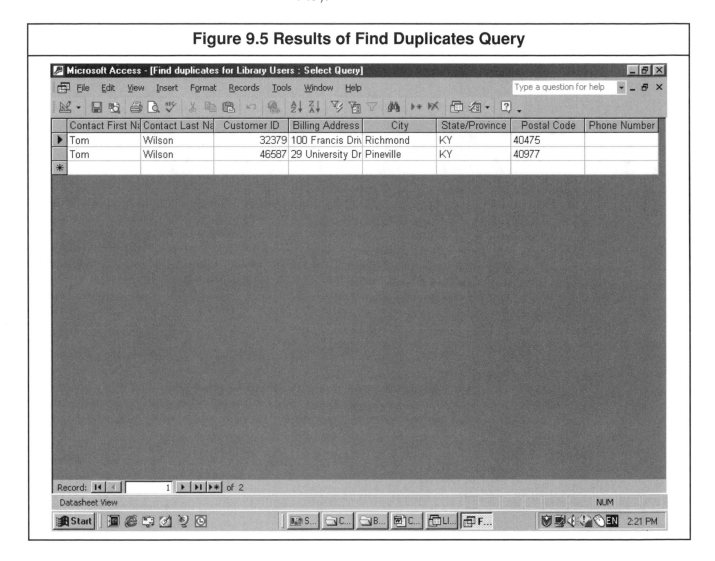

The results of the query show that there are two library users named Tom Wilson. Notice that each user has a different address. It is possible that there are two library users named Tom Wilson. It is also possible that this is the same person who has lived at both addresses. The database cannot determine which scenario is correct.

The query we ran, however, did find the duplicate values for first name and last name and now we can investigate to determine if this is the same library user or two separate library users.

For our example, let's assume these are two library users with the same name who live at different addresses.

16. Close the results of the query and return to the database window.

9.2 FIND UNMATCHED QUERY WIZARD

1. Click the **Queries** object button.
2. Click the **New** button.
3. Select **Find Unmatched Query Wizard** (see Figure 9.6).

Figure 9.6 Find Unmatched Query Wizard

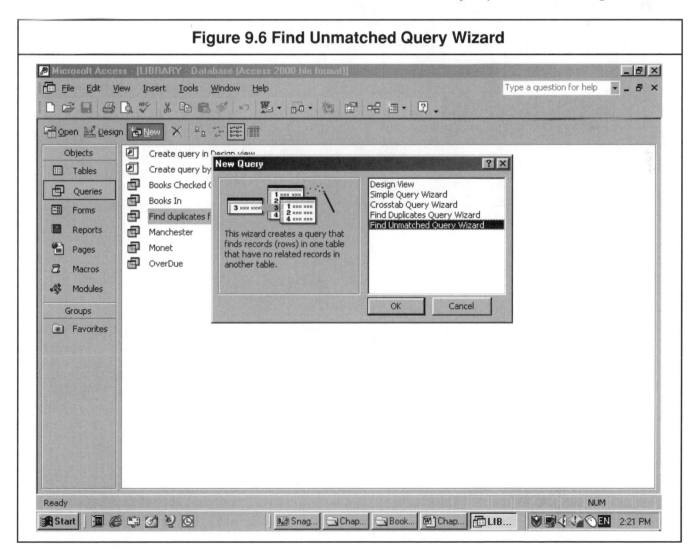

4. Click **OK**.
5. Select **Table: Library Users**. Make sure the **View Tables** option button is selected (see Figure 9.7).

Figure 9.7 Table Select

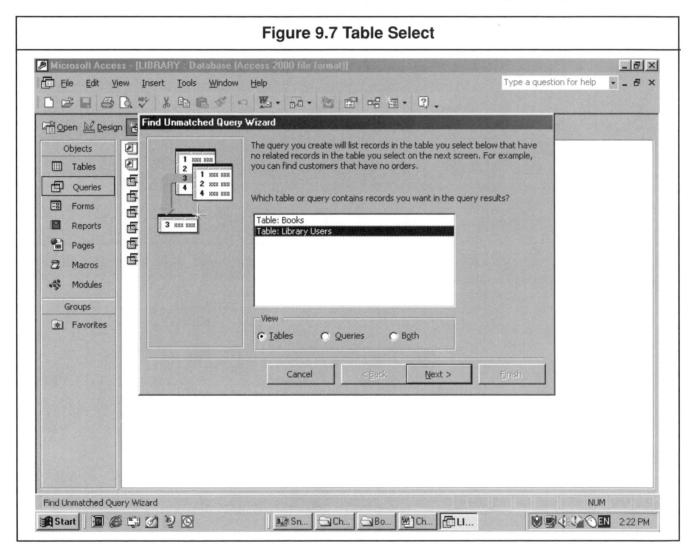

6. Click **Next**.

7. Select **Table: Books.** Make sure the **View Tables** option button is selected (see Figure 9.8).

Figure 9.8 Related Records Table

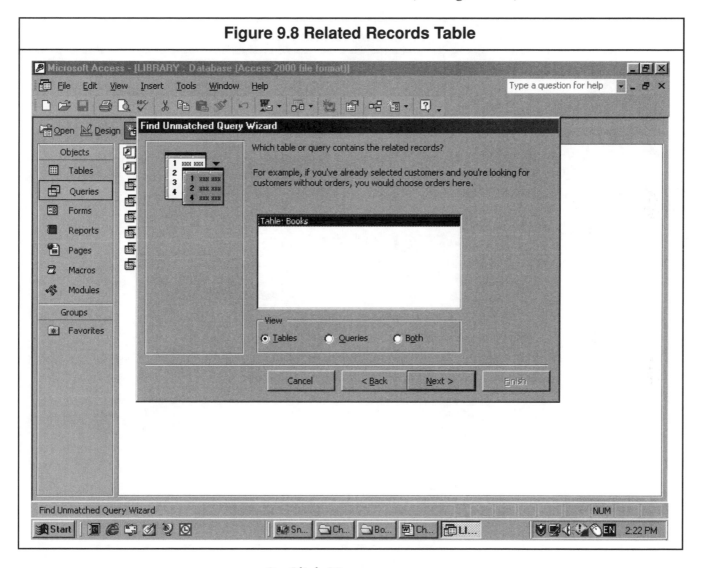

8. Click **Next.**
9. Click **CustomerID** in the Fields in Library Users list (if it is not already selected).
10. Click **User_No** in the Fields in Books list (if it is not already selected).

11. Make sure the Matching fields box reads "CustomerID <=> User_No" (see Figure 9.9).

Figure 9.9 Matching Fields

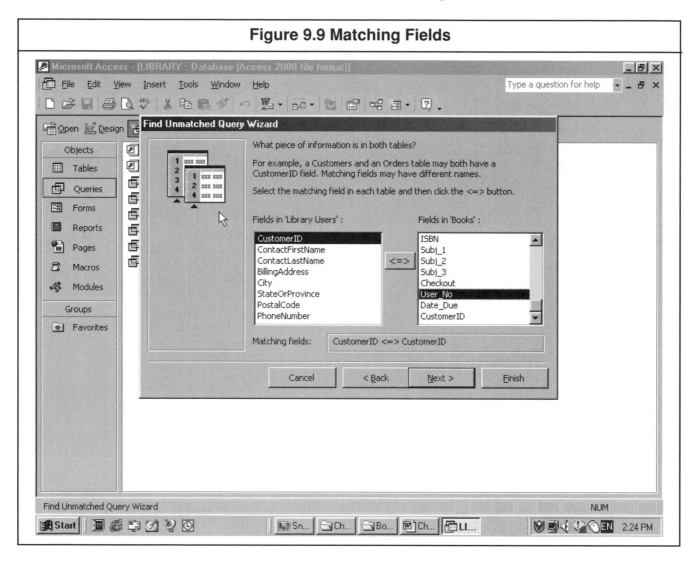

12. Click **Next**.

13. Add all of the remaining fields to the Selected Fields list (see Figure 9.10).

Figure 9.10 Selected Fields

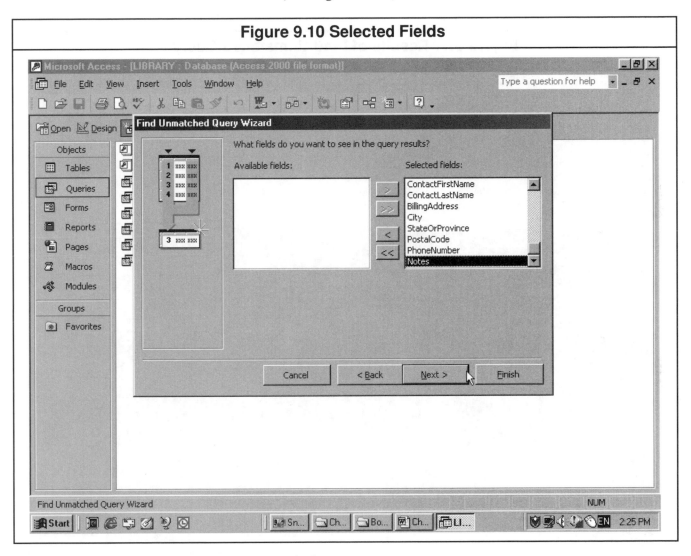

14. Click **Next**.

15. Accept the name **Library Users Without Matching Books**. Make sure **View the Results** is selected. Click **Finish** (see Figure 9.11).

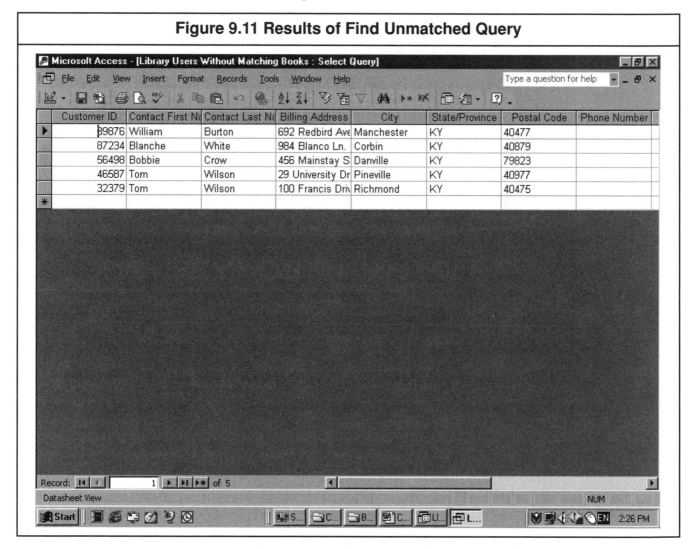

Figure 9.11 Results of Find Unmatched Query

Customer ID	Contact First Na	Contact Last Na	Billing Address	City	State/Province	Postal Code	Phone Number
89876	William	Burton	692 Redbird Ave	Manchester	KY	40477	
87234	Blanche	White	984 Blanco Ln.	Corbin	KY	40879	
56498	Bobbie	Crow	456 Mainstay S	Danville	KY	79823	
46587	Tom	Wilson	29 University Dr	Pineville	KY	40977	
32379	Tom	Wilson	100 Francis Driv	Richmond	KY	40475	

The results of the query show those library users who do not currently have any books checked out of the library. The query compared the **CustomerID** field (primary key) in the **Library Users** table to the **User_No** field (foreign key) in the **Books** table.

Each time a matching value was not found, the related record for that particular library user was included in the results of the query. Therefore, there were six library users who did not have library books checked out at this time.

16. Close the results of the query and return to the database window.

9.3 CROSSTAB QUERY

Next we are going to create a Crosstab Query that will show all of the library users and the cities in which they live. This will allow us to see the areas in which our library serves.

1. Click the **Queries** object button.
2. Click the **New** button.
3. Select **Crosstab Query Wizard** (see Figure 9.12).

Figure 9.12 Select Query Wizard

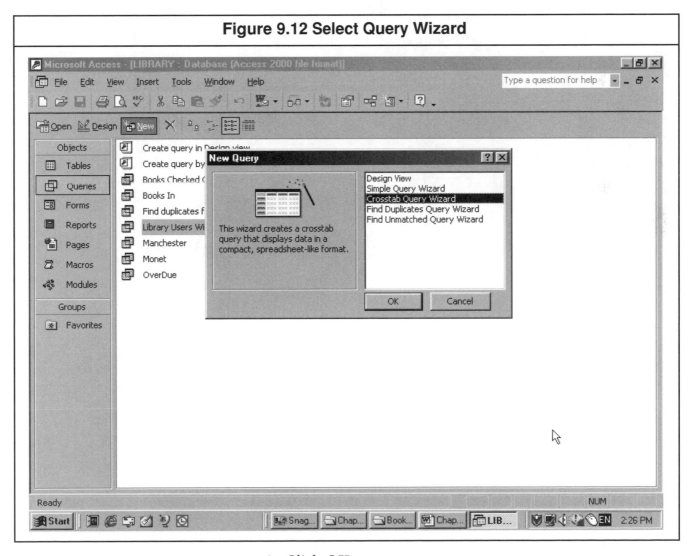

4. Click **OK**.
5. Click **Tables** in the **View** section (if it is not already selected).

6. Select **Table: Library Users** (see Figure 9.13).

Figure 9.13 Crosstab Table Selection

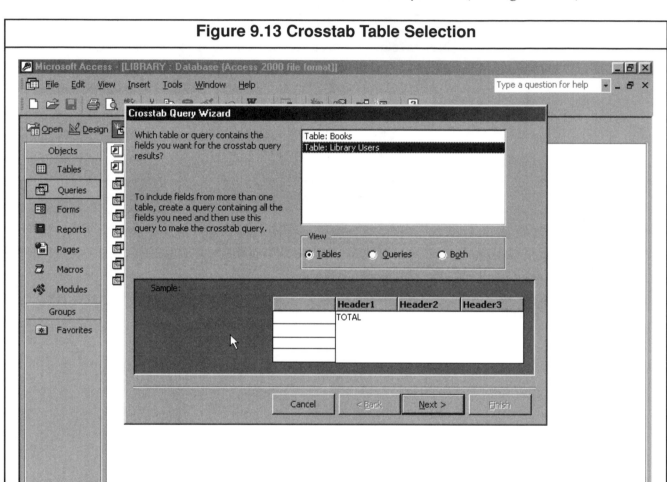

7. Click **Next**.

8. Add the following Available Fields to the Selected Fields list (see Figure 9.14):

CustomerID
FirstName
LastName

Figure 9.14 Crosstab Row Headings

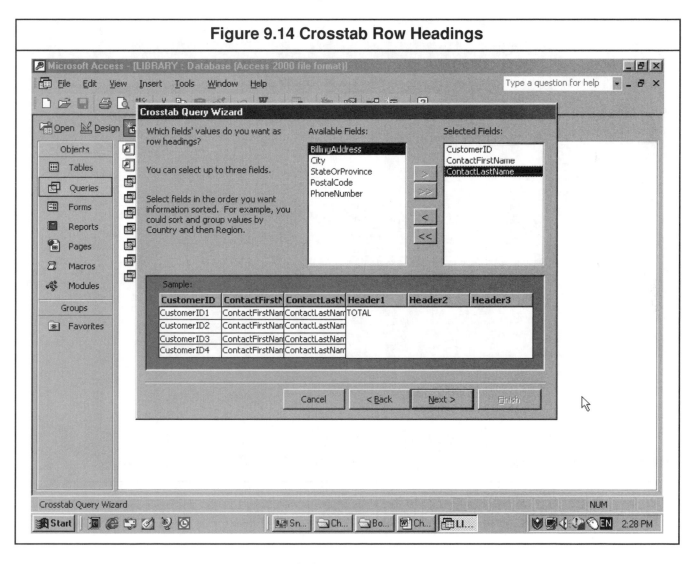

9. Click **Next**.

10. Select **City** from the field list to specify **City** as the **Crosstab Column Heading** (see Figure 9.15).

Figure 9.15 Crosstab Column Heading

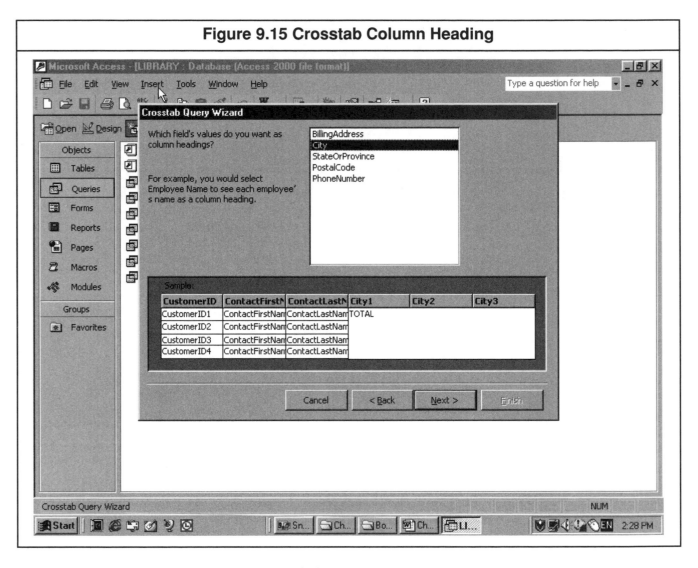

11. Click **Next**.

12. Click in the check box to deselect the option to include summary rows (see Figure 9.16).

Figure 9.16 Crosstab Row Summary Option

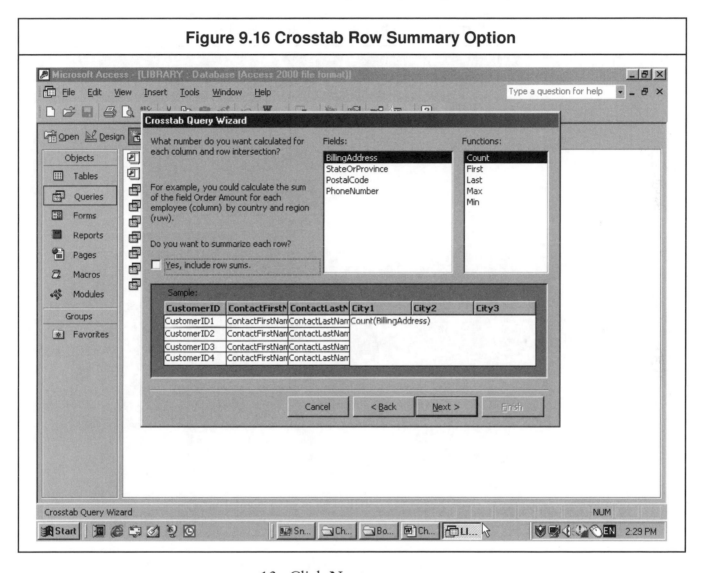

13. Click **Next**.
14. Accept the Query name **Library Users_Crosstab** and make sure the **View the query** option is selected.

15. Click **Finish** and the query results are displayed (see Figure 9.17).

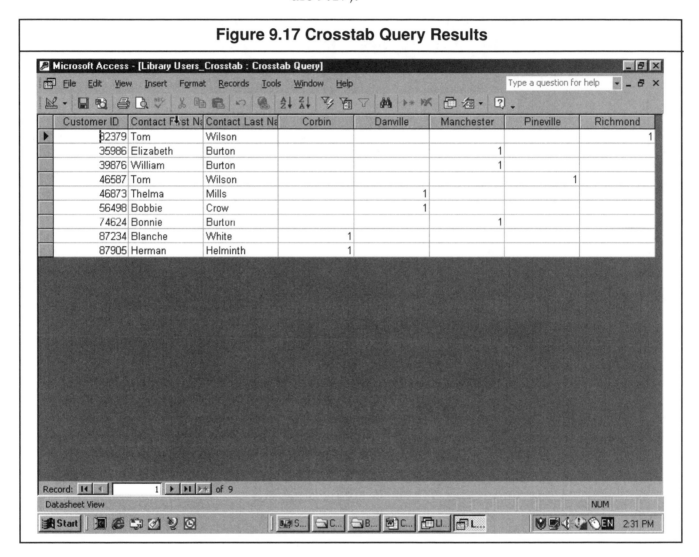

Figure 9.17 Crosstab Query Results

The query lists each library user by row. Each library user is identified by their **CustomerID, FirstName,** and **LastName.** The column headings are labeled by city. Here we can view how many library users live in each city.

16. Close the Crosstab Query and return to the database window.

9.4 PARAMETER QUERY

Suppose you want to check to see if a particular book is checked out. Instead of creating a query that displays the entire list of books checked out, we can create a query that will allow us to search for a single book. This will save time as we won't need to search through the entire list of checked-out books. The type of query that allows us to do this is a Parameter Query.

A Parameter Query will search a query for a record or records that meet specific criteria. For example, if we want to search to see if a book is checked out of the library, we can search the **Books Checked Out** query for a particular book. In our example we will search by **Call No**.

1. Click the **Queries** object.
2. Click the **Books Checked Out** query.
3. Click the **Design** button.
4. Click in the **Criteria** field for the **Call_No** field.
5. Enter the following (with the brackets):
   [**Enter Call No**] (scc Figure 9.18).

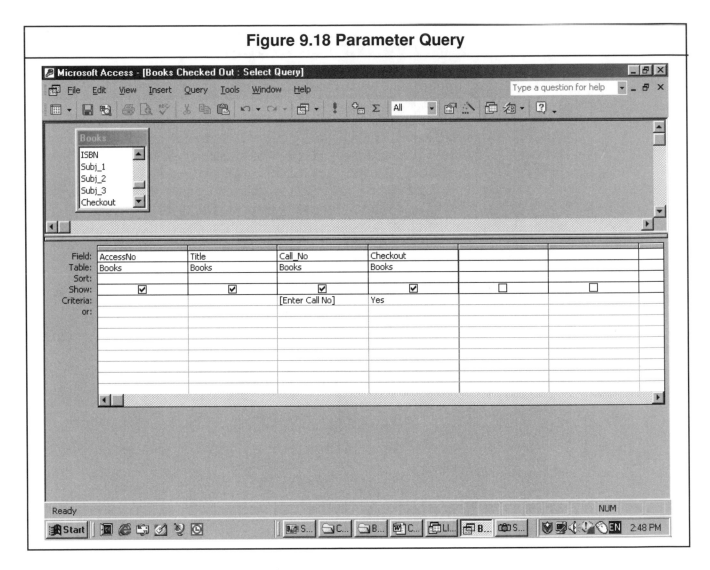

Figure 9.18 Parameter Query

6. Click **File, Save As.**

7. Save the query as **Books Checked Out Parameter Query** (see Figure 9.19).
8. Click **OK**.

Figure 9.19 Saving Parameter Query

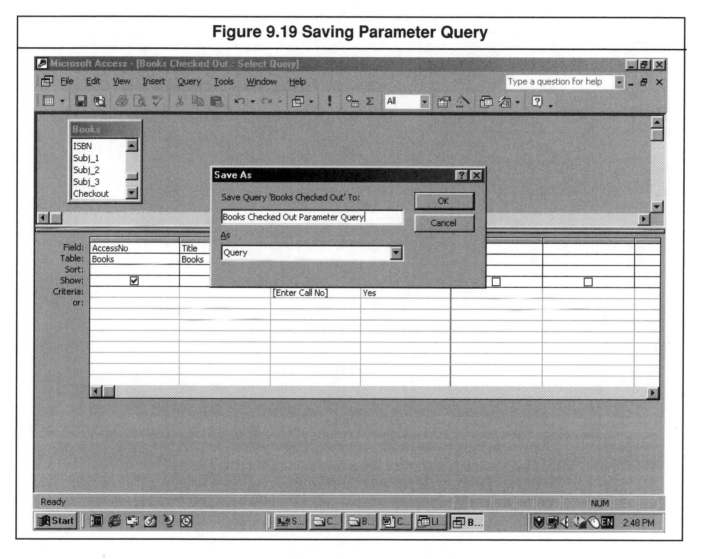

9. Close the query.

10. Open the **Books Checked Out Parameter Query** and you are prompted for a call no. (see Figure 9.20).

Figure 9.20 Run Parameter Query

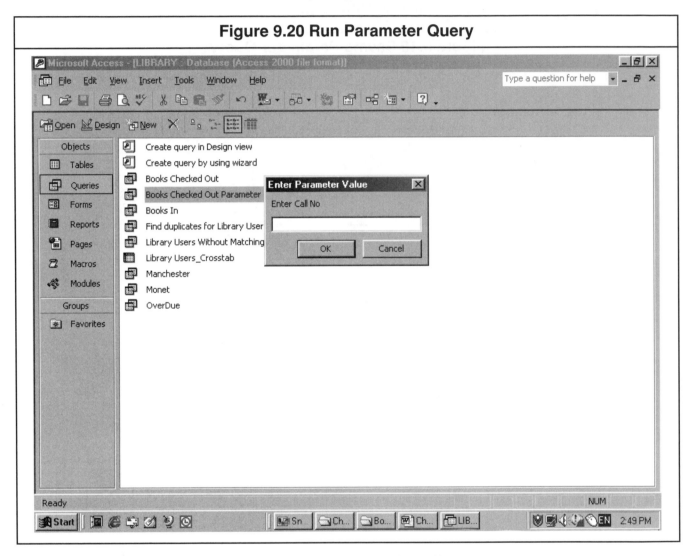

11. Enter **F FIN** as the call no.
12. Click **OK**.
13. The book **Seven Gothic Tales** appears. The query only returns the book with the same call no. as what we entered when prompted (see Figure 9.21).

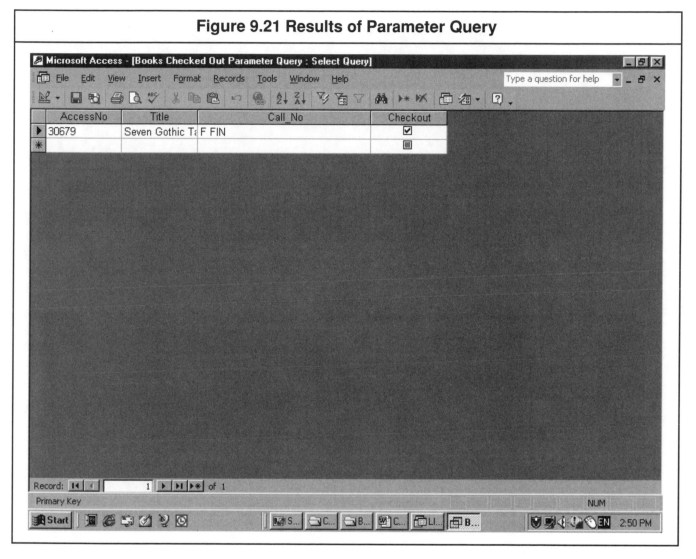

Figure 9.21 Results of Parameter Query

14. Close the query and return to the database window.

10 REPORTS

OBJECTIVES

10.1 PRINTING FROM A DATABASE
10.2 REPORT BASED ON DATES
10.3 MAILING LABELS

You have learned many things about Access leading up to this chapter:

- How to create tables and store data.
- How to create queries to join tables.
- How to create forms to input data.

In this chapter we are going to look at how to create reports to print information from the database. You will learn to do the following:

- How to create and print reports from a table or a query.
- How to create and print a report for an overdue notice.
- How to create mailing labels.

10.1 PRINTING FROM A DATABASE

Our first report will print a list of all library users. We will generate the report directly from the **Library Users** table.

1. Open the **LIBRARY.mdb** database.
2. Click on the **Reports** object.
3. Click on the **New** button and the **New Report** window opens (see Figure 10.1).

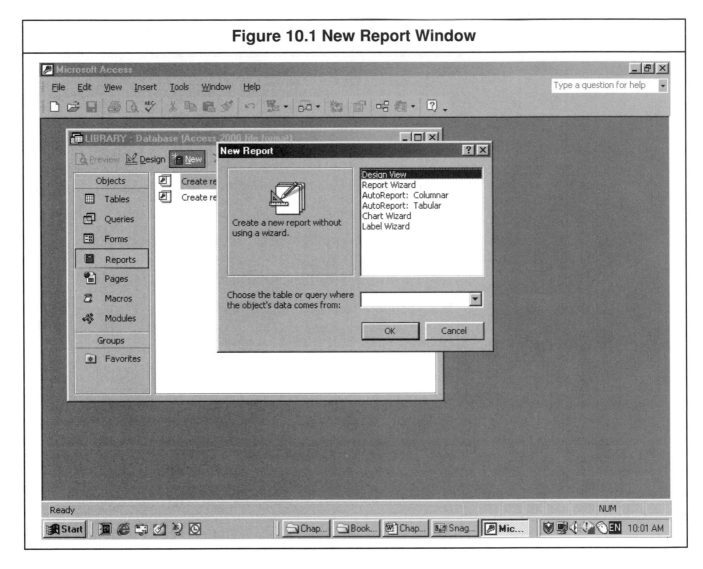

Figure 10.1 New Report Window

4. Click **Report Wizard**.

5. Select **Library Users** from the **Choose the table or query where the object's data comes from** list box (see Figure 10.2).

Figure 10.2 New Report Criteria

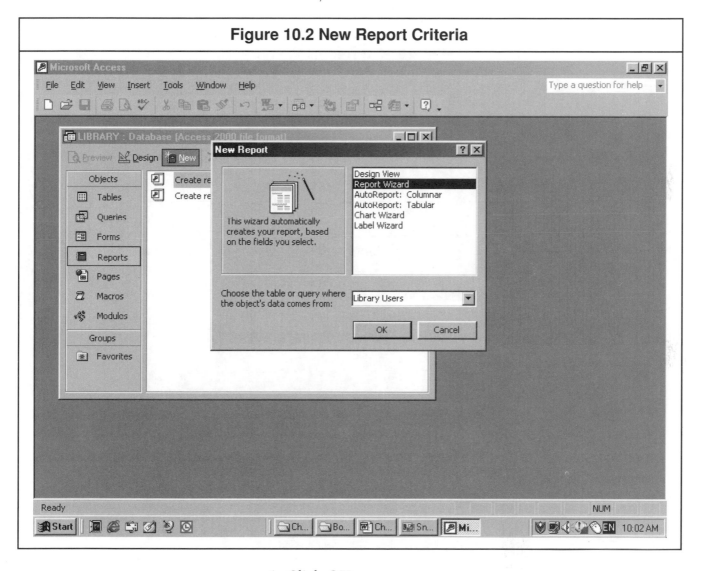

6. Click **OK**.

7. When the Report Wizard window opens, add the following fields to the Selected Fields list: **FirstName**, **LastName**, **BillingAddress**, **City**, **StateOrProvince**, and **PostalCode** (see Figure 10.3).

Figure 10.3 Report Fields

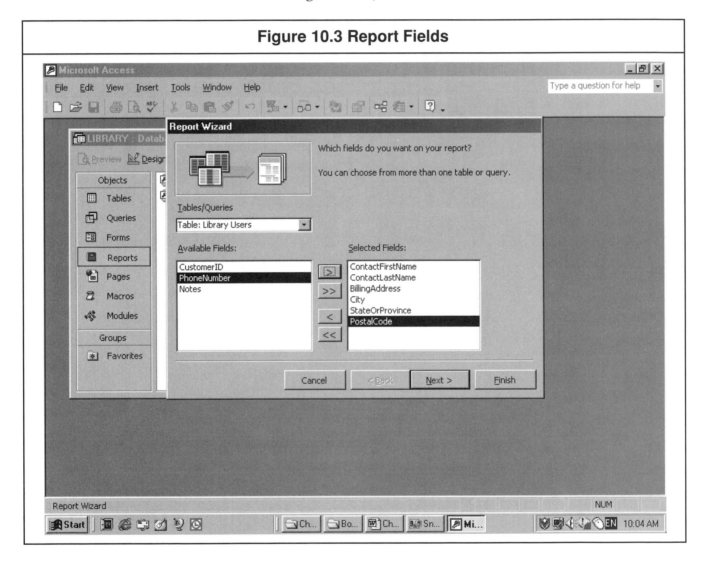

8. Click **Next**.
9. Click **Next** since we do not want to add any grouping levels.

10. Select **LastName** from the first sort order list box (see Figure 10.4).

Figure 10.4 Sort Order

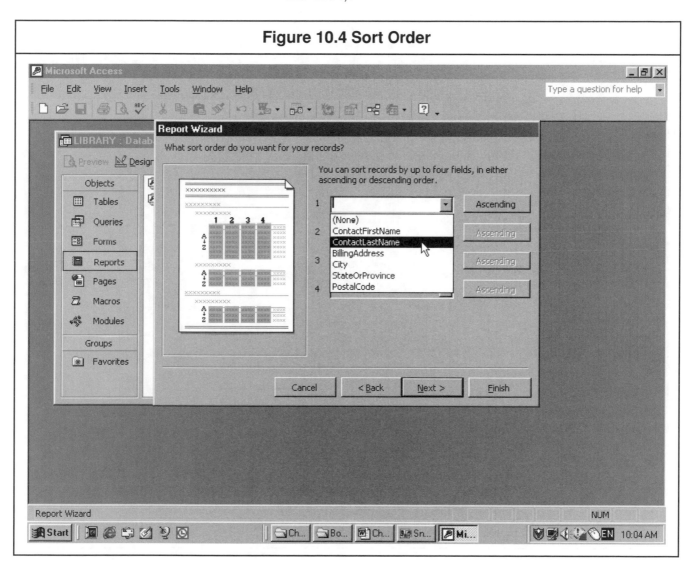

11. Select **FirstName** in the second sort order list box (see Figure 10.5).

Figure 10.5 Multiple Sort Fields

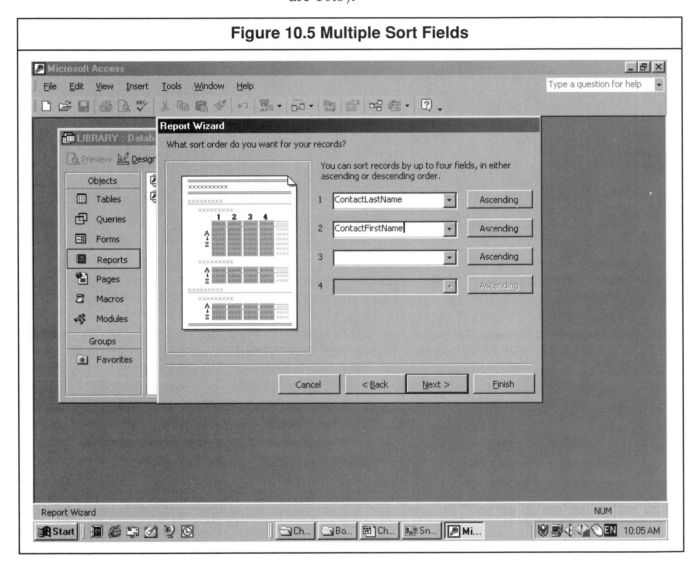

12. Click **Next**.
13. Click **Next** to accept **Tabular Layout** and **Portrait Orientation**.
14. Click **Next** to accept **Corporate Style**.
15. Enter **Library Users** as the title of the Report, if necessary.

16. Make sure the **Preview the Report** option button is selected (see Figure 10.6).

Figure 10.6 Report Wizard Conclusion

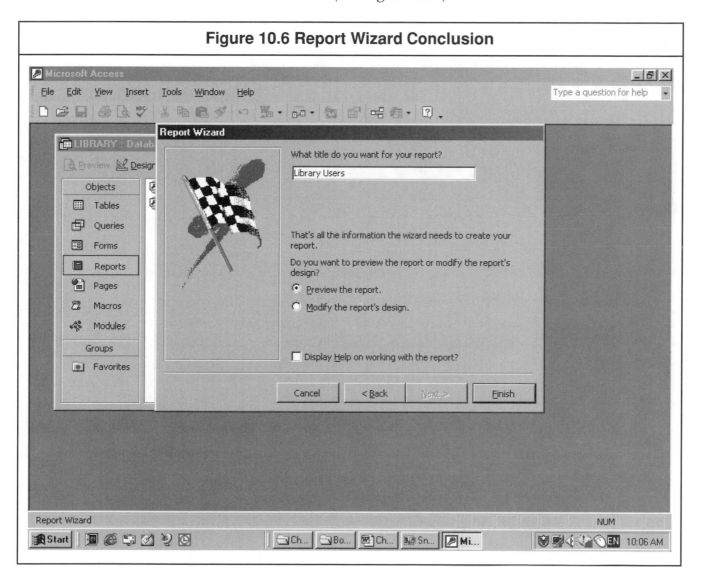

17. Click **Finish**. The report opens and is now ready to print (see Figure 10.7).

Figure 10.7 Library Users Report

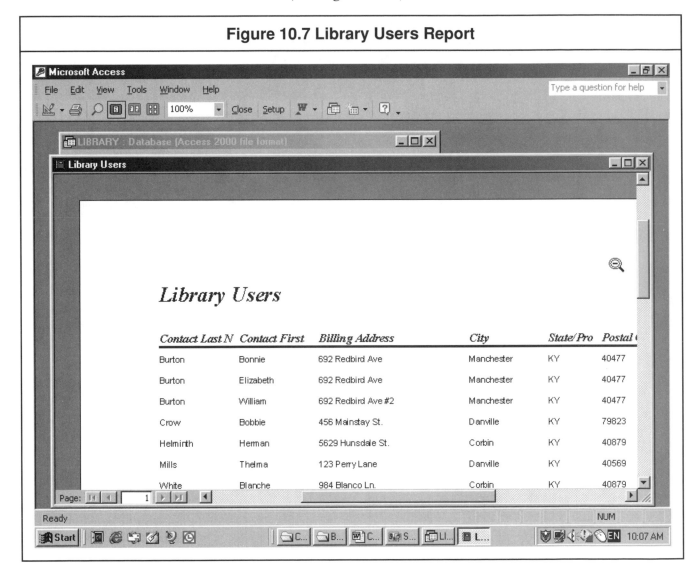

18. Click **File**, then **Print**.
19. The Print window appears. The name box at the top of the window shows which printer you will print to. You should already be set up to a printer, but you can always choose a different printer.
20. **Print to file** means the query will be saved as a file. This option allows you to print the file later without running Microsoft Access. Choosing this option will require you to specify a location and filename for the new file.
21. The **Print Range** box defines exactly what will be printed:

- **All** will print the entire report.
- **Pages From:** will print a range of pages.

22. **Copies** allows you to choose the number of copies that will be printed (1 is the default).
23. Click **OK** and the report will print.

Complete steps 3–17 above to create a report with the same information, but this time use the **Justified Layout**. Save this report as **Library Users Justified** (See Figure 10.8).

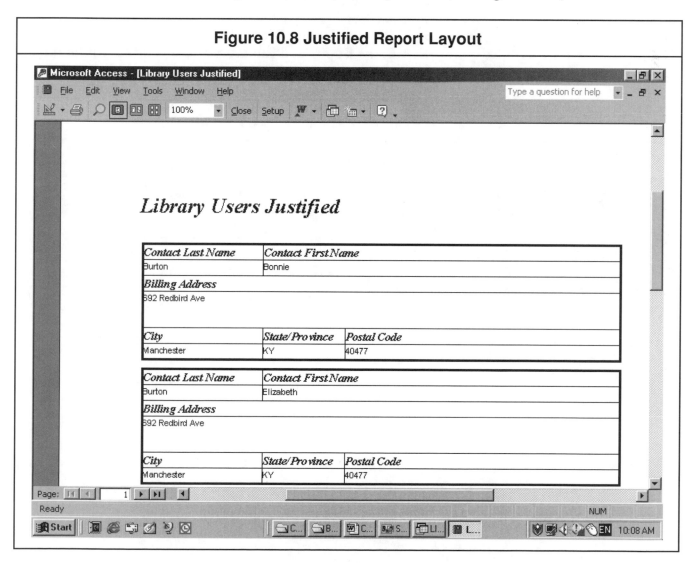

Figure 10.8 Justified Report Layout

Print both pages and close the report.

10.2 REPORT BASED ON DATES

In this section we are going to create a report that prints only those records that meet certain criteria. For example, we will print a list of records that include those books that are past due.

Before we create the report, we need to create a query that retrieves data from both the **Books** and the **Library Users** tables.

1. Click the **Queries** object button.
2. Click **New**.
3. Make sure **Design View** is selected and click **OK**.
4. Add the **Books** and the **Library Users** tables to the query.
5. Close the **Show Table** window.
6. Add **Date_Due**, **Title**, and **Call_No** from the **Books** table.
7. Add **ContactFirstName** and **ContactLastName** from the **Library Users** table (see Figure 10.9).

Figure 10.9 Multi-table Query for Report

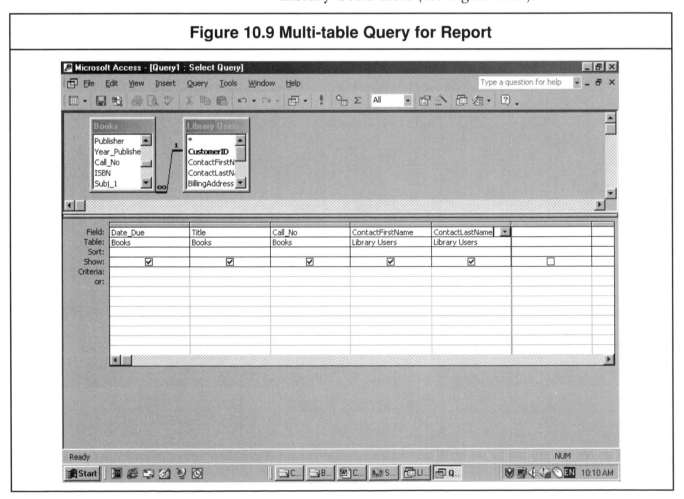

8. Close the query window.
9. Click **Yes** when asked to save.
10. Enter the Title **Users With OverDue Books.**
11. Click **OK.**
12. Click the **Reports** object.
13. Click **New.**
14. Click **Report Wizard** on the **New Report** window.
15. Select **Users With OverDue Books** from the **Choose the table or query where the object's data comes from** list (see Figure 10.10).

Figure 10.10 New Report Window

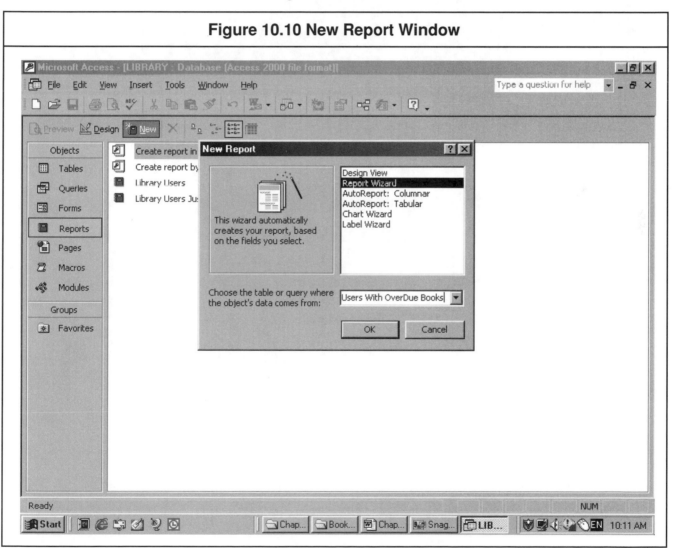

16. Click **OK.**

17. Select all of the fields for the report (see Figure 10.11).

Figure 10.11 Selected Fields for Report

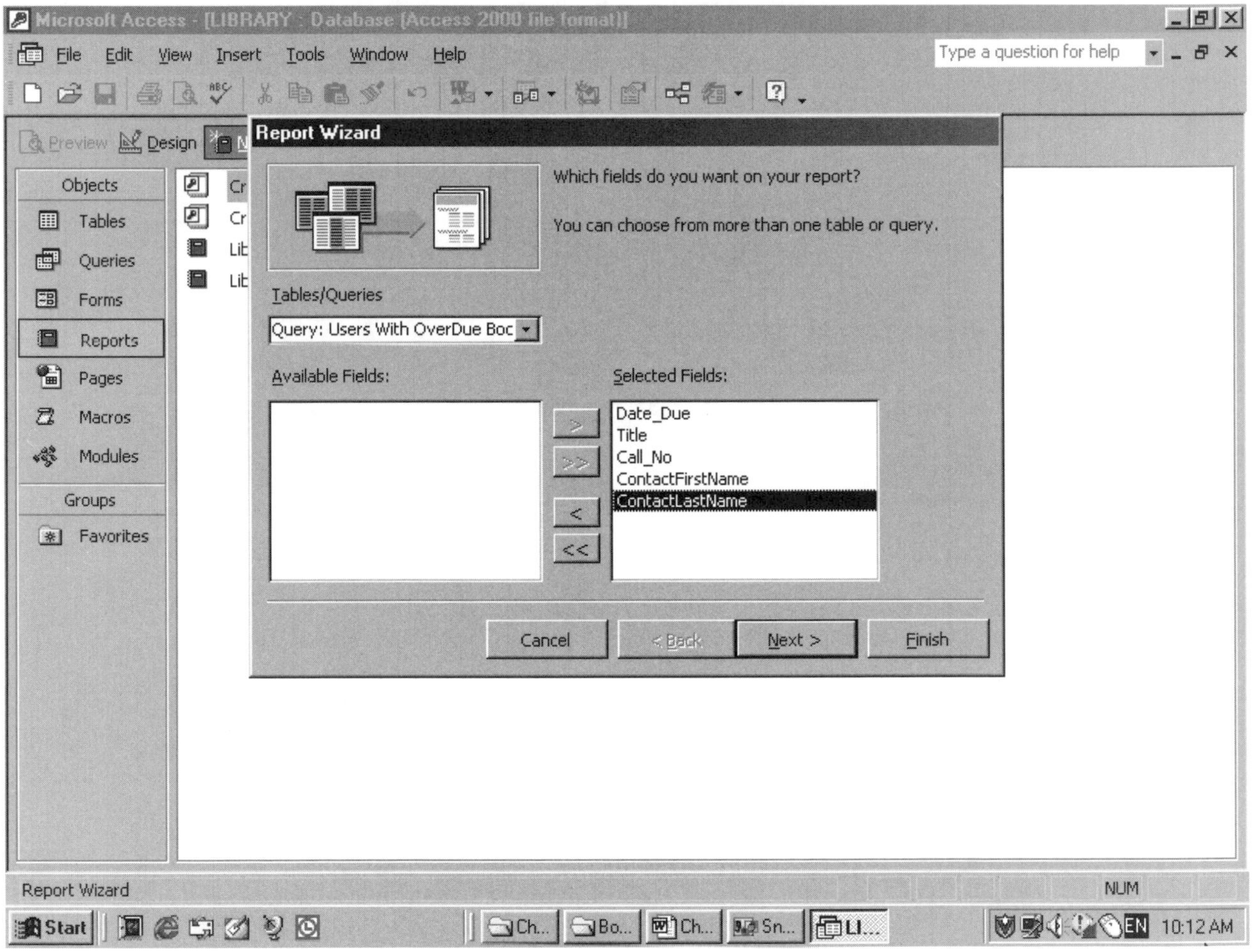

18. Click **Next**.
19. Click **Next**.

20. When the report sort order window opens, select **Date_Due** as the primary sort field (see Figure 10.12).

Figure 10.12 Sort by Date Due

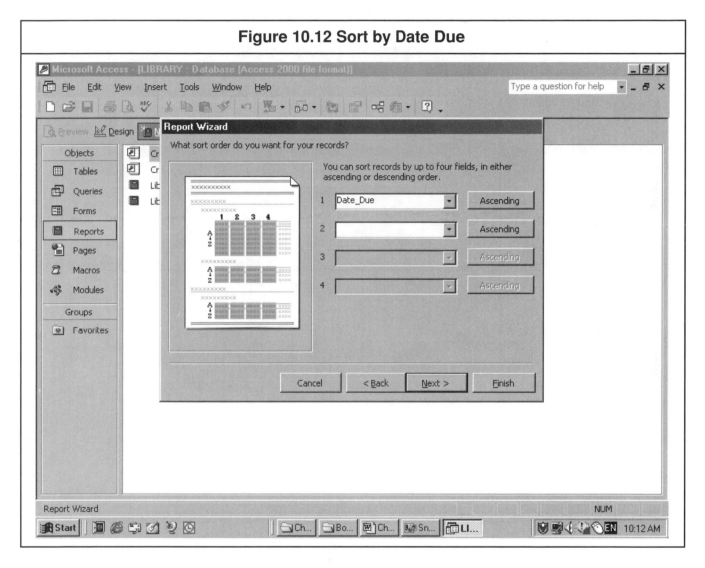

21. Click **Next**.
22. Click **Next** to accept the Tabular Layout and Portrait Orientation.
23. Click **Next**.
24. Enter **Users With Books Overdue** as the Title of the report.

25. Click **Finish** (see Figure 10.13).

Figure 10.13 Users With Books Overdue Report

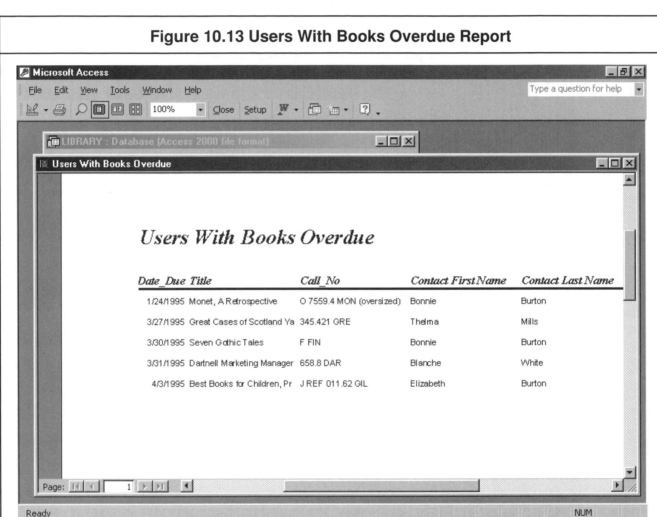

As you can see, this report returned all books that are checked out, regardless of the due date. We are now going to set a condition that will query the database only for books that are actually overdue.

26. Close the **Books Overdue** report.
27. Open **Users With Books Overdue** in design view.

28. Click to open the properties window if it is not already open (see Figure 10.14).

Figure 10.14 Books Overdue Report in Design View

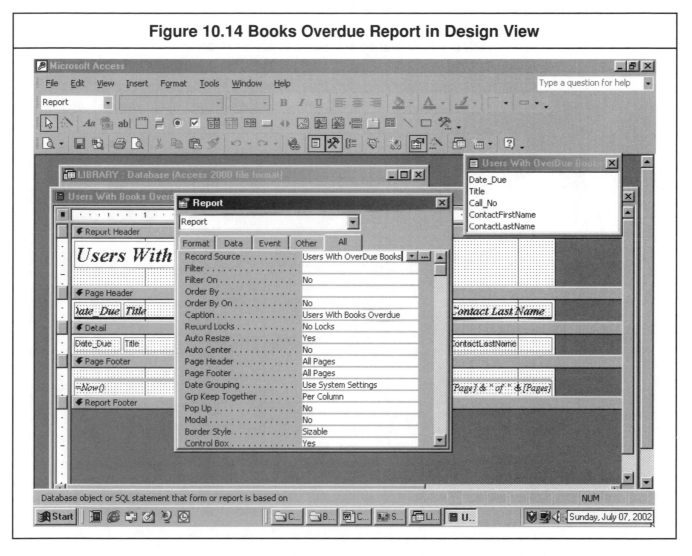

29. Make sure the **All** tab is selected in the properties window.
30. Click the **Record Source** textbox (which currently has **Users With Books Overdue** as the record source).

31. Click the box that appears to the right of the record source that has three dots and a message should appear (see Figure 10.15).

Figure 10.15 Using a Query With a Report

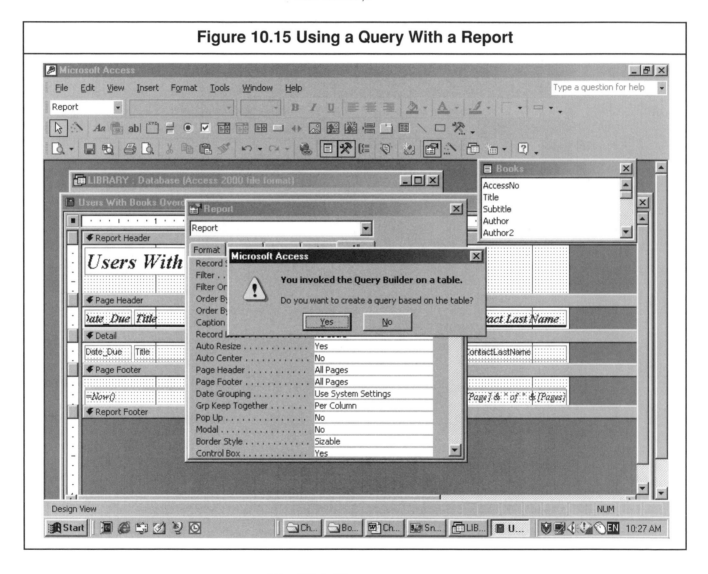

32. Click **Yes.**

33. Enter "=3/30/1995" (without the parenthesis) in the criteria field for **Date_Due** (see Figure 10.16).

Figure 10.16 Report With Query Condition

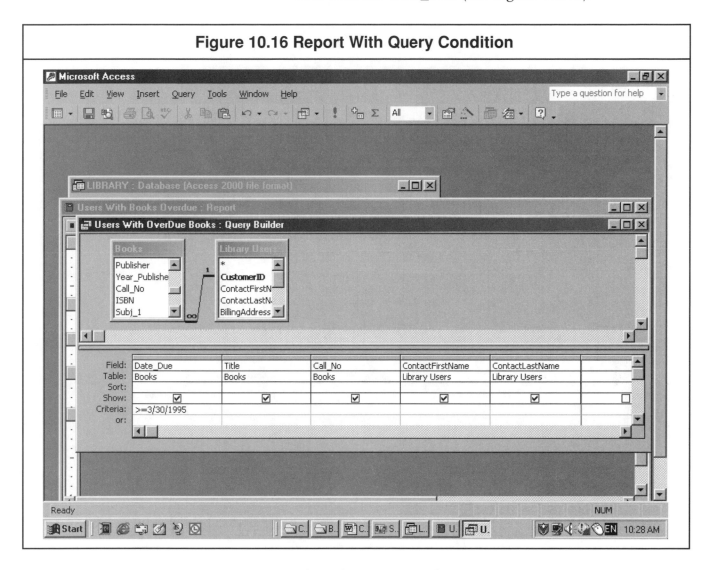

34. Close the query window.
35. Click **Yes** to save and exit.

36. Click the **Preview Report** button to see the report that shows only those books overdue (see Figure 10.17).

Figure 10.17 Updated Book Overdue Report

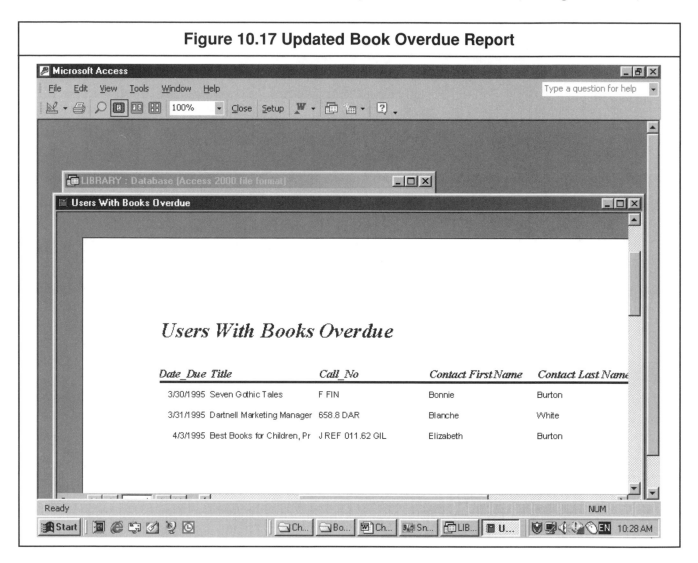

37. Close the report.
38. Click **Yes** to save.

10.3 MAILING LABELS

1. Click the **Report** object button.
2. Click **New**.
3. Click **Label Wizard**.
4. Select the table **Library Users** (see Figure 10.18).

Figure 10.18 Label Wizard

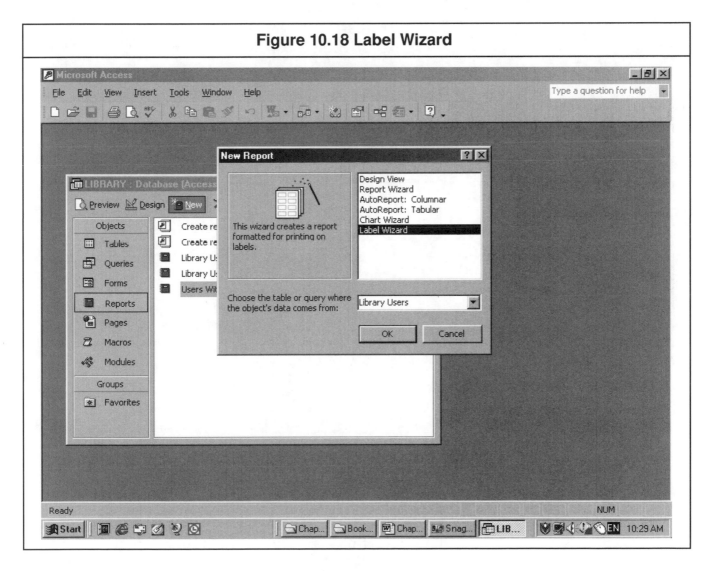

5. Click **OK**.
6. Click **English** for the Unit of Measure.
7. Select **Avery** to Filter by Manufacturer.

8. Click Product Number **5161** (see Figure 10.19).

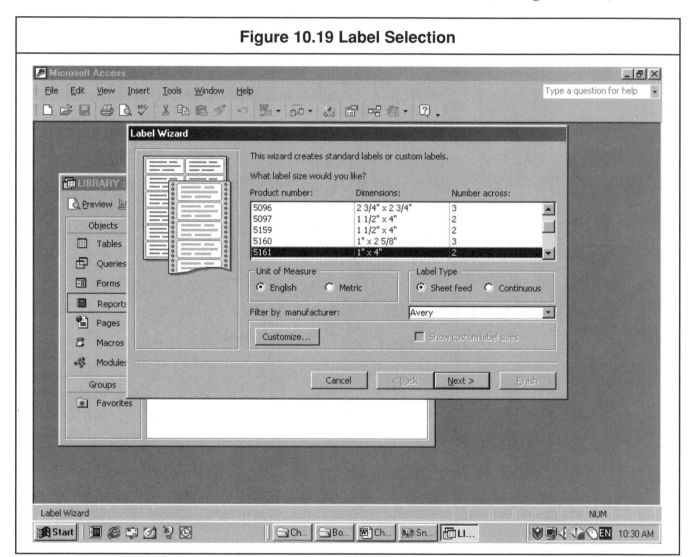

Figure 10.19 Label Selection

9. Click **Next**.
10. Click **Next** to accept the default font and color.
11. Click on the **Select** button to add **ContactFirstName** to the label.
12. Press the <spacebar> to add a space, then add **ContactLastName** to the label.
13. Press the <enter> key on your keyboard to move to the next line.

14. Add the remaining fields to the label. Remember to space between the fields and to also add a comma after the city field (see Figure 10.20).

Figure 10.20 Label Fields

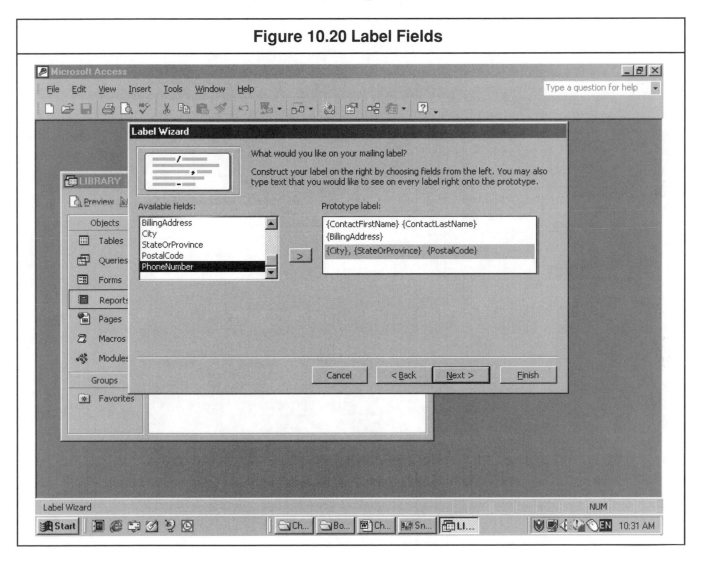

15. Click **Next**.

16. Sort by **ContactLastName** (see Figure 10.21).

Figure 10.21 Sorted Field

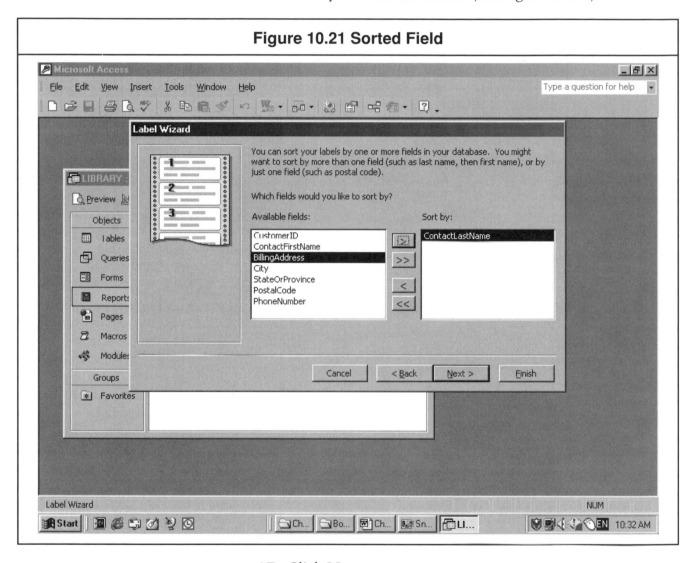

17. Click **Next**.

18. Accept the name **Label Library Users**. Click **Finish** (see Figure 10.22).

Figure 10.22 Library Users Labels

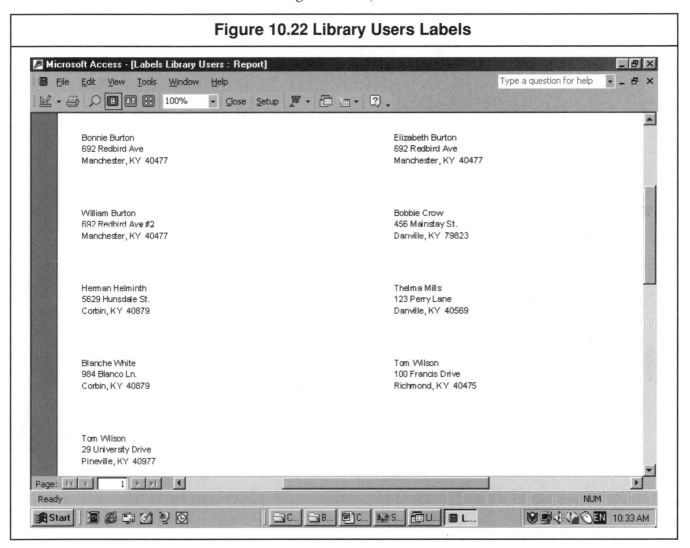

19. Close the **Labels** report.
20. Exit the database.

11 MACROS

In this chapter we are going to work with macros. A macro is created to perform one or more operations. For example, we can use a macro to open a query or to print a report. Macros allow us to perform these types of operations without having to program these types of operations into our database using visual basic for applications.

We are going to create macros that will open queries. Then we will create a macro that will open a form. After that we will create a macro that will automatically print a report. Finally, we will create a macro that will allow us to exit our database.

11.1 OPEN QUERY MACRO

Here we are creating a macro that will automatically open a query. We will use a macro to open the query and get the same results as if we had opened the query itself. We are going to create a macro to open the query so that we can utilize the advantages of using macros when creating a switchboard (Chapter 12).

1. Click the **Macros** object button.
2. Click the **New** button. The Macro window opens (see Figure 11.1).

Figure 11.1 Macro Window

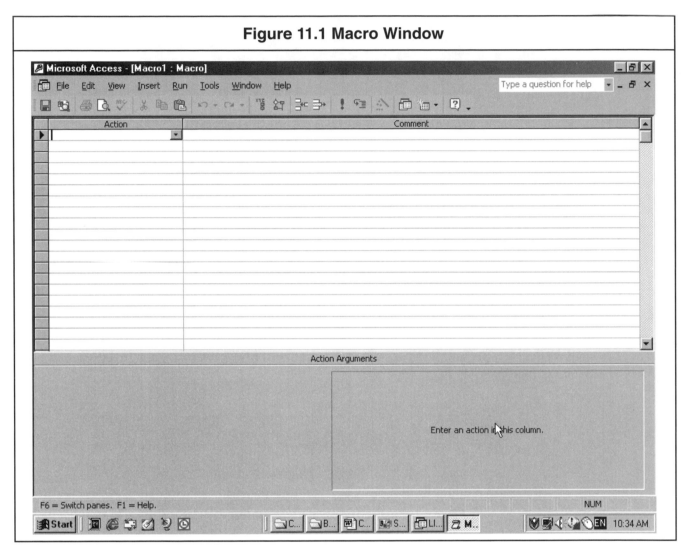

3. In the first Action field, select **OpenQuery**.

4. Select **Books Checked Out** in the Query Name field. Make sure View is equal to **Datasheet** and Data Mode is equal to **Edit** (see Figure 11.2).

Figure 11.2 Open Query Macro

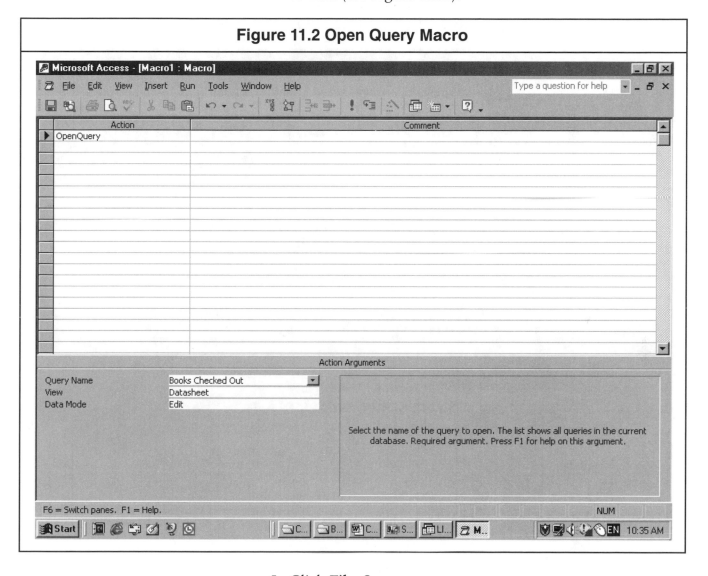

5. Click **File, Save**.
6. Enter **Books Checked Out** as the Macro Name.
7. Click **OK**.
8. Close the macro window.

9. Run the **Books Checked Out** macro. The Books Checked Out query opens (see Figure 11.3).

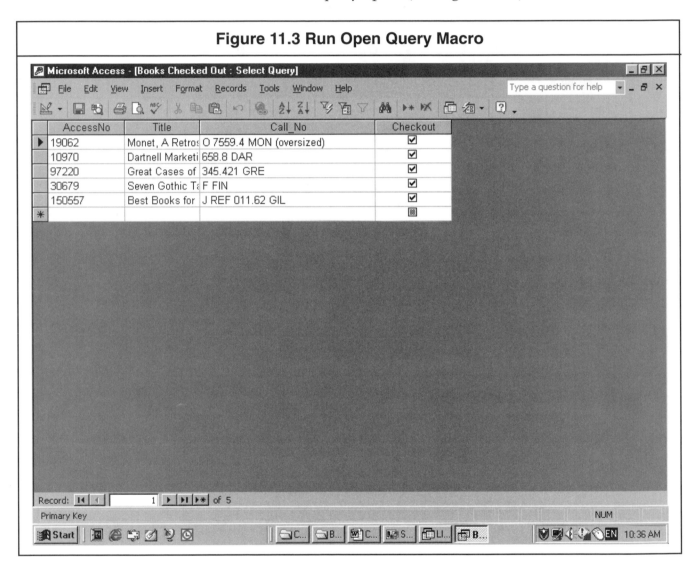

Figure 11.3 Run Open Query Macro

10. Close the query window.

11. Create a macro to open each of the queries we have created thus far. Follow steps 2 through 8 above. There should be a total of nine macros to equal the nine queries. Give the macros the same names as the queries (see Figure 11.4).

Figure 11.4 Macros Created

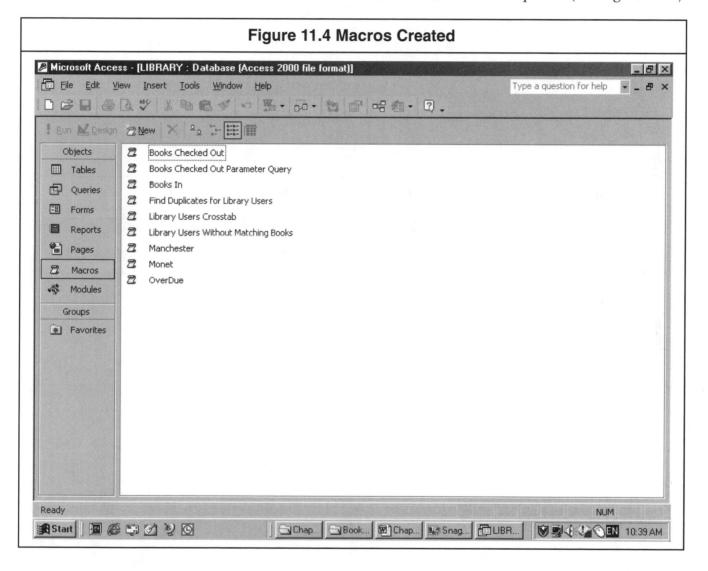

11.2 OPEN FORM MACRO

Here we are creating a macro that will automatically open a form. We will use a macro to open the form and get the same results as if we had opened the form itself.

1. Click the **Macros** object button.
2. Click the **New** button. The Macro window opens.
3. In the first Action field, select **OpenForm**.
4. Select **Books** in the Form Name field. Make sure View is equal to **Form** and Window Mode is equal to **Normal** (see Figure 11.5).

Figure 11.5 Open Form Macro

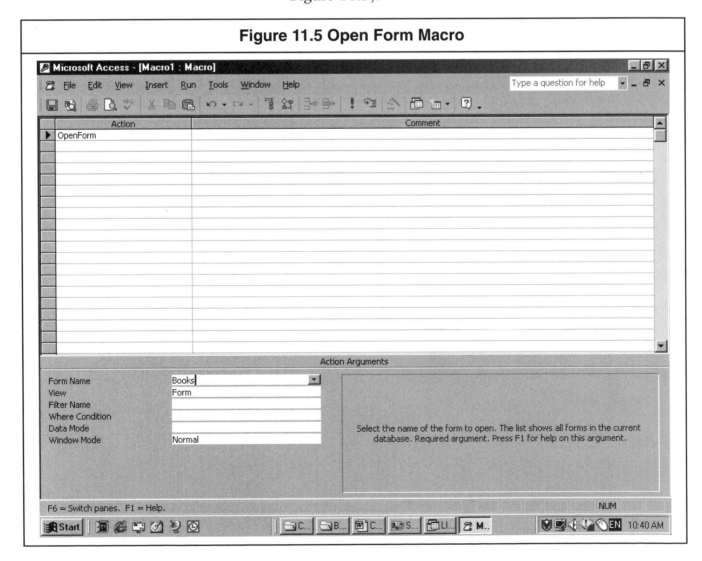

5. Click **File, Save**.
6. Enter **Books** as the Macro Name.
7. Click **OK**.
8. Close the macro window.
9. Run the **Books** macro. The Books form opens (see Figure 11.6).

Figure 11.6 Run Open Form Macro

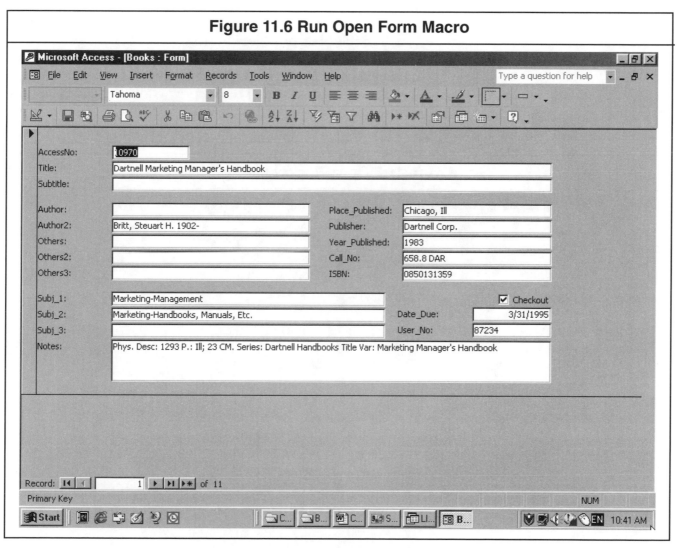

10. Close the form window.

11.3 PRINT REPORT MACRO

Here we are creating a macro that will automatically print a report. We will use a macro to print the report and we will get the same results as if we had opened the report and gave the print command.

1. Click the **Macros** object button.
2. Click the **New** button. The Macro window opens.
3. In the first Action field, select **OpenReport**.
4. Select **Library Users** in the Report Name field. Make sure View is equal to **Print** and Window Mode is equal to **Normal** (see Figure 11.7).

Figure 11.7 Open Report Macro

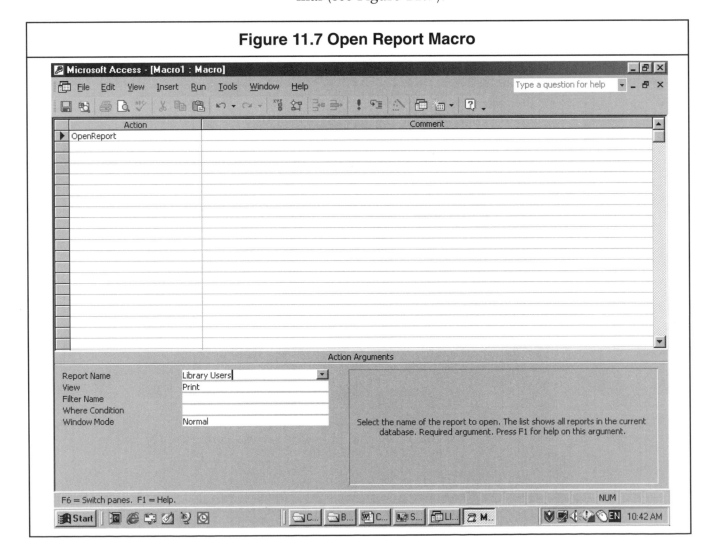

5. Click **File, Save**.
6. Enter **Library Users** as the Macro Name.
7. Click **OK**.
8. Close the macro window.
9. Run the **Library Users** macro. The **Library Users** report prints.
10. Close any open windows and return to the database window.

11.4 EXIT DATABASE MACRO

Here we are creating a macro that will automatically close the **LIBRARY.mdb** database and exit from Access. We will use a macro to exit the database and get the same results as if we had manually closed the **Library** database and exited from Access.

1. Click the **Macros** object button.
2. Click the **New** button. The Macro window opens.
3. In the first Action field, select **Quit**.
4. Make sure Options is equal to Save All (see Figure 11.8).

Figure 11.8 Exit Database Macro

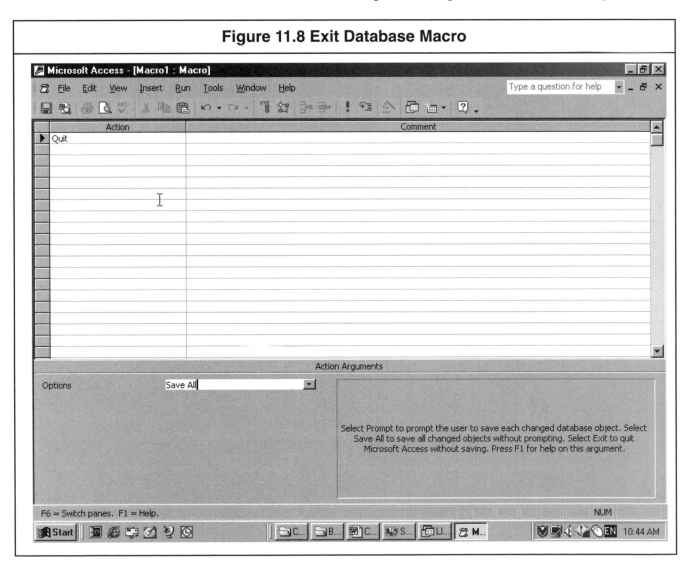

5. Click **File, Save**.
6. Enter **Exit Database** as the Macro Name.
7. Click **OK**.
8. Close the macro window.
9. Run the **Exit Database** macro. The **LIBRARY.mdb** database and the Access program close.

12 SWITCHBOARD MANAGER

OBJECTIVES

12.1 CREATING THE DEFAULT SWITCHBOARD
12.2 CREATING SWITCHBOARD PAGES
12.3 MODIFYING SWITCHBOARD PAGES
12.4 MAIN PAGE STARTUP

So far we have created many different types of objects that include tables, forms, queries, and reports. The database, as it is, would be considered to be in a usable format. We need, however, to specify the environment and the specific objects that we want the database users to be able to access. We need to create an environment where the objects that can be accessed by the users are already determined.

We can manage our database objects by using the Switchboard Manager. We can create switchboard forms that will allow us to access all of the objects we have created in our database. Our switchboard will have different forms that will manage our objects pertaining to the books in the library as well as objects pertaining to the library users.

We will begin by creating the switchboard manager. Then we will specify the different pages that we will use in the switchboard. After that we can determine what we want to include on each switchboard page. Finally, we will set up the Main Switchboard page to open automatically when we open the **LIBRARY.mdb** database.

12.1 CREATING THE DEFAULT SWITCHBOARD

1. Click **Tools** on the menu bar.
2. Click **Database Utilities.**

3. Click **Switchboard Manager** (see Figure 12.1).

Figure 12.1 Accessing Switchboard Manager

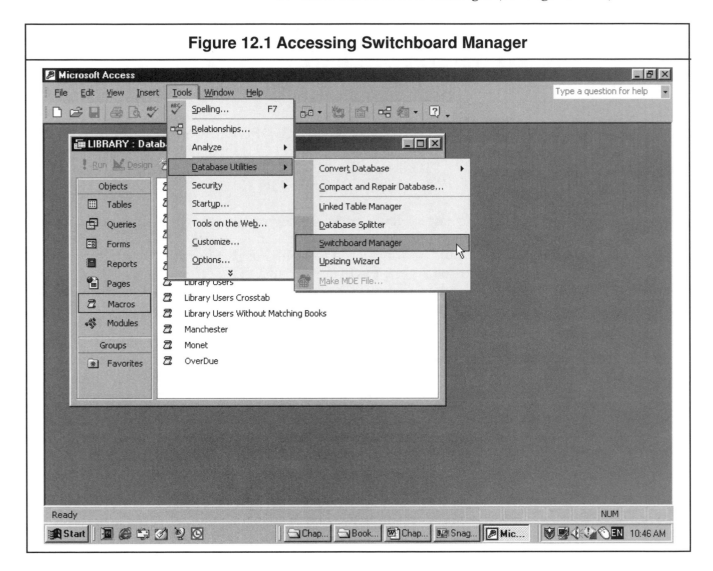

4. Click **Yes** when the warning message appears. The message states that we do not currently have a switchboard in our database. We click **Yes** to specify that we wish to create a switchboard. The switchboard manager now opens (see Figure 12.2).

Figure 12.2 Switchboard Manager

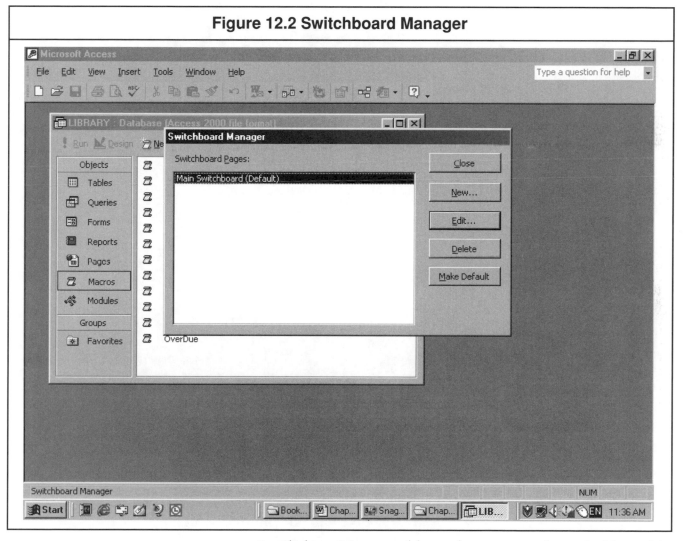

5. Click on **New** to add another page to the switchboard in addition to the Main Switchboard (default) page.

6. Enter **Books** as the Switchboard Page Name (see Figure 12.3).

Figure 12.3 Creating New Switchboard Page

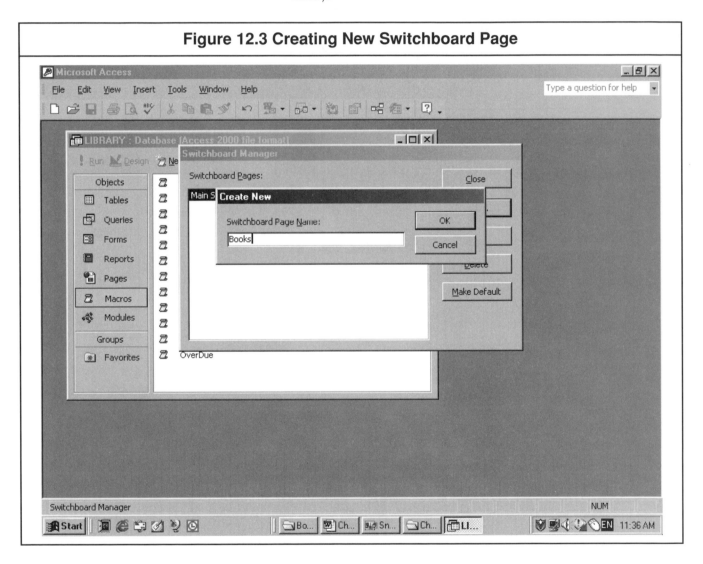

7. Click **OK**.
8. Click **New** to add another switchboard page.
9. Enter **Library Users** as the switchboard page name.

10. Click **OK**. We now have three switchboard pages (see Figure 12.4).

Figure 12.4 Switchboard Pages

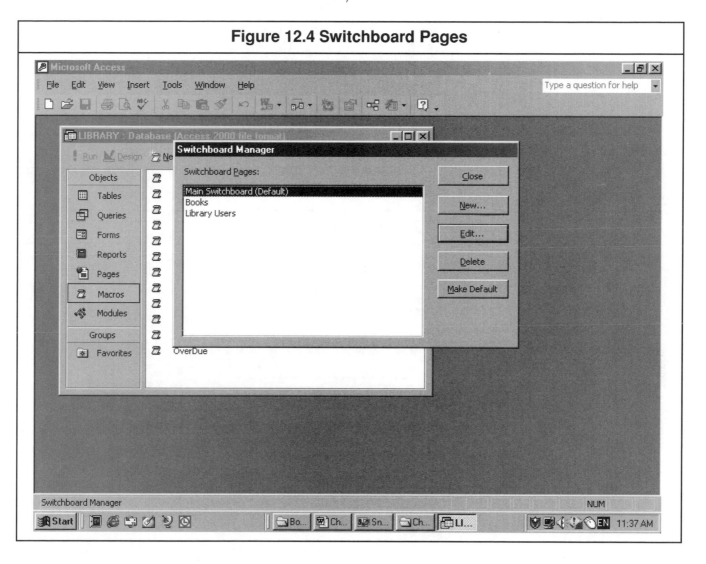

12.2 CREATING SWITCHBOARD PAGES

We want to be able to access both the **Books** and the **Library Users** information from the Main Switchboard Page. The next step is to add those two pages so that they will appear whenever we access the switchboard's main page. We will have to edit the Main Switchboard to create this environment.

1. Click **Main Switchboard** (default) if it is not already selected.
2. Click **Edit**. This opens the Edit Switchboard Page (see Figure 12.5).

Figure 12.5 Edit Switchboard Page

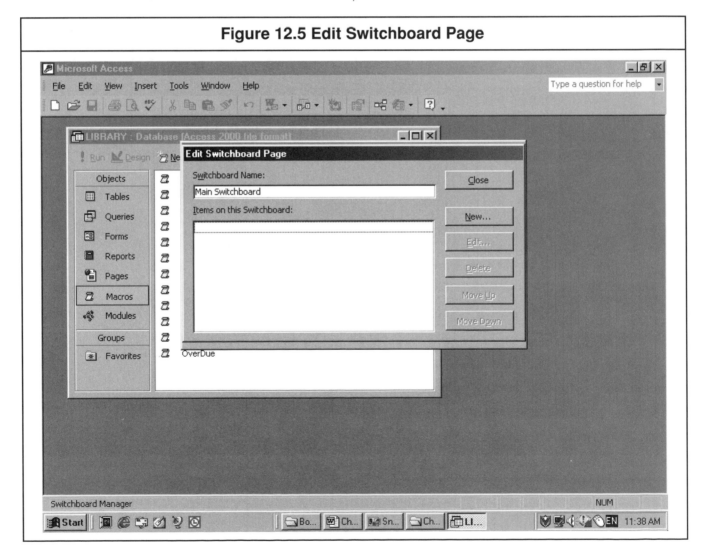

Notice that it is blank under **Items on this Switchboard.** Here we can add the pages that we want to be able to access from the Main Switchboard.

    3. Click **New.**
    4. Change Text to **Books.**
    5. Select **Go to Switchboard** from the Command list if it is not already selected.
    6. Select **Books** from the Switchboard list (see Figure 12.6).

Figure 12.6 Edit Switchboard Item

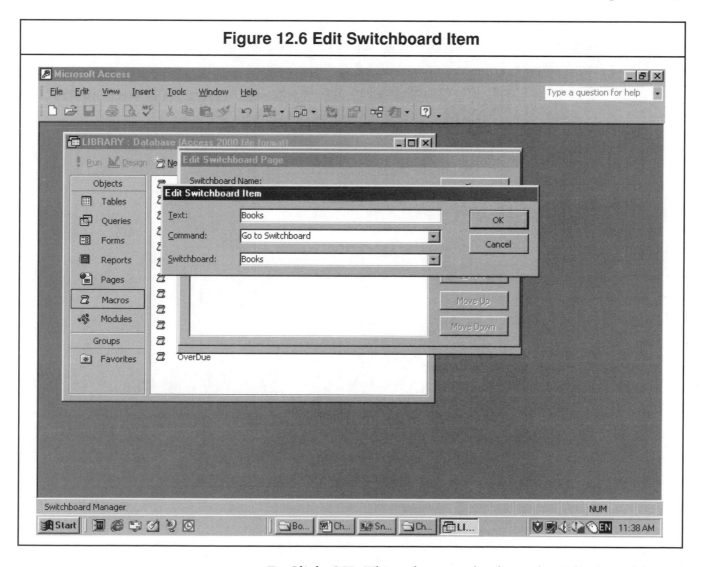

    7. Click **OK.** This takes you back to the Edit Switchboard Page.
    8. Click **New.**

9. Change Text to **Library Users**.
10. Select **Go to Switchboard** from the Command list if it is not already selected.
11. Select **Library Users** from the Switchboard list (see Figure 12.7).

Figure 12.7 Edit Switchboard Item

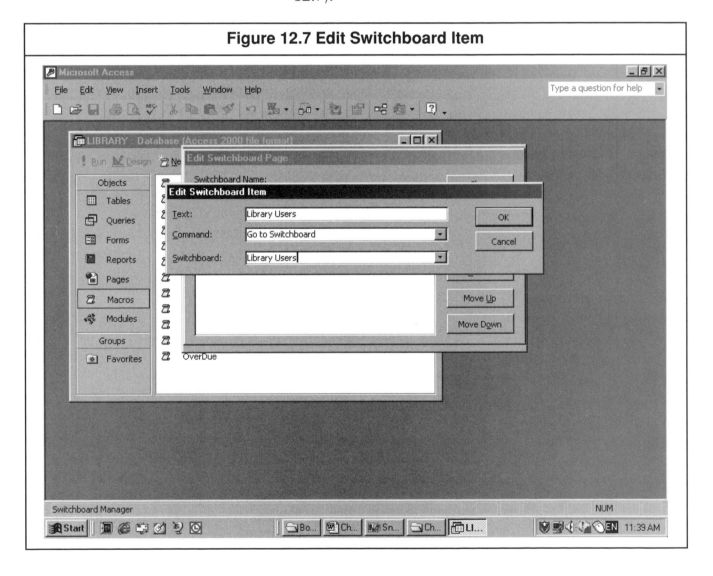

12. Click **OK**. This takes you back to the Edit Switchboard Page (see Figure 12.8).

Figure 12.8 Edit Switchboard Page

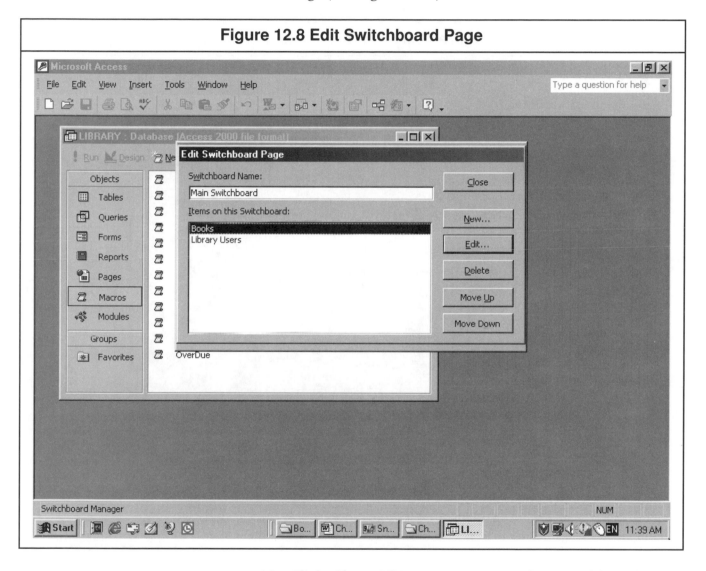

13. Click **Close**. This returns you to the Switchboard Manager.
14. Click **Close**.
15. Click the **Tables** object button.

16. Open the Switchboard Items table that was created when you created the switchboard (see Figure 12.9).

Figure 12.9 Switchboard Items Table

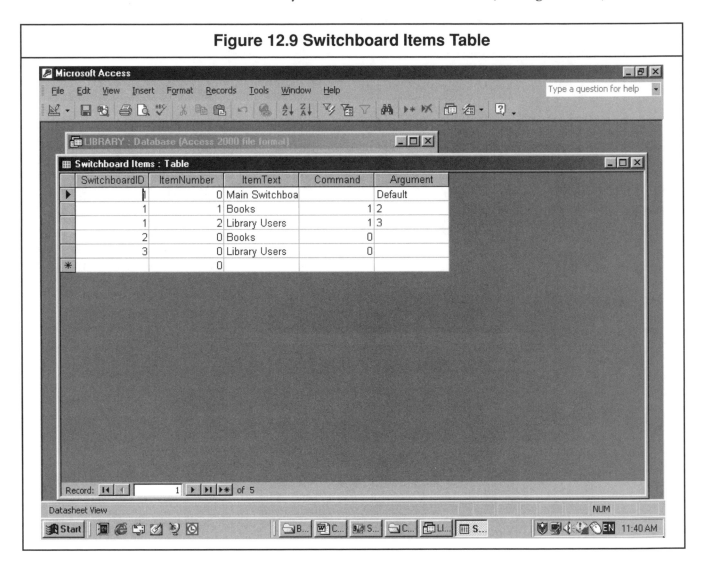

---

17. Close the table.
18. Click the **Forms** object button.

19. Open the Switchboard form (see Figure 12.10).

Figure 12.10 Switchboard Form

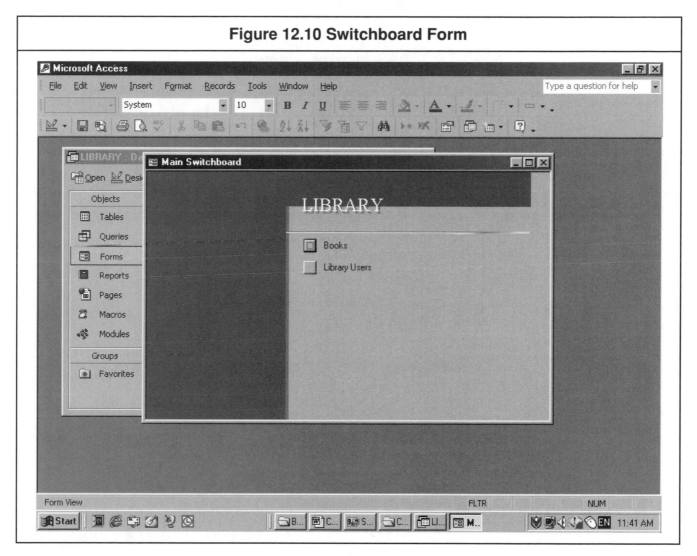

20. Click on the **Books** button.

There are no links on the **Books** switchboard page. We will add links to both the **Books** and the **Library Users** pages in the next exercise.

21. Close the Switchboard.

12.3 MODIFYING SWITCHBOARD PAGES

1. Click **Tools** on the menu bar.
2. Click **Database Utilities**.
3. Click **Switchboard Manager**.
4. Click **Books** under Switchboard Pages.
5. Click **Edit** and the Edit Switchboard Page opens (see Figure 12.11).

Figure 12.11 Edit Switchboard Page

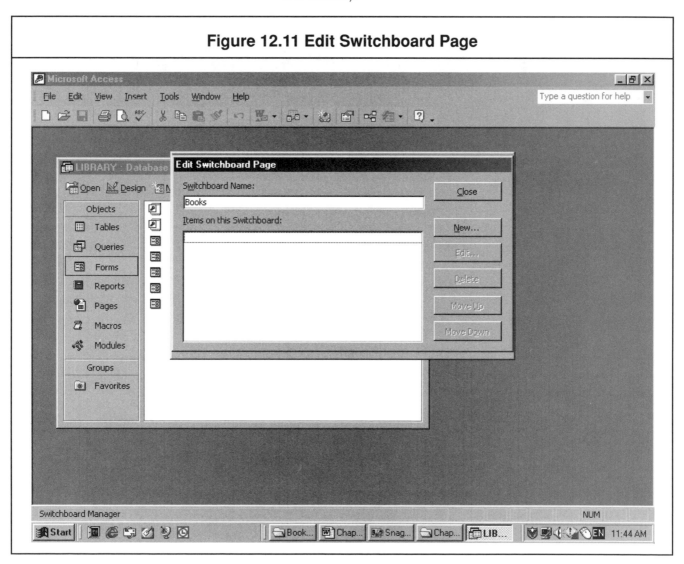

6. Click **New.**
7. Change Text to **Books.**

8. Select **Open Form in Edit Mode** from the Command list.
9. Select **Books** from the Switchboard list (see Figure 12.12).

Figure 12.12 Open Form Switchboard Item

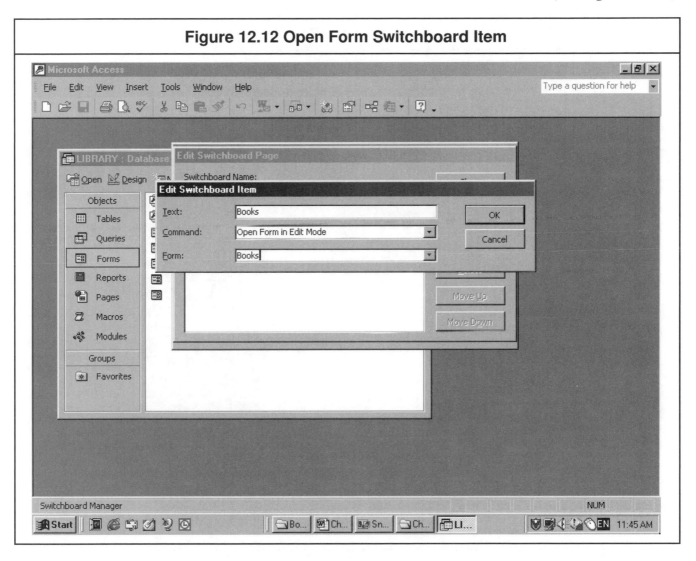

10. Click **OK**.

We have just added a link on the **Books** page that will open the **Books** form when we click on the adjacent button. We also have several queries that are related to the book inventory in the library. Now we are going to add these queries to the **Books** page.

11. Click **New**.
12. Change Text to **Books Checked Out**.
13. Select **Run Macro** from the Command list.

14. Select **Books Checked Out** from the Switchboard list (see Figure 12.13).

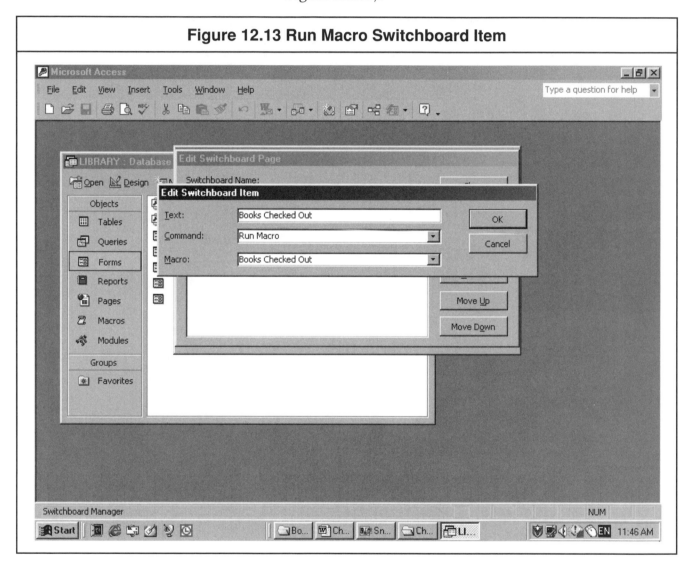

Figure 12.13 Run Macro Switchboard Item

15. Click **OK**.

Follow steps 11–15 above to add the following macros to the Books Switchboard Page (see Figure 12.14):

- Books Checked Out Parameter Query
- Books In
- Monet
- Overdue

Figure 12.14 Books Switchboard Page

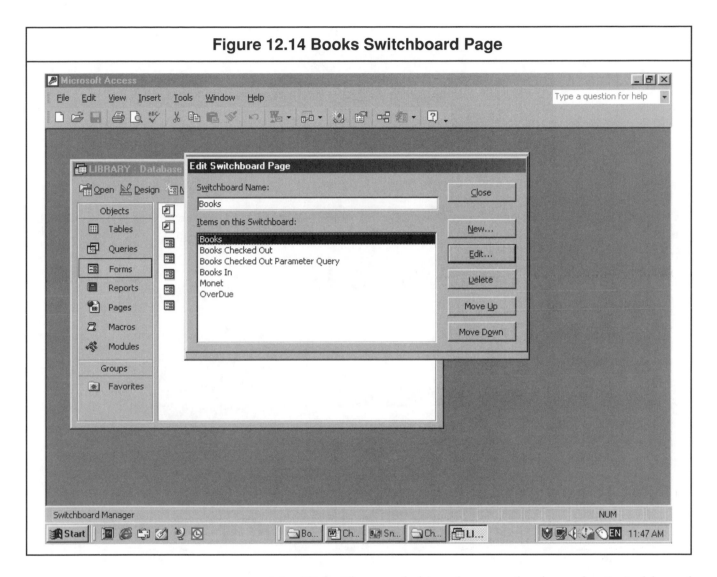

16. Click **Close** and this takes you back to the Switchboard Manager.

Now that we have created the Books Switchboard Page, we can also create the Library Users Page. The Library Users Page will include a form, several queries, and two reports.

17. Click **Library Users** under Switchboard Pages.
18. Click **Edit** and the Edit Switchboard Page opens.

Follow steps 6–10 above to add the **Library Users** form to the Library Users Page (see Figure 12.15).

Figure 12.15 Library Users Switchboard Page

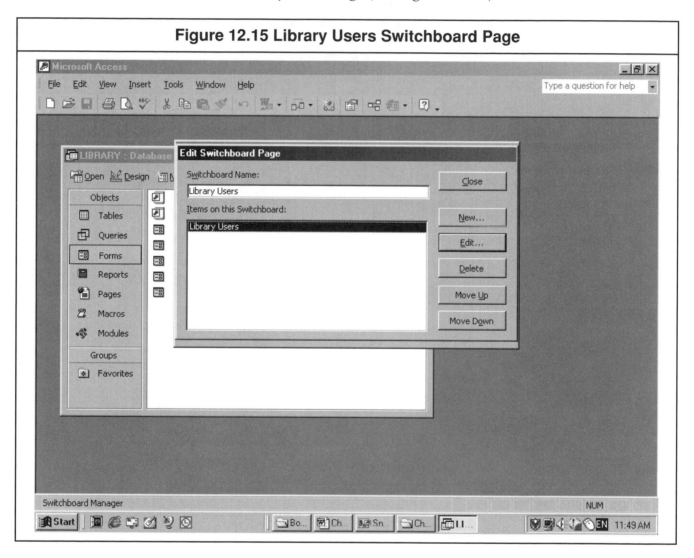

Follow steps 11–15 above to add the following macros to the Library Users Switchboard Page (see Figure 12.16):

- Find Duplicates for Library Users
- Library Users Without Matching Books
- Library Users Crosstab
- Manchester

Figure 12.16 Modified Library Users Switchboard Page

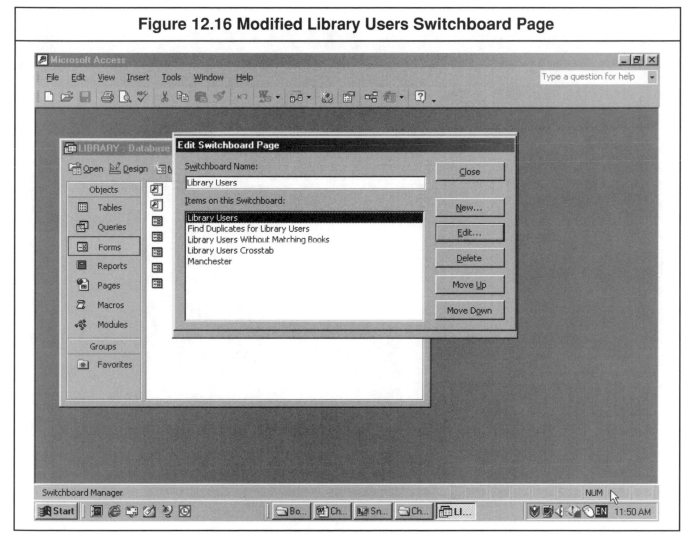

Now that we have added the necessary form and queries to the Library Users Switchboard Page, let's add the reports to this page to complete the page.

19. Click **New**.
20. Change Text to **Library Users Report**.
21. Select **Open Report** from the Command list.

22. Select **Library Users** from the Switchboard list (see Figure 12.17).

Figure 12.17 Open Report Switchboard Item

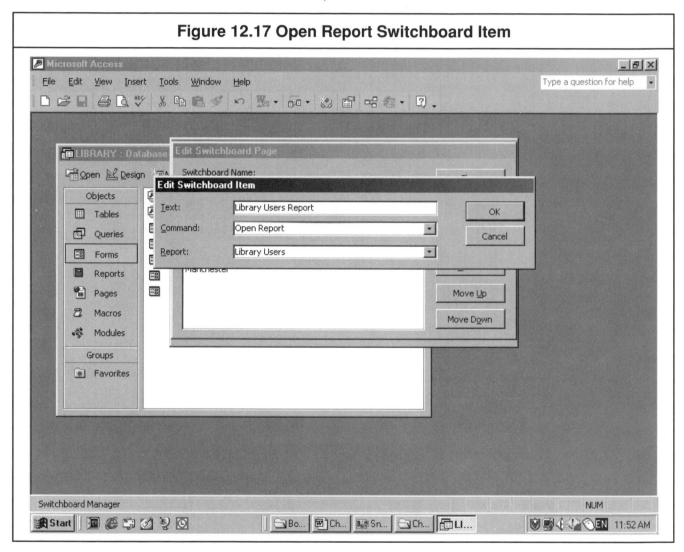

23. Click **OK.**

Follow steps 19–23 above to add the **Library Users Justified** report to the Library Users Page (see Figure 12.18).

Figure 12.18 Completed Library Users Switchboard Page

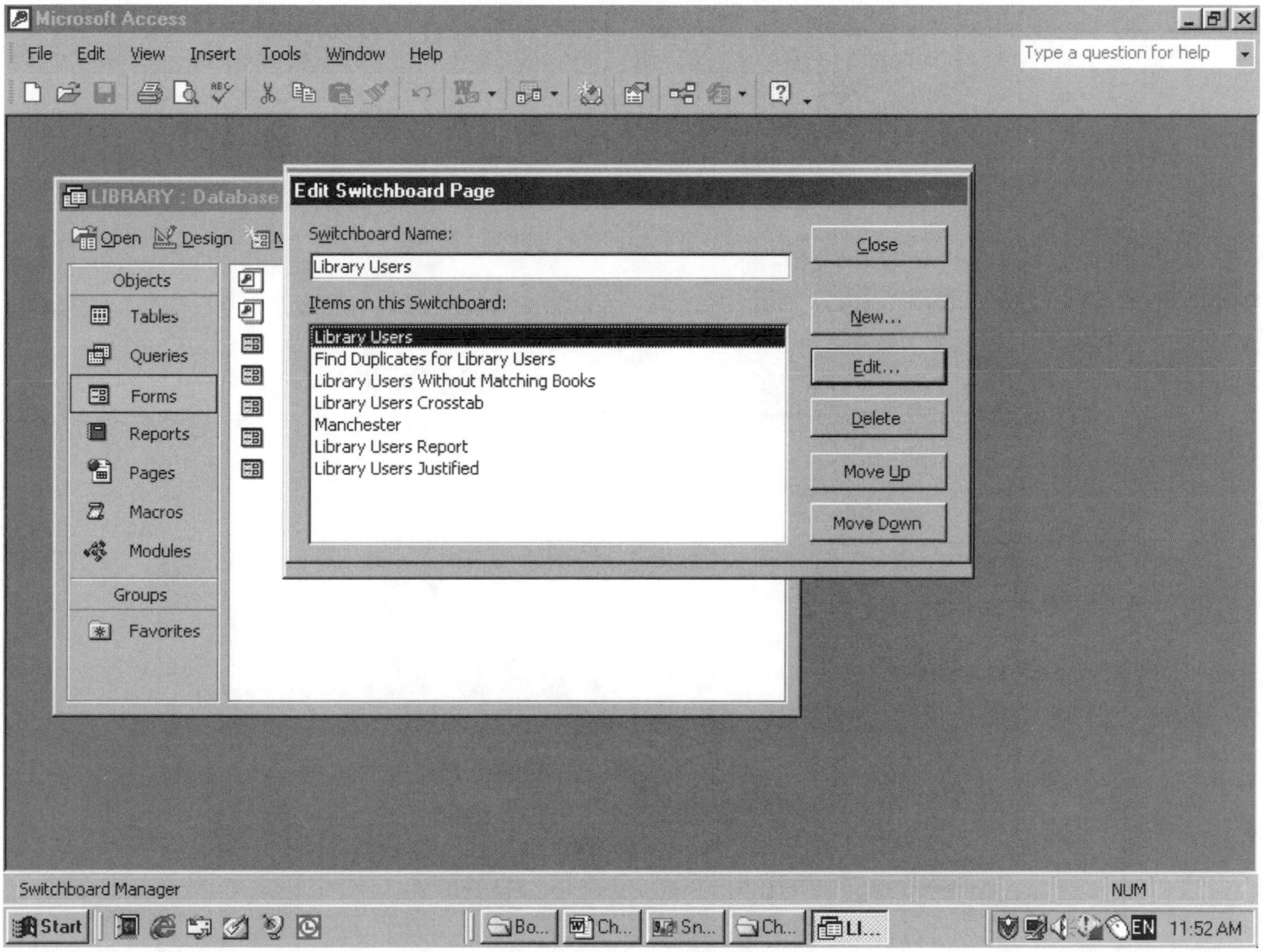

---

24. Close the Edit Switchboard Page window.

We now need to add links to the **Books** and **Library Users** pages that will take us back to the Main Switchboard Page. We also need to add a link that will allow us to exit our database.

25. Click **Books** under Switchboard Pages.
26. Click **Edit**.
27. Click **New**.
28. Repeat step 20.

28. Select **Go to Switchboard** from the Command list.
29. Select **Main Switchboard** from the Switchboard list (see Figure 12.19).

Figure 12.19 Edit Switchboard Item

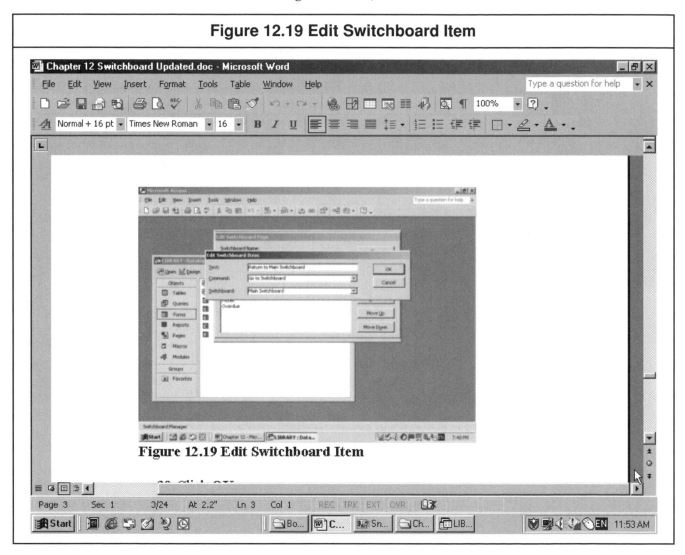

Figure 12.19 Edit Switchboard Item

---

30. Click **OK**.
31. Click **Close** to return to the Main Switchboard Page.

Follow steps 25–31 above to add the same **Return to Main Switchboard** page to the Library Users Page.

32. Click **Main Switchboard (default)** under Switchboard Pages.
33. Click **Edit**.

34. Click **New.**
35. Change Text to **Exit the Database.**
36. Select **Run Macro** from the Command list.
37. Select **Exit Database** from the Switchboard list (see Figure 12.20).

Figure 12.20 Exit Database Switchboard Item

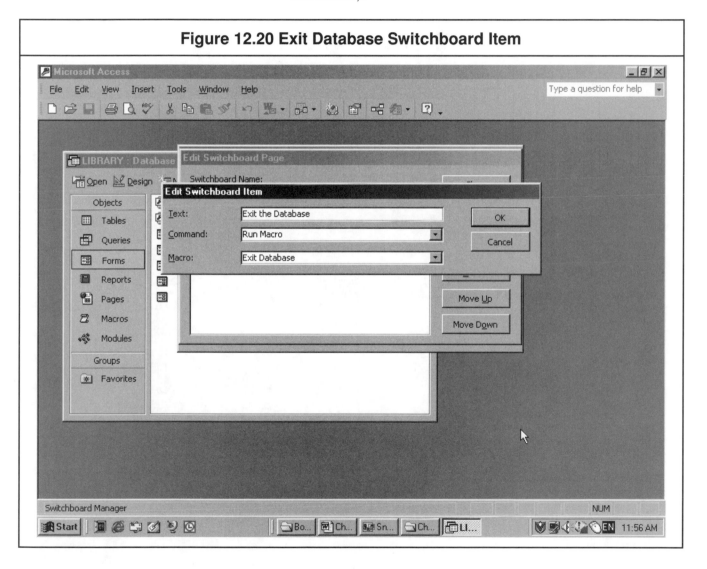

38. Click **OK.**
39. Click **Close** to return to the Main Switchboard Page.
40. Click **Close** to return to the database window.

Open the switchboard form and click on the different links.

Finally, click on the **Exit the Database** button to exit the database. Then open the **LIBRARY.mdb** database to continue with the following exercises.

12.4 MAIN PAGE STARTUP

1. Click **Tools** on the menu bar.
2. Click **Startup**.
3. Select **Switchboard** from the Display Form/Page list. Do not change any of the other settings at this time (see Figure 12.21).

Figure 12.21 Startup Screen

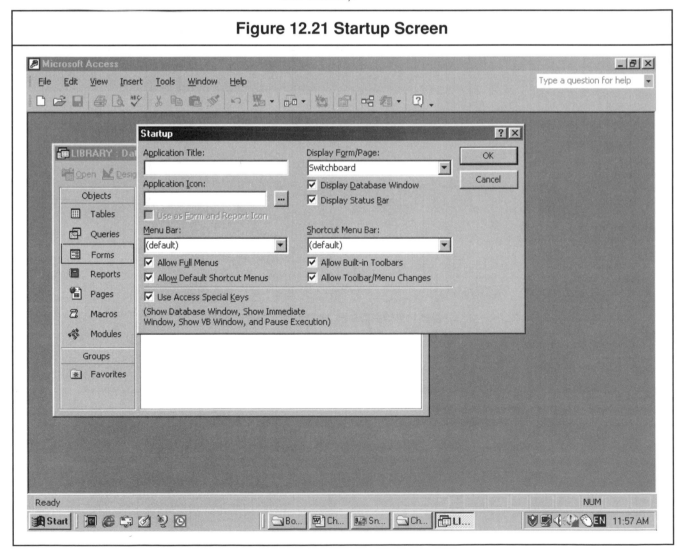

4. Click **OK**.
5. Open the **Switchboard** form.
6. Click **Exit the Database**.
7. Open the **LIBRARY.mdb** database. The Main Switchboard opens (see Figure 12.22).

Figure 12.22 Main Switchboard at Startup

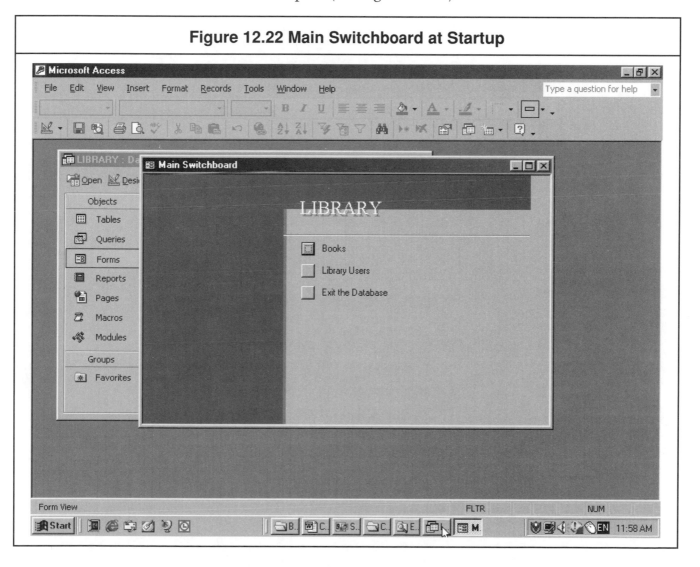

Navigate through the switchboard manager and make sure that the links are all working properly. Using the switchboard manager to navigate through forms, queries, and reports is just one way to set up the database for the user. Another way is to manually link the objects. We will take a look at manually linking the objects to command buttons on forms in the next chapter.

13 LINKING WITHOUT THE SWITCHBOARD MANAGER

OBJECTIVES

13.1 CREATING THE FORMS
13.2 CREATING THE LINKS
13.3 ADDITIONAL FORM LINKS
13.4 CREATING QUERY LINKS
13.5 CREATING REPORT LINKS
13.6 MODIFYING FORMS

In this chapter we are going to link database objects by creating our own forms and manually creating each object link. We used the assistance of the switchboard manager in Chapter 12 to link the objects in the **LIBRARY.mdb** database. In this chapter we are going to replace the switchboard manager with the forms that we will create.

We will create a standard form format that will be used to contain the object links. Then we will create links to the forms, reports, and macros in the **LIBRARY.mdb** database. Let's get started.

13.1 CREATING THE FORMS

1. Open the **LIBRARY.mdb** database.
2. Close the **Main Switchboard**.
3. Click the **Forms** object (if it is not already selected).
4. Click **New**.
5. Make sure **Design View** is selected and click the **OK** button (see Figure 13.1).

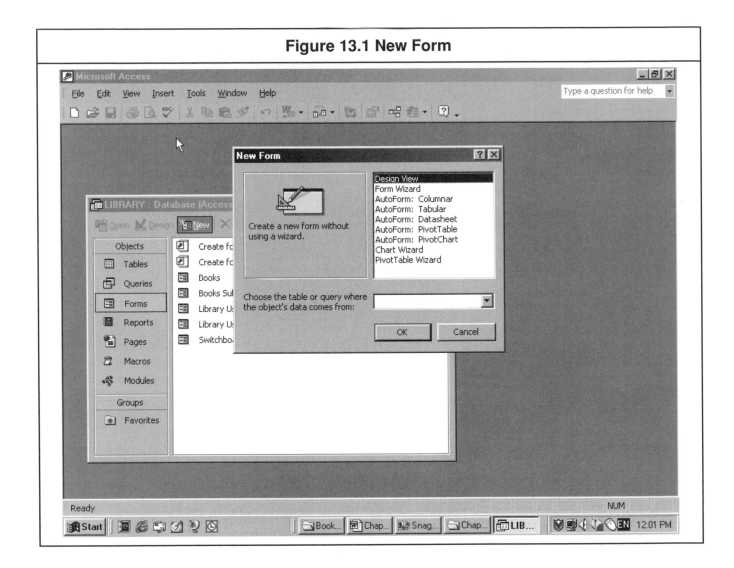

Figure 13.1 New Form

This opens the Form in Design View. We created forms in design view in a previous chapter, so we will jump right in to creating forms here.

6. Click **File, Save As**.
7. Enter **Main Library Links** in the Save Form 'Form1' To: box.
8. Click the **OK** button.
9. Close the form.

Now create two more forms following steps 4–9 above. Name the forms **Books Links** and **Library Users Links**.

10. You should now see the new forms that you just created (see figure 13.2).

Figure 13.2 New Forms

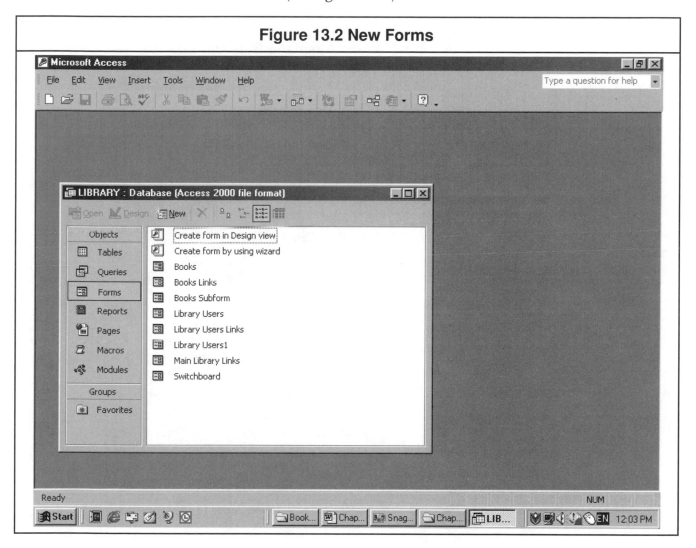

Now we are ready to link the forms and the objects.

13.2 CREATING THE LINKS

1. Open the **Main Library Links** form in **Design View**.
2. Click the **Command Button** on the Toolbox toolbar (see Figure 13.3).

Figure 13.3 Command Button

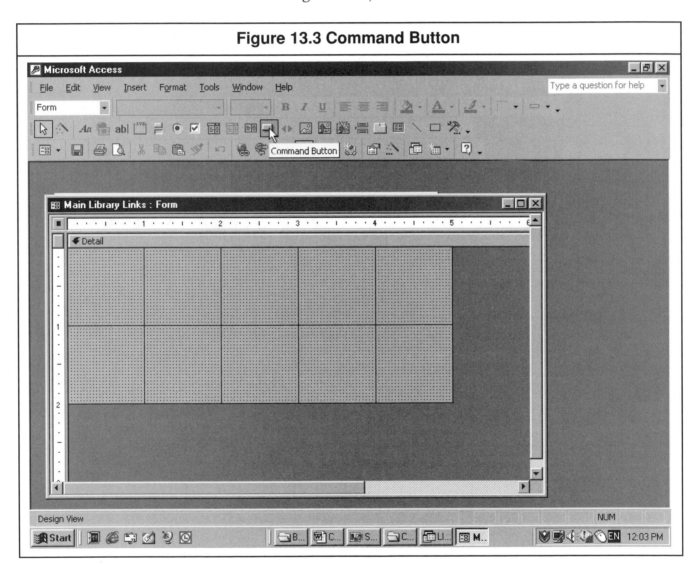

3. Click on the form one inch from the top and one inch from the left of the border of the form. This places a command button on your form and also opens the **Command Button Wizard** (see Figure 13.4).

Figure 13.4 Command Button Wizard

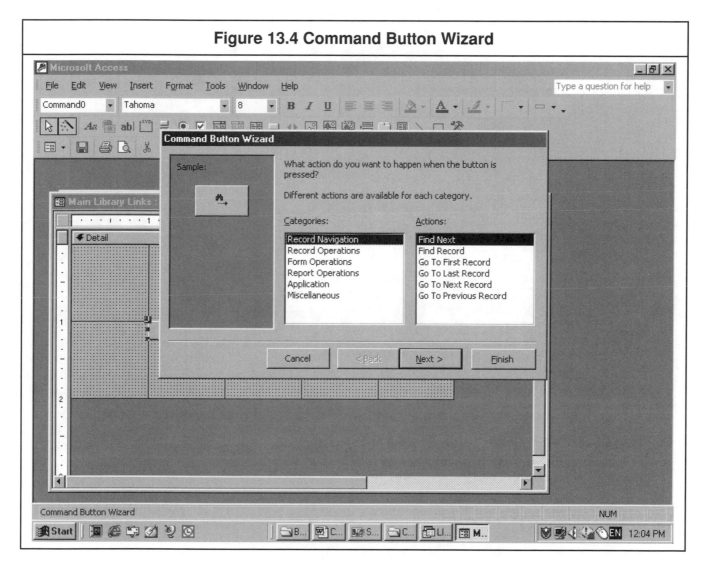

There are many operations that can be performed using the Command Button Wizard. The operations are separated into categories. When you select a category you will find a list of related operations that can be performed.

4. Select **Form Operations** in the **Categories** list.

5. Select **Open Form** in the **Actions** list (see Figure 13.5).

Figure 13.5 Command Button Wizard Selections

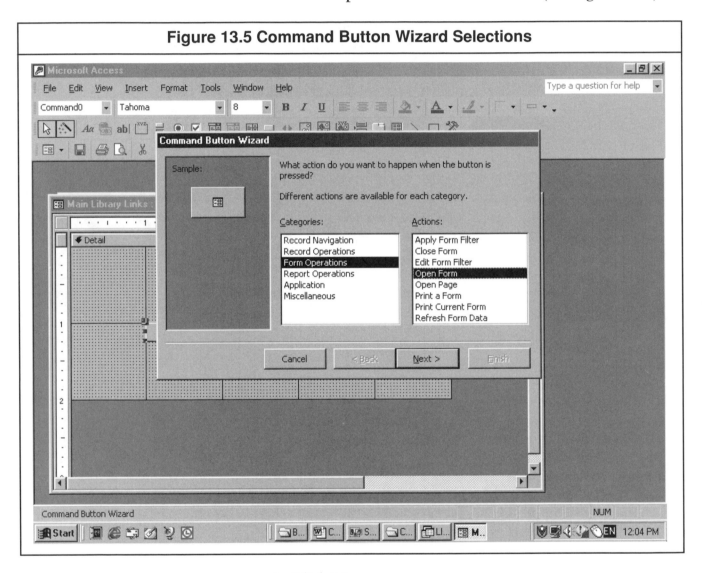

6. Click **Next**.

7. Select **Books Links** from the list (see Figure 13.6).

Figure 13.6 Form Selection

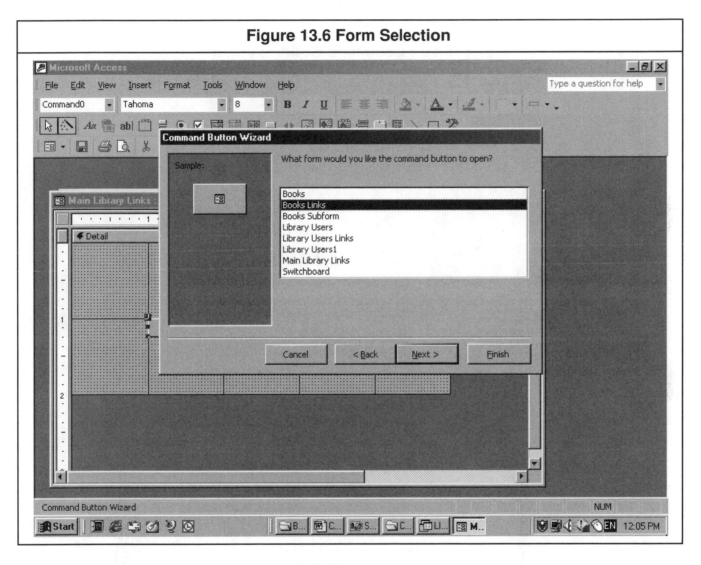

8. Click **Next**.

9. Click the Text radio button. Enter **Books Links** in the textbox beside **Text** (see Figure 13.7).

Figure 13.7 Command Button Caption

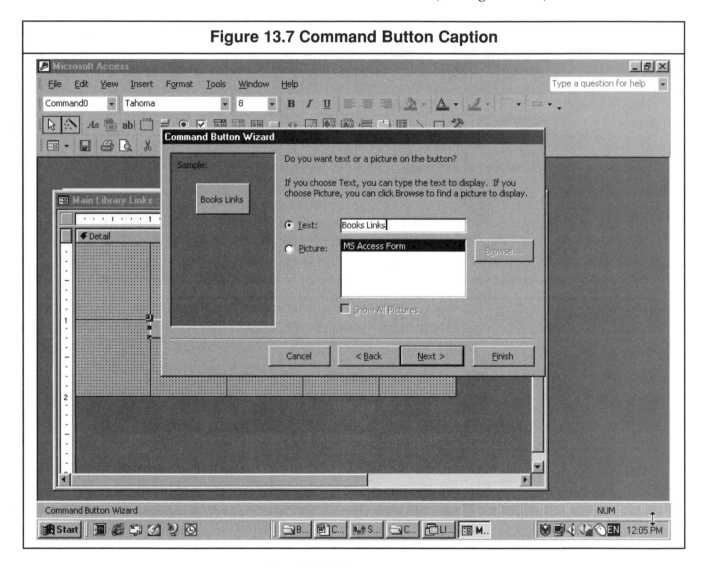

10. Click **Next**.
11. Enter **cmdBooksLinks** as the name for the command button.
12. Click **Finish**.

Follow steps 2–12 above to create a command button link to the **Main Library Links** form. Place the command button one inch from the top and two inches from the left border of the form. Enter **Library Users Links** as the Text Caption (see step 9 above). Enter **cmdLibraryUsersLinks** as the name for the command button (see step 11 above). Your form should now contain two command buttons (see Figure 13.8).

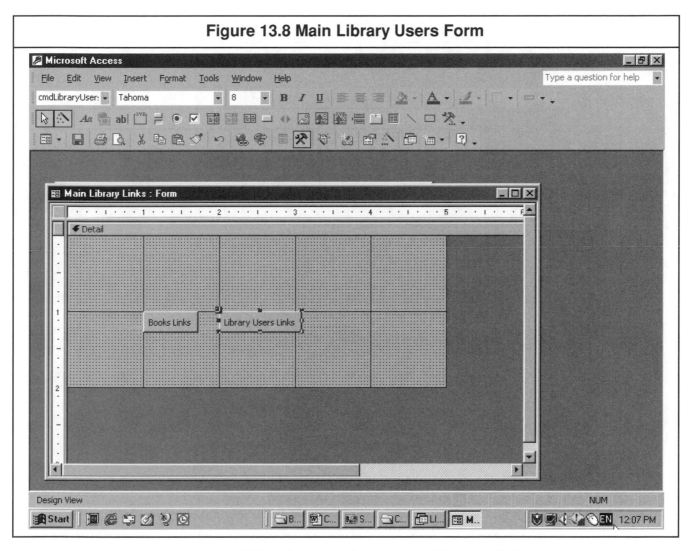

Figure 13.8 Main Library Users Form

Now let's test the command button links.

13. Click the **Form View** button on the Toolbox (see Figure 13.9).

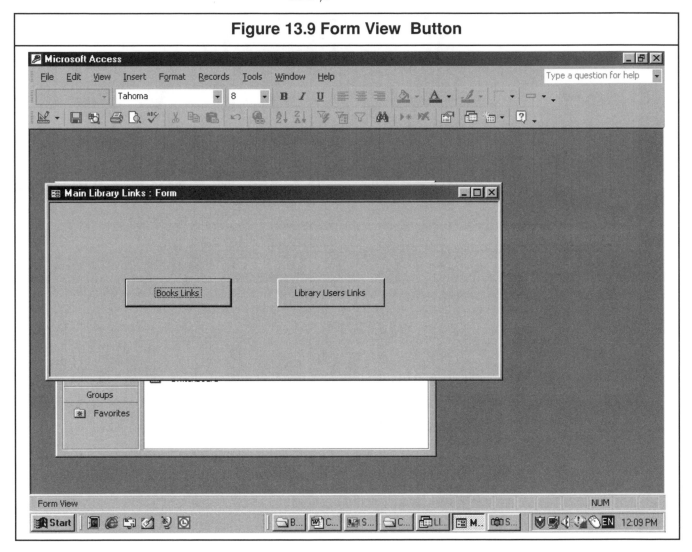

Figure 13.9 Form View Button

14. Click the **Books Links** command button to open the **Books Links** form.
15. Close the **Books Links** form.
16. Click the **Library Users Links** command button to open the **Library Users Links** form.
17. Close the **Library Users Links** form.

13.3 ADDITIONAL FORM LINKS

Now we are going to create links to all of the books and library users forms, queries, and reports. We will create the same links that we created in Chapter 12 when we used the switchboard manager.

1. Open the **Books Links** form in **Design View**.
2. Click the **Command Button** on the Toolbox toolbar.
3. Click on the form one inch from the top and one inch from the left of the border of the form. This places a command button on your form and also opens the **Command Button Wizard**.
4. Select **Form Operations** in the **Categories** list.
5. Select **Open Form** in the **Actions** list.
6. Click **Next**.
7. Select **Books** from the list.
8. Click **Next**.
9. Make sure "Open the form and show all the records" is selected (see Figure 13.10).

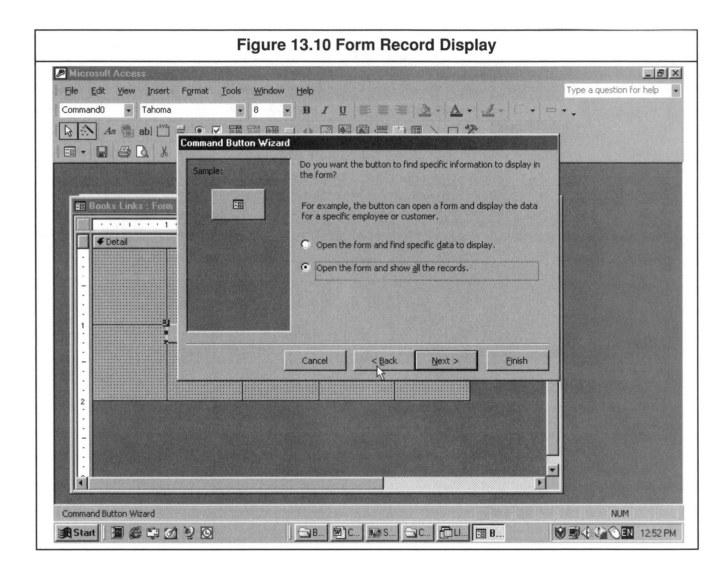

Figure 13.10 Form Record Display

10. Click **Next**.
11. Click the **Text** radio button. Enter **Books** in the textbox beside Text.
12. Click **Next**.
13. Enter **cmdBooks** as the name for the command button.
14. Click **Finish**.

13.4 CREATING QUERY LINKS

1. Click the **Command Button** on the Toolbox toolbar.
2. Click on the form one inch from the top and two inches from the left of the border of the form. This places a command button on your form and also opens the **Command Button Wizard**.
3. Select **Miscellaneous** in the **Categories** list.
4. Select **Run Query** in the **Actions** list (see Figure 13.11).

Figure 13.11 Run Query Action

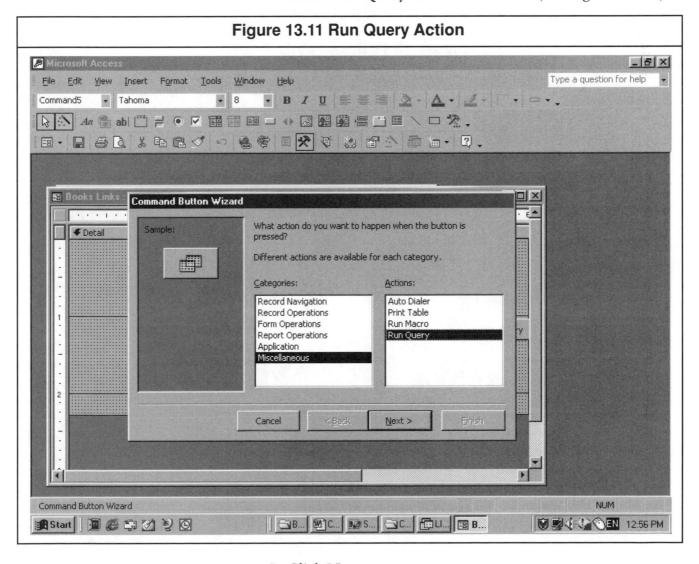

5. Click **Next**.
6. Select **Books Checked Out** from the list (if it is not already selected).

7. Click **Next**.
8. Click the **Text** radio button. Enter **Books Checked Out** in the textbox beside Text.
9. Click **Next**.
10. Enter **cmdBooksCheckedOut** as the name for the command button.
11. Click **Finish**.

Follow steps 1–11 above to add the following query links to the **Books Links** form. Place the command buttons on the form as you see in Figure 13.12:

Figure 13.12 Books Links Form

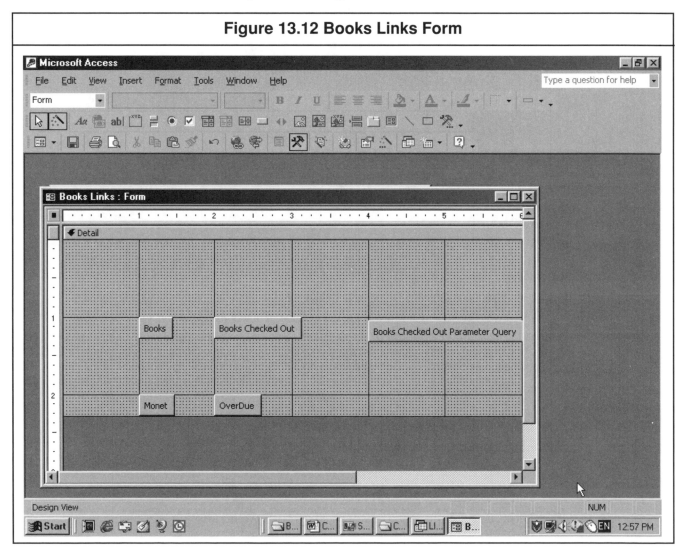

Books Checked Out Parameter Query
Books In

Monet
Overdue

12. Close the **Books Links** form.
13. Click **Yes** to save the form.

Don't worry about the appearance of the form right now. We are going to change the appearance later. For now we need to create the **Library Users Links** form just like we created the **Books Links** form.

Follow the steps above to add the following form link to the **Library Users Links** form:

Library Users

Follow the steps above to add the following query links to the **Library Users Links** form (see Figure 13.13):

Figure 13.13 Library Users Links Form

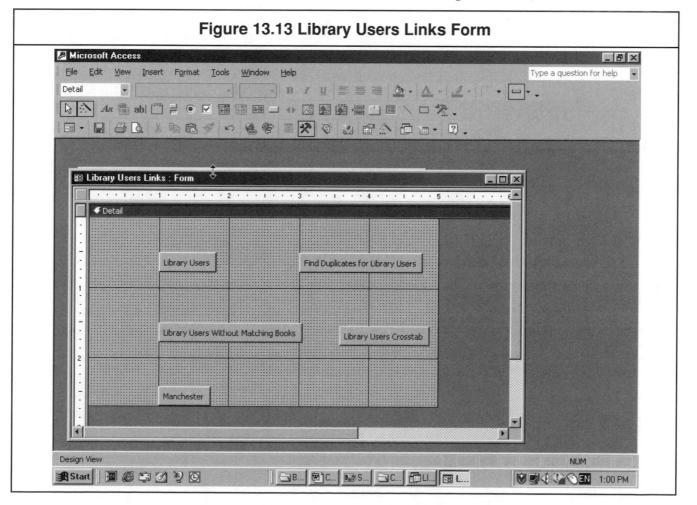

Find Duplicates for Library Users
Library Users Without Matching Books
Library Users Crosstab
Manchester

We still need to add two report links to the **Library Users Links** form. The next section will show you how to do this.

13.5 CREATING REPORT LINKS

Open the **Library Users Links** form if it is not already open. Then follow the steps below to add report links to the form.

1. Click the **Command Button** on the Toolbox toolbar.
2. Click on the form to add the command button link. This places a command button on your form and also opens the **Command Button Wizard**.
3. Select **Report Operations** in the **Categories** list.
4. Select **Preview Report** in the **Actions** list (see Figure 13.14).

Figure 13.14 Preview Report Action

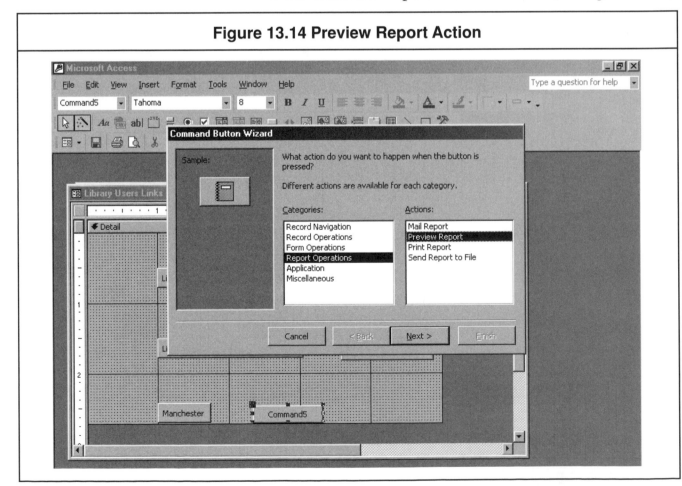

5. Click **Next**.
6. Select **Library Users** from the list (if it is not already selected).
7. Click **Next**.
8. Click the **Text** radio button. Enter **Library Users Report** in the textbox beside Text.
9. Click **Next**.
10. Enter **cmdLibraryUsersReport** as the name for the command button.
11. Click **Finish**.

Follow steps 1–11 to add the **Library Users Justified** report to the **Library Users Links** form (see Figure 13.15).

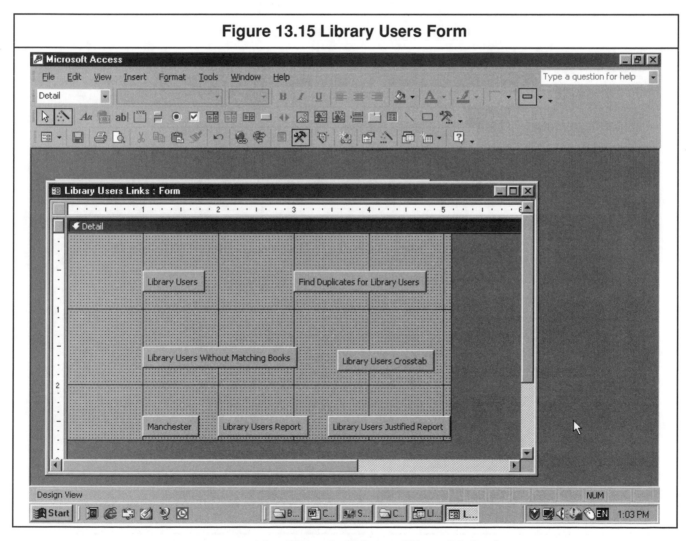

Figure 13.15 Library Users Form

12. Close the **Library Users Links** form.
13. Click **Yes** to save the form.

13.6 MODIFYING FORMS

Before the forms are ready to use, we need to modify some of the form options. First, let's modify the command buttons.

1. Open the **Main Library Links** form in **Design View**.
2. Hold down the <shift> key and click both <command> buttons.
3. Right-click either of the selected <command> buttons and a shortcut menu appears.
4. Click **Properties** (see Figure 13.16).

Figure 13.16 Selecting Properties

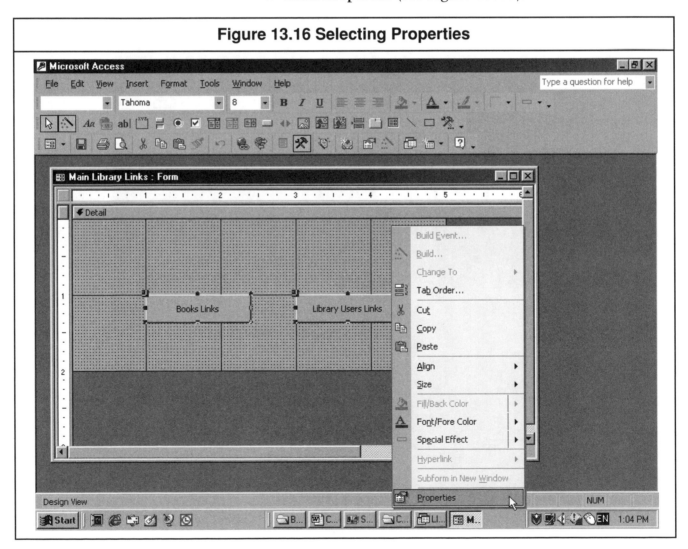

5. Change the width to 1.5 inches and the height to .5 inches.

6. Close the Properties window.
7. Rearrange the command buttons on the form (see Figure 13.17).

Figure 13.17 Main Library Form

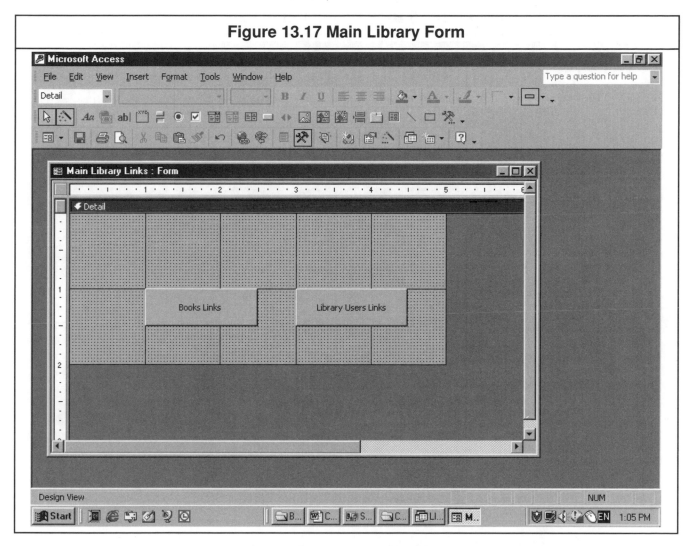

Now let's change the background color of the form.

8. Right-click a blank area on the form and a shortcut menu appears.

9. Choose **Fill/Back Color** and select the "dark blue" color (see Figure 13.18).

Figure 13.18 Background Color Selection

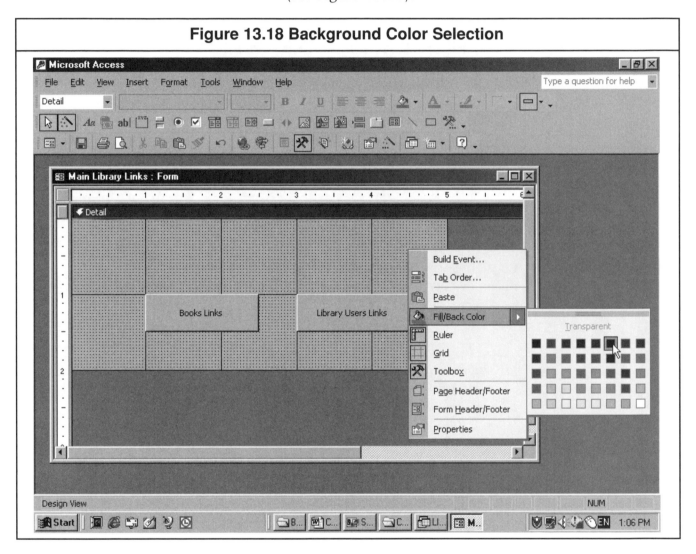

Now let's modify the form properties.

10. Click **Edit**.
11. Click **Select Form**.

12. Click the **Properties** button on the **Form Design** toolbar (see Figure 13.19).

Figure 13.19 Properties Option

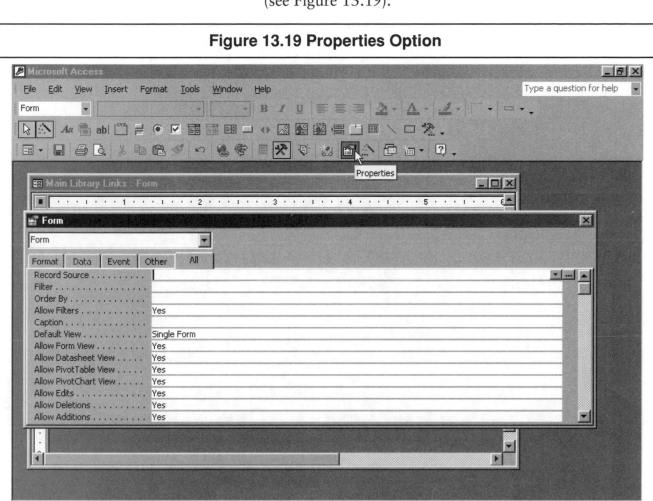

13. Change the following form settings to **No: Record Selectors, Navigation Buttons,** and **Dividing Lines**.
14. Close the form Properties window.
15. Click the **Maximize** button on the **Main Library Links** form.
16. Close the **Main Library Links** form.
17. Click **Yes** to save the form.

Follow steps 1–17 above to modify the **Books Links** form and the **Library Users Links** form.

Figure 13.20 shows an example of how the **Main Library Links** form might look in form view.

Figure 13.20 Main Library Links Form

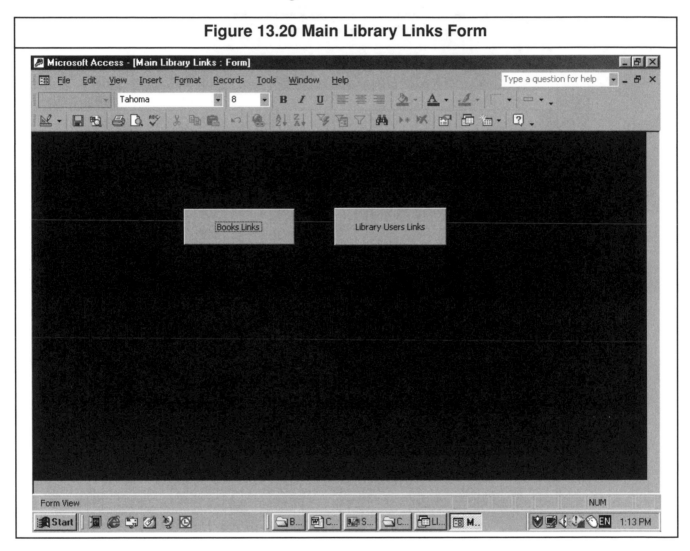

Figure 13.21 shows an example of how the **Books Links** form might look in form view.

Figure 13.21 Books Links Form

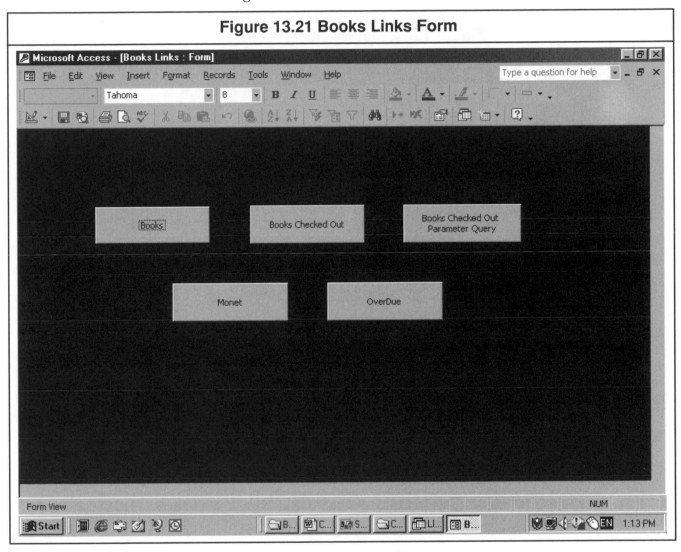

Figure 13.22 shows an example of how the **Library Users Links** form might look in form view.

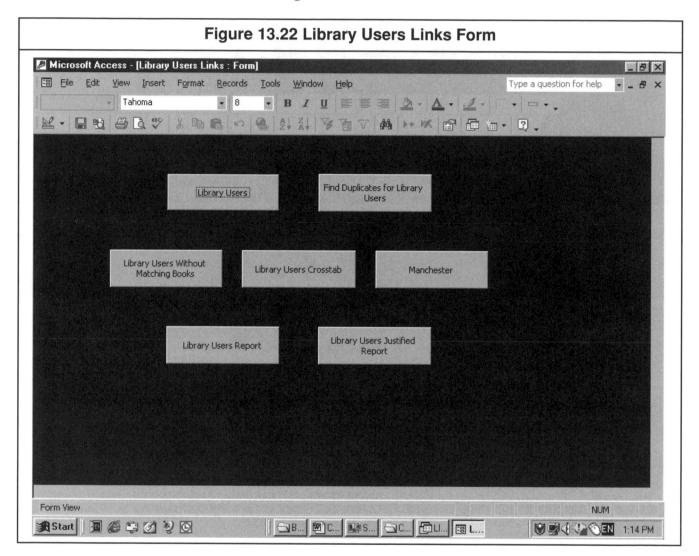

Figure 13.22 Library Users Links Form

Open the **Main Library Links** form and click on the <command> buttons to open the other forms we just created. Click on each of the <command> buttons to test the links.

The last thing we need to do is to assign the **Main Library Links** form as the form to display when the database is opened. Follow the directions in Chapter 12 to make this change.

14   SECURITY

OBJECTIVES

14.1 ASSIGNING A DATABASE PASSWORD
14.2 HIDING THE DATABASE WINDOW
14.3 HIDING DATABASE OBJECTS

It is important to restrict access of unwanted users to your database. There are various measures of security that the Access program offers for your safety. In this chapter we will look at a couple of those security measures. There are security features, however, in the Access program that go far beyond what we will discuss in this chapter.

Keep in mind that you may have additional security measures set up by your network administrator. This level of security is actually the first-line of defense against intruders. After getting past the network security measures in place, you can have security features set up within your database program. If additional security is needed, please look into more advanced Access security options or contact your network administrator for tighter network security.

In this chapter we are going to look at two different types of security we can apply to our database. First, we will assign a password that is necessary in order to open the program. Second, we will see how to hide the database window so that when users are working within the program they can't see or access any of the other objects.

14.1 ASSIGNING A DATABASE PASSWORD

In order to set a database password the database must be opened exclusively. To open a database exclusively you must first open the Access program, then choose **File, Open**. In the Open dialog box, you click the arrow to the right of the **Open** button and choose **Open Exclusive**. Now let's set the database password:

1. Click the **Start** button.
2. Click **Programs**.
3. Click **Microsoft Access**.
4. Click **File**.

5. Click **Open**.
6. Navigate to the **LIBRARY.mdb** database and click it once to select it.
7. Click to the right of the **Open** button and select **Open Exclusive**.
8. Click **Tools**.
9. Click **Security**.
10. Click **Set Database Password** (see Figure 14.1).

Figure 14.1 Set Database Password

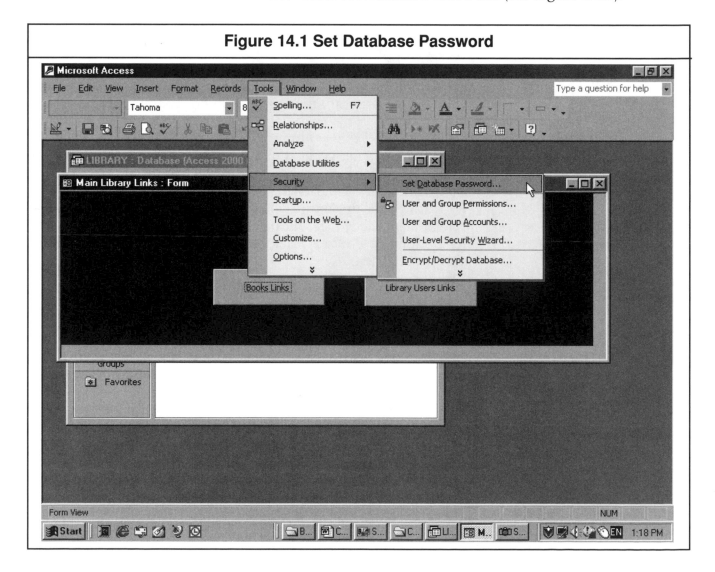

11. Enter **Library** as the password. Passwords are case sensitive, so make sure that you type the password exactly as you will type it to open the database.
12. Enter **Library** again to verify the password.

13. Click **OK**.
14. Close the database.
15. Exit the Access program.

Now let's test the password to see that it works.

16. Open the **LIBRARY.mdb** database. The database password window opens (see Figure 14.2).

Figure 14.2 Database Password

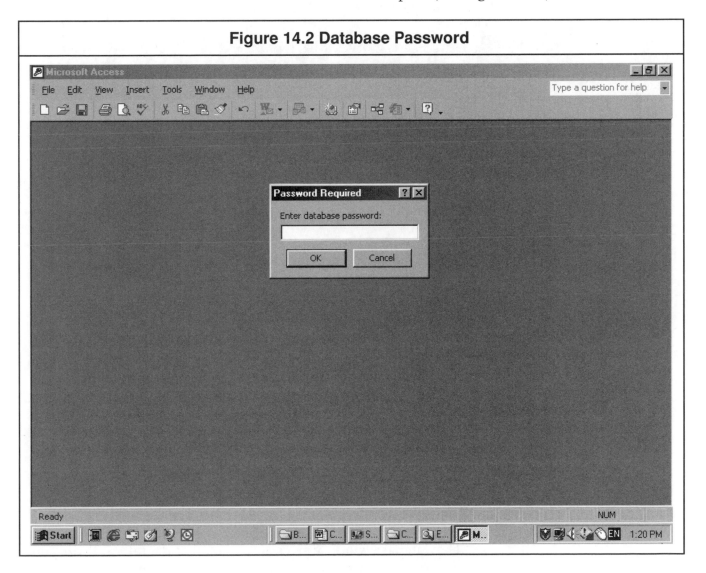

Let's enter an incorrect password to see what happens.

17. Type **Books**.
18. Click **OK** and a warning message box displays (see Figure 14.3).

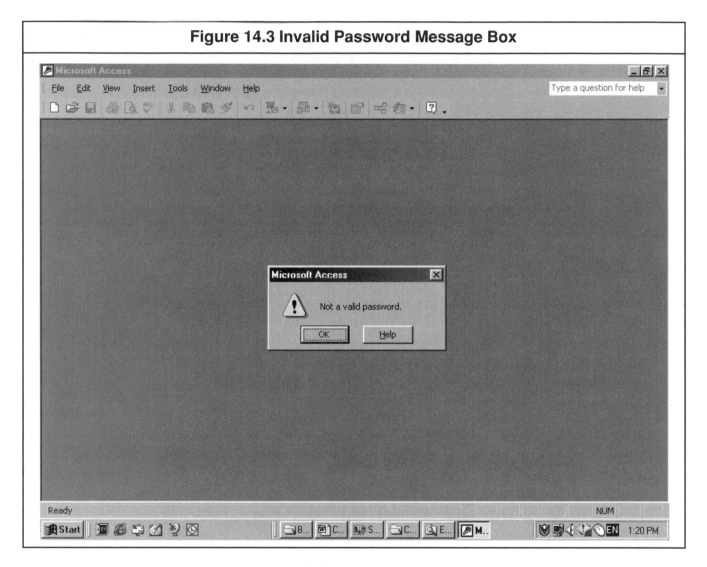

Figure 14.3 Invalid Password Message Box

19. Click **OK**.
20. Type **Library**.
21. Click **OK**. The database opens

Notice that when the database opens you can see the **Main Library Links** form and also the database window. Most likely you will not want database users to view the database window. The database window gives access to all of the tables, forms, queries, reports, macros, pages, and modules in the database. If we take away access to these objects, then it is less likely that the database users will be able to access them.

14.2 HIDING THE DATABASE WINDOW

1. Close the **Main Library Links** form.
2. Click **Tools**.
3. Click **Startup** and the startup window opens (see Figure 14.4).

Figure 14.4 Startup Window

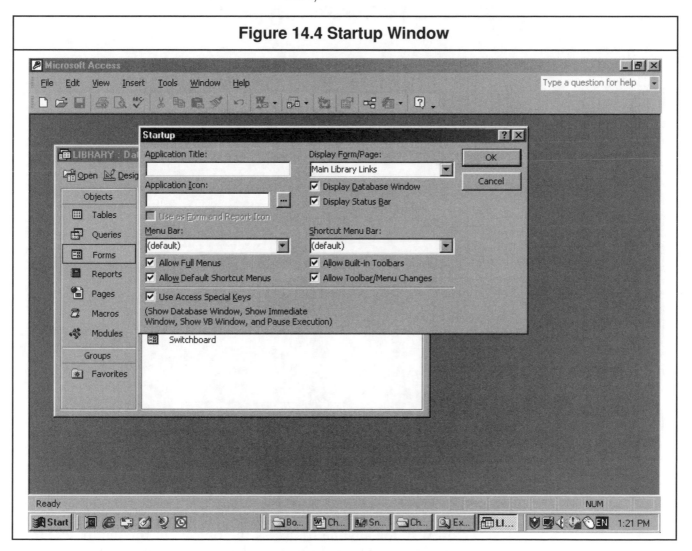

4. Click the check box to remove the check mark from the **Display Database Window** option.
5. Click **OK**.
6. Close the database window. When you open the database again the database window will not be displayed.

7. Exit Access.
8. Open the **LIBRARY.mdb** database and enter the password.
9. Close the **Main Library Links** form. The database window does not display (see Figure 14.5).

Figure 14.5 Hidden Database Window

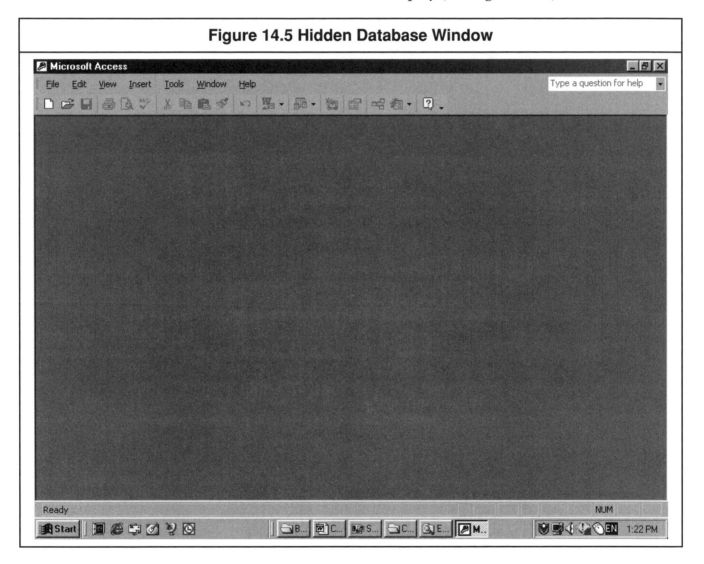

By not displaying the database window, you see that there is no way for anyone to access the objects in the database. However, if you need to access the database window, just follow steps 1–9 above and check the **Display Database Window** to enable that feature.

14.3 HIDING DATABASE OBJECTS

Tables contain all of the information in your database. It may be vital, therefore, for you to create additional security to protect the tables and their data. You may want users to be able to modify queries or reports and, therefore, you may only want to hide the table objects. Now let's take a look at how to accomplish this task.

1. Open the **LIBRARY.mdb** database.
2. Close the **Main Library Links** form.
3. Click the **Books** table to select it.
4. Click the **Properties** button on the toolbar.
5. Click the **Hidden** check box.
6. Click **OK.**

Follow steps 3–6 to hide the **Library Users** table.

7. Close the **LIBRARY.mdb** database.
8. Exit Access.
9. Open the **LIBRARY.mdb** database
10. Click the **Tables** object button. The tables do not display in the database window (see Figure 14.6).

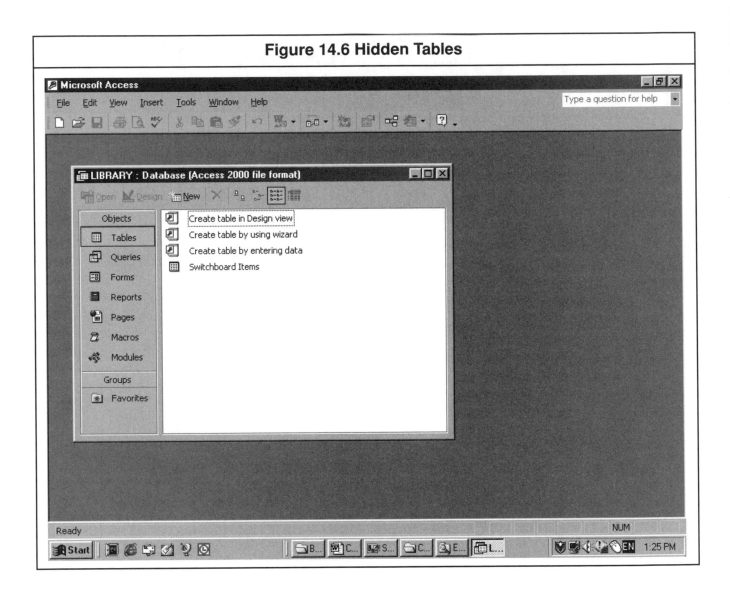

Figure 14.6 Hidden Tables

Suppose you decide you need to view the tables to modify their design. Follow the steps below to unhide the tables.

11. Click **Tools**.

12. Click **Options** and the Options window opens (see Figure 14.7).

Figure 14.7 Options Window

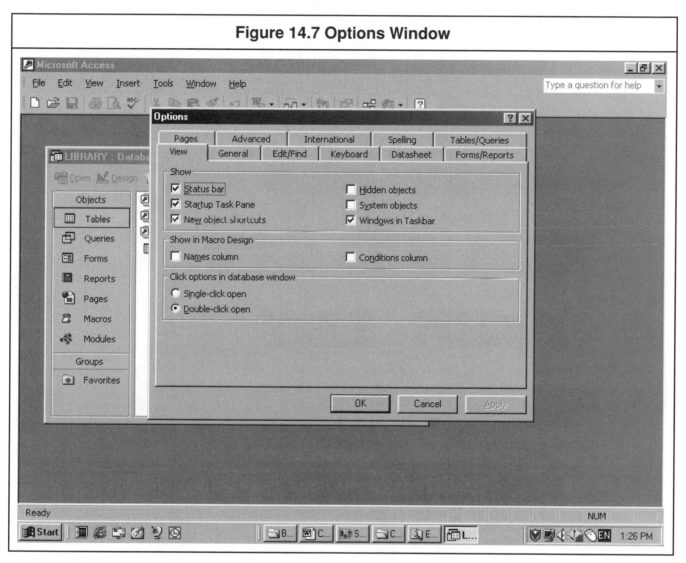

13. Make sure the **View** tab is selected and click the **Hidden Objects** check box.
14. Click **OK**.

The tables display but they are still considered hidden objects. You will need to perform one more task to permanently unhide these tables.

15. Right-click the **Books** table and a shortcut menu appears.
16. Click **Properties**.

17. Click the **Hidden** check box.
18. Click **OK**.

Follow steps 15–18 to permanently unhide the **Library Users** table.

19. Close the **LIBRARY.mdb** database.
20. Open the **LIBRARY.mdb** database and the tables should appear.
21. Close the database.
22. Exit Access.

15 WORKING ON THE WEB

OBJECTIVES

15.1 CREATING THE DATABASE FOLDER
15.2 CREATING THE DATA ACCESS PAGE
15.3 USING THE DATA ACCESS PAGE

In this chapter we are going to create data access pages that will allow us to give Internet access to our database. Data access pages are HTML (Hypertext Markup Language) documents that can be bound directly to data stored in the database. Microsoft Access 2002 allows us to create and use data access pages.

In our example, we are going to create a data access page and view it using the Internet Explorer Web browser. Keep in mind that we will be using the browser to display the data access page. The browser is creating an interactive environment for access to our data. Using the data access page we can add, delete, and modify the data stored in our database.

In our example we will create a folder on our hard drive that will store both our data access page and the **LIBRARY.mdb** database. If we actually wanted to allow Internet access to our database, we would need to move the data access page and the **LIBRARY.mdb** database to a server that would be available to the Internet.

We will need to create a folder that will contain our data access page and the **LIBRARY.mdb** database. Then we will create the data access page and store it in the folder we created. Once we have the data access page created we will test it using Internet Explorer. Finally, we will check our database to check that the updates are processed.

15.1 CREATING THE DATABASE FOLDER

We will create a folder on our hard drive to store the data access page and the **LIBRARY.mdb** database. We will use Windows Explorer to create the folder.

1. Click the **Start** button.
2. Move your mouse pointer over **Programs** and a submenu will appear.

3. Move your mouse pointer over **Accessories** and a submenu will appear (see Figure 15.1).

Figure 15.1 Opening Windows Explorer

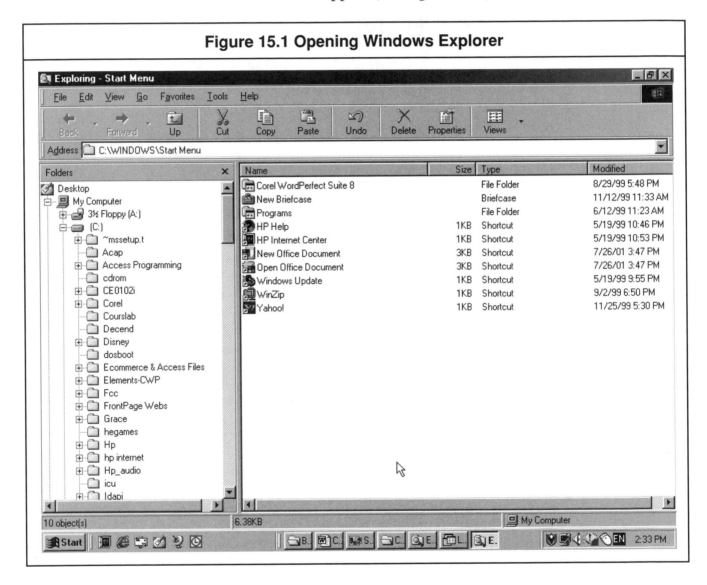

4. Click **Windows Explorer**.
5. Click **Desktop** in the left pane of the Windows Explorer window. (We will place our folder on our desktop.)
6. Click **File**.
7. Click **New**.
8. Click **Folder** (see Figure 15.2).

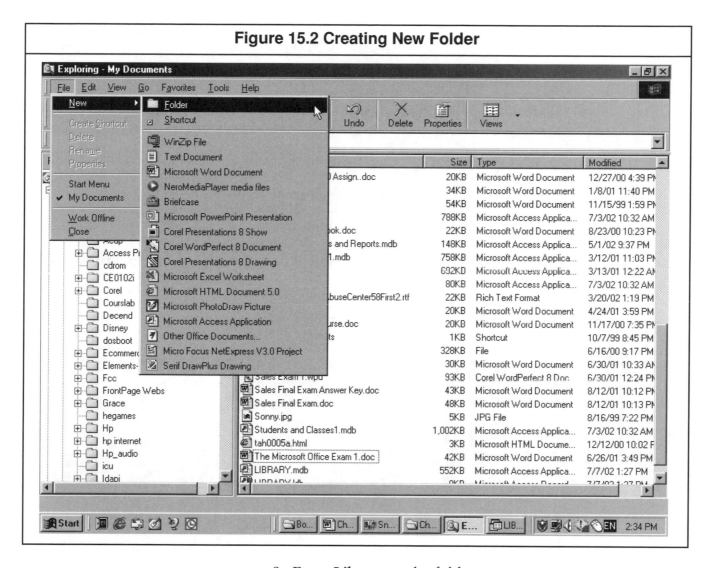

Figure 15.2 Creating New Folder

9. Enter **Library** as the folder name.
10. Press the <Enter> key to accept the folder name.
11. Now locate the **LIBRARY.mdb** database on your computer's hard drive and move it to the **Library** folder.
12. Close **Windows Explorer.**

15.2 CREATING THE DATA ACCESS PAGE

We are now ready to create the data access page. We will save the data access page in the **Library** folder along with the **LIBRARY.mdb** database.

1. Open the **LIBRARY.mdb** database that you just moved to the **Library** folder (remember the password that you created in the previous chapter, "Library").
2. Close the **Main Library Links** form.
3. Click the **Tables** object.
4. Click the **Library Users** table.
5. Click the **New Object: AutoForm** button arrow on the Database Toolbar.
6. Click **Page** (see Figure 15.3).

Figure 15.3 Selecting Page AutoForm

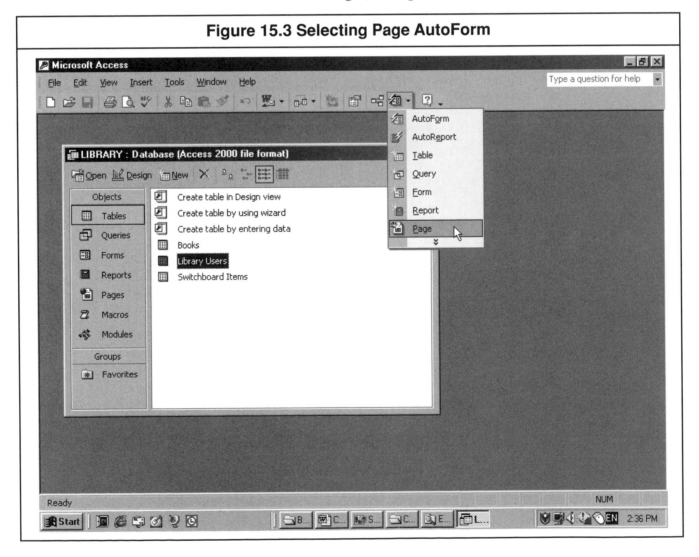

7. When the **New Data Access Page** window opens, select **Page Wizard**.
8. Make sure **Library Users** is selected in the **Choose the table or query where the object's data comes from** field (see Figure 15.4).

Figure 15.4 New Data Access Page

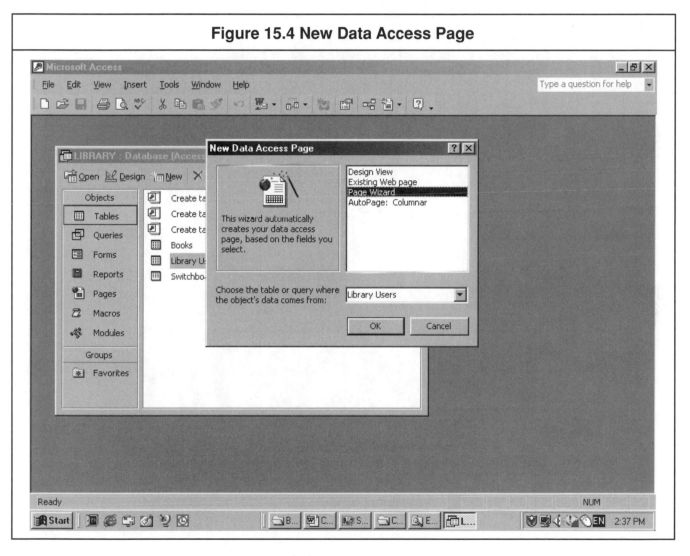

9. Click **OK**.

10. Add all of the fields in the Available Field list to the Selected Field list (see Figure 15.5).

Figure 15.5 Selected Fields

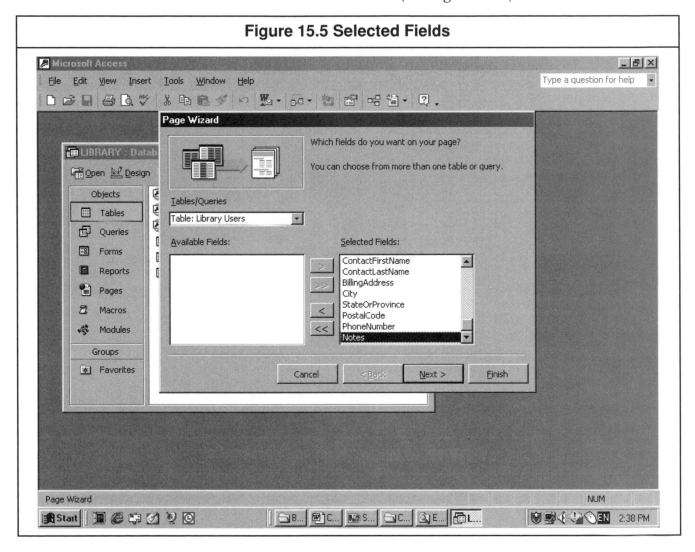

11. Click **Next**.
12. Click the **Next** button on the screen that asks "Do you want to add any grouping levels" (we do not want any grouping levels for this page).
13. Click the **Next** button on the screen that asks "What sort order do you want for your records" (we do not want to sort our records).
14. Enter **Library Users** as the title for the data access page.

15. Make sure the option to "Modify the page's design" option is selected (see Figure 15.6).

Figure 15.6 Page Wizard Finish Screen

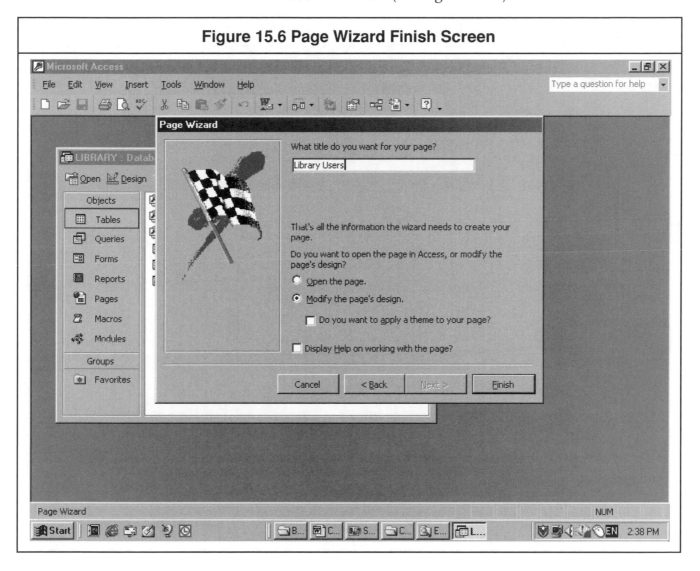

16. Click the **Finish** button and the data access page opens (see Figure 15.7).

Figure 15.7 Data Access Page

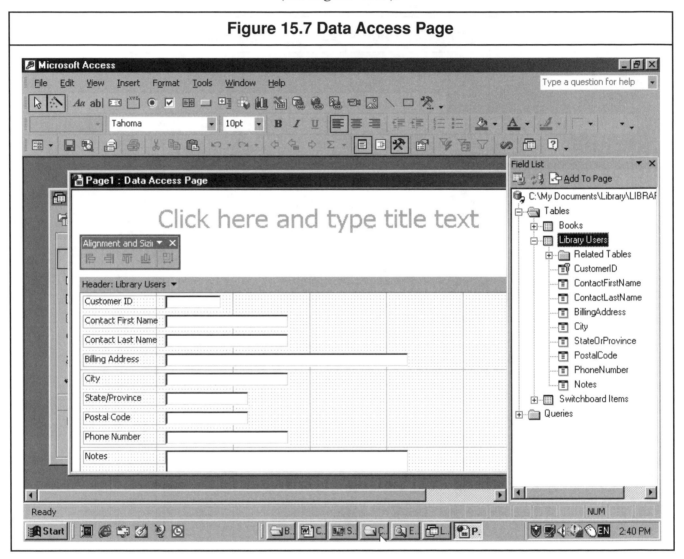

17. Click in the section labeled "Click here and type title text" and enter **Library Users** (see Figure 15.8).

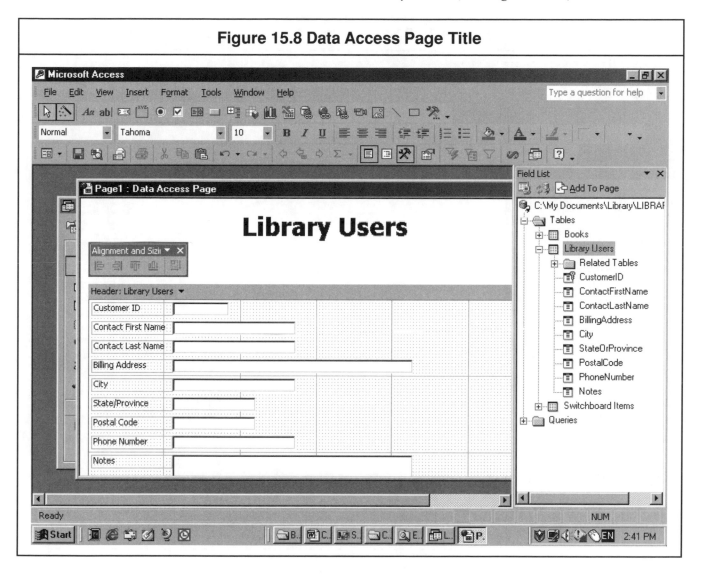

Figure 15.8 Data Access Page Title

Now we are ready to save our data access page.

18. Click **File**.
19. Click **Close**.
20. Click **Yes** to save the data access page.
21. Make sure the **Library** folder is selected in the "Save in" box.

22. Make sure the name **Library Users** is entered as the File Name (see Figure 15.9).

Figure 15.9 Saving Data Access Page

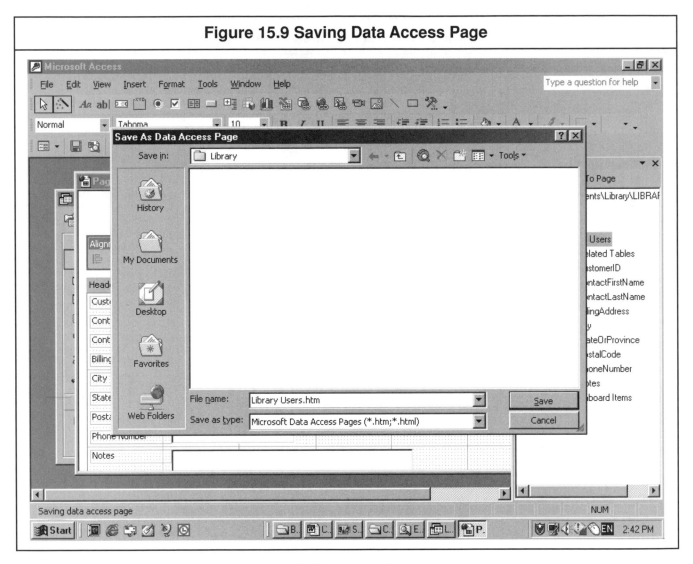

23. Click the **Save** button.

24. Click **OK** if you get the following message: This message is notifying us that we need to use a naming convention if we are going to be using our data access page on a network (see Figure 15.10).

Figure 15.10 Network Access Message

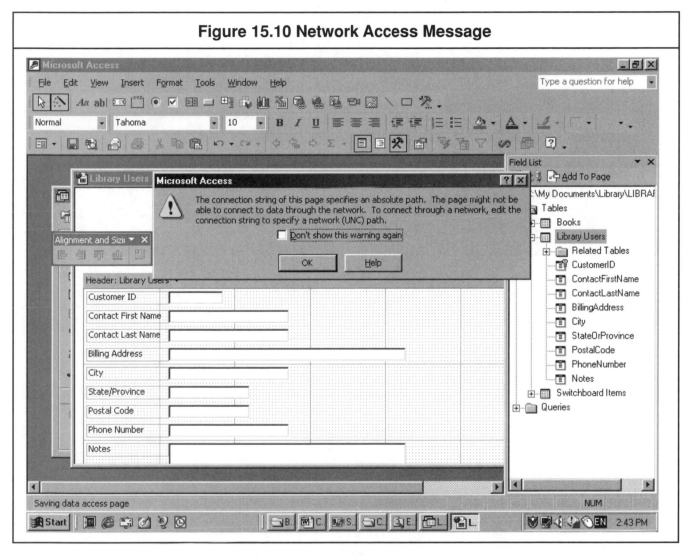

25. When you are returned to the Database Window, click the **Pages** object and you should see the data access page we created.

Now we are ready to test our data access page to modify the data in the **Library Users** table.

15.3 USING THE DATA ACCESS PAGE

1. Open **Windows Explorer**.
2. Navigate to the **Library** folder.
3. Double-click on the **Library Users** data access page and it will open in Internet Explorer. You will need to enter the password to access the **Library** database (password = "Library"). Internet Explorer opens and displays the data access page (see Figure 15.11).

Figure 15.11 Data Access Page in Internet Explorer

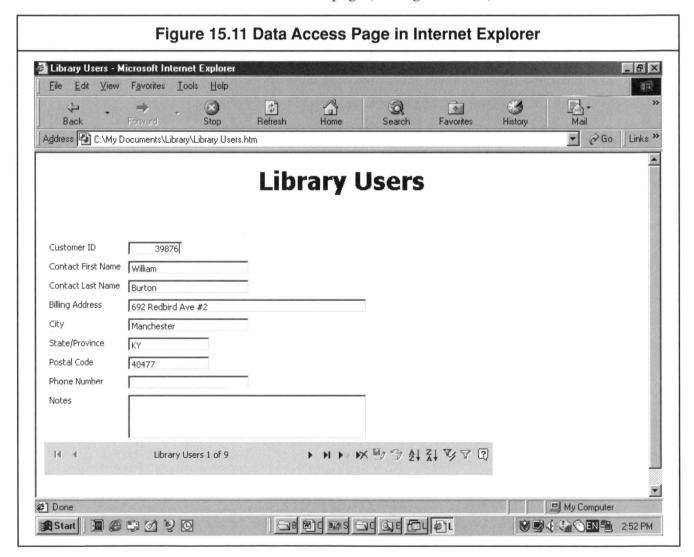

4. Navigate through the records using the record navigation buttons at the bottom of the screen.
5. Click the **Add New** button to add a new Library User (see Figure 15.12).

Figure 15.12 Add New Button

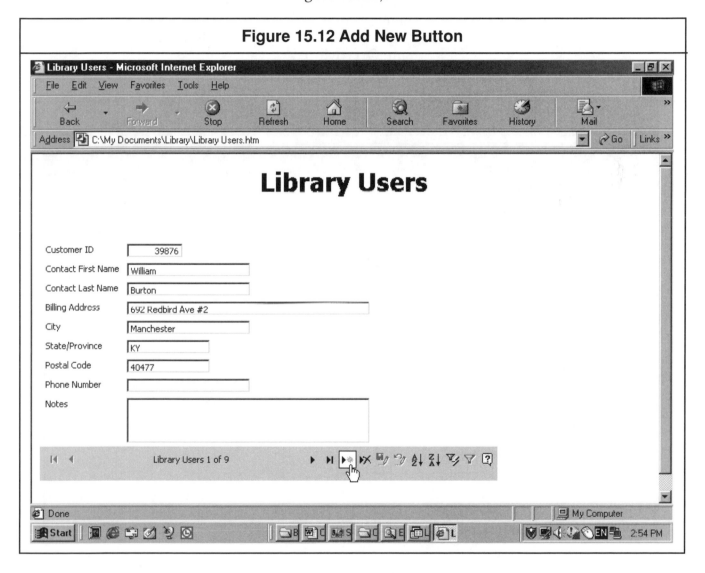

6. Enter the following record (see Figure 15.13):

CustomerID	12345
ContactFirstName	Sherry
ContactLastName	Brants
BillingAddress	131 East Main
City	Richmond
StateOrProvince	KY
PostalCode	40475

Figure 15.13 New Record Added

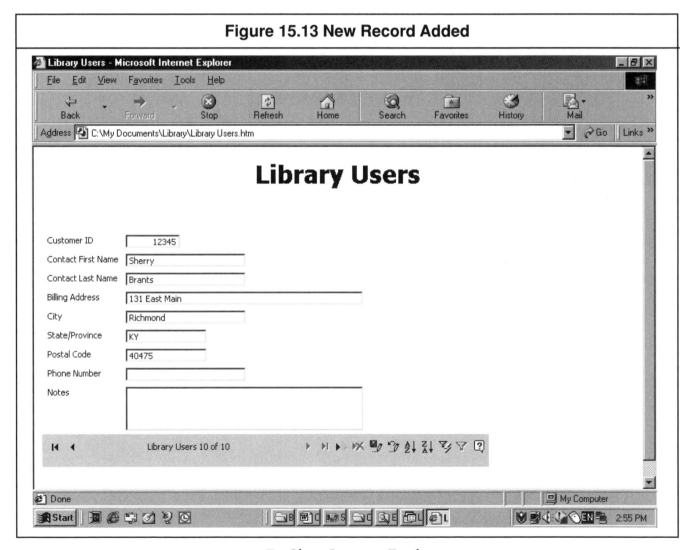

7. Close Internet Explorer.

Now we are going to check the **Library Users** table in our database for the added record. The **LIBRARY.mdb** database should still be open.

8. Click the **Tables** object button.
9. Double-click the **Library Users** table to open it and see that the new record has been added to the table (see Figure 15.14).

Figure 15.14 Record Added to Table

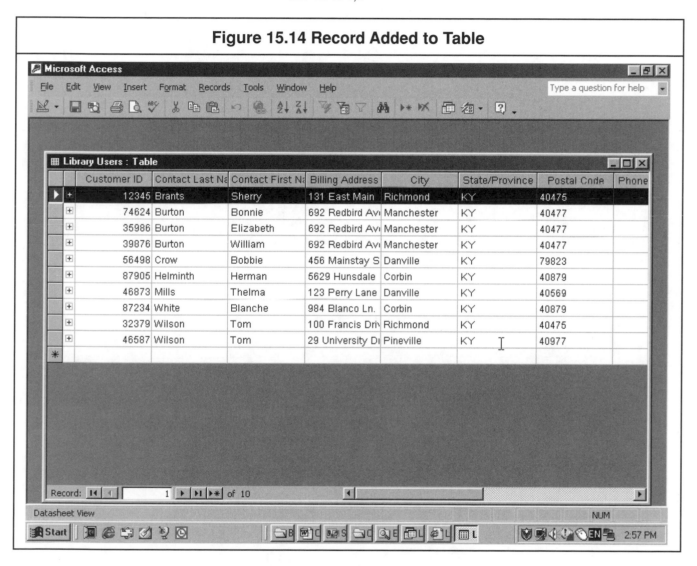

10. Close the **Library Users** table.
11. Close the **LIBRARY.mdb** database.
12. Exit Access.
13. Close **Windows Explorer**.

This concludes the session on data access pages. Hopefully you have learned much from this chapter and from the entire book. This book was designed to cover many different areas of designing, developing, and using the Microsoft Access program to show the user the program's numerous capabilities.

The authors really enjoyed writing this book and hopefully you enjoyed reading it. So that is it for now . . . until the next version of Microsoft Access. See you then. Thank you.

GLOSSARY

Access XP (2002)
A database program developed by Microsoft.

Alphanumeric field
A field that contains any combination of letters, numbers, and/or special characters.

Ascending
Ordering data in a field in ASCII order, numbers from smallest to largest, dates from earliest to latest; and letters from A to Z, with uppercase and lowercase letters considered separate lists.

Data
Alphanumeric characters that are grouped together in fields.

Database
An organized collection of information in the form of tables, records, and fields.

Database Management System (DBMS)
A software program that facilitates storage, organization, and retrieval of large amounts of related information.

Data Entry
A technique for entering records of data into a table.

Default
A value or setting that the system or software assumes if no other is specified.

Delete
To remove from existence; to *remove* a record from a table.

Edit
The process of changing data.

Field
A column in a table; an item of information in a record.

Field Type
The kind of information permitted in a specific location in a record. Basic field types include text, memo, number, date/time, currency, autonumber, yes/no, OLE object, hyperlink, and Lookup Wizard.

Index
> Reorganizing the order of fields in a table without changing the table structure

Index field
> The designated field(s) that controls the order of records.

Linking tables
> Linking tables together to form a relational database, which is, essentially, a database that stores data in multiple tables that you can relate in useful ways. Linking two or more tables lets Access draw information from these tables to create forms, queries, and reports.

Menu
> A list of options from which to choose in a software program.

Menu bar
> At the top of the screen, divisions that indicate the commands available when using Access for specific reasons.

Modify
> To change the structure of a table or to update data stored in the table.

Number field
> A field that can only contain numbers, or numbers with decimals.

Object
> The different parts of a database. These include tables, queries, forms, reports, pages, macros, and modules.

Operator(s)
> A feature used to find a range of values rather than an exact match; also called relational operator(s).

Query
> A question asked about the data stored in a table or group of tables.

Record
> A row in a table; it contains all the fields for an entity.

Relational Database
A database in which common fields create relationships between tables to allow data to be retrieved from more than one table.

Report
A designation that determines how information retrieved from the system displays or prints.

Sort
The process of changing the order of the records in a table.

Table
A database structure in which data is arranged in columns and rows; columns contain fields, and rows contain records.

View
Different displays for different types of objects.